THE FAILURES OF AMERICAN
AND EUROPEAN CLIMATE POLICY

SUNY series in Global Environmental Policy
Uday Desai, Editor

THE FAILURES OF AMERICAN AND EUROPEAN CLIMATE POLICY

International Norms, Domestic Politics,
and Unachievable Commitments

Loren R. Cass

State University of New York Press

Published by
State University of New York Press, Albany

For information, address State University of New York Press,
194 Washington Avenue, Suite 305, Albany, NY 12210-2384

Production by Judith Block
Marketing by Anne M. Valentine

Library of Congress Cataloging-in-Publication Data

Cass, Loren R., 1968–
    The failures of American and European climate policy : international
norms, domestic politics, and unachievable commitments / Loren R. Cass.
        p. cm. — (SUNY series in global environmental policy)
    Includes bibiographical references and index.
    ISBN 0-7914-6855-0 (hardcover : alk. paper)
    1. Climatic changes—Government policy—United States. 2. Climatic
changes—Government policy—Europe. I. Title. II. Series.

QC981.8.C5C377 2006
363.738'740973—dc22   2005033338

ISBN-13: 978-0-7914-6855-5 (hardcover : alk. paper)

10 9 8 7 6 5 4 3 2 1

Contents

CHAPTER ONE

Climate Policy and the Domestic Salience of International Norms

Climate change emerged as a major political issue in the late 1980s. As a recently identified environmental threat, the science was not well understood, and the economic consequences were uncertain. Scientists, political leaders, business executives, and the general public had to examine the threat, evaluate its potential economic and ecological implications, and develop strategies to respond both domestically and in cooperation with other states. The international and domestic responses to climate change present an important opportunity to analyze the process of problem definition and policy response in both a comparative and longitudinal context. By the late 1980s, even though every developed country acknowledged that climate change, at a minimum, required additional study and potentially demanded coordinated international action to address the threat, there was still significant variation in the domestic political responses and foreign policy positions adopted by the developed states. What explains this variation?

The conventional answer to this question is that differences in national cost-benefit calculations of the domestic effects of climate change and the policies to reduce greenhouse gas (GHG) emissions explain the variation. The potential economic effects of climate change, as well as the redistributive consequences of policies to address it, have heavily influenced both the international negotiations and the domestic policy debates. However, the rationalist material explanation does not appear to provide a sufficient explanation for the variation. Several states accepted emission reduction commitments that would be extremely difficult to achieve, and other states rejected commitments that would appear to be easy to meet. The larger normative context of the climate negotiations appears to have influenced the positions adopted by many states. The domestic and international deliberations produced contentious normative debates related to how political leaders should respond to the problem. The international and related domestic responses to climate change provide an important opportunity to explore the interrelated processes of international norm emergence and domestic political

1

responses to a new problem. To what extent did the debates over norms influence state interests and behavior, and conversely to what extent did domestic politics affect the emergence of international norms?

Norms are defined as collective expectations about the proper behavior for a given actor.[1] Most international relations scholars accept that norms exist, but there has been a growing debate surrounding the questions of when and how international norms affect state behavior. Materialist approaches to international relations theory have tended to treat norms as merely reflecting the interests and power positions of the dominant states. From this perspective, powerful states promote norms to justify and legitimate their preferred policies. It is the underlying pursuit of material interests that explains the process of norm selection and affirmation. The most powerful states create incentive structures that provide benefits for the affirmation of preferred norms and costs for norm violation. Thus, norms have no independent effect on national interests or behavior; they are tools utilized by the dominant states to pursue their interests. However, constructivist and liberal scholars have challenged the exclusive focus on material interests. They argue that actors do not define their interests exclusively in material terms, but rather they pursue a complex mix of interests that reflects normative as well as material foundations. Ideas matter. The social construction of the problem and the process of determining appropriate responses profoundly affect the formation, evolution, and pursuit of national preferences.

The constructivist literature on international norms has tended to emphasize the role of persuasion and social learning among political leaders in the process of international norm emergence. However, recently several scholars have begun to focus on the relationship between domestic politics and international norms.[2] Particularly in international environmental affairs, it is typically not sufficient for political leaders to be persuaded of the appropriateness of a norm for it to alter state behavior. Rather, the norm must become embedded in domestic political discourse and eventually be incorporated into the foreign and domestic policies of the state. National leaders play a vital role in this process, but in most cases the norm must be accepted by domestic political actors for it to significantly alter national behavior. This suggests that domestic institutional structures, political culture, and historically contingent choices will be critical intervening variables in the translation of international norms into domestic policy.

International norm emergence is by definition a process of social interaction. National leaders as well as private norm entrepreneurs compete to shape norms. International norms develop concurrently with domestic and foreign policy formulation. The processes are intimately connected. States seek to establish international norms that are consistent with domestic norms and interests in order to minimize adjustment costs. Norm entrepreneurs seek to alter international norms as a means to influence domestic policy. It is thus important to view the contested process of norm emergence as a two-level game involving both domestic and international actors. The theoretical focus of this book is not primarily on the process of international norm emergence but rather on the relationship between international norms and domestic policy. Which norms will be translated into domestic policy and why? When is a norm likely to influence the formulation of domestic and foreign policy responses to climate change? These questions point to the problem of determining domestic norm salience.[3] Norm salience refers to the norm's level of domestic political influence.[4] To what extent does an international norm constrain national behavior or create obligations for action? To what extent do political actors appeal to the norm to justify domestic policies or to block policy changes? In other words, how influential is the norm in shaping national political dialogue and behavior?

The starting point for studying norm salience is to analyze domestic political rhetoric. Rhetorical norm affirmation provides early evidence of the promotion of a preferred norm or the acknowledgement of an emergent international norm, which may later be more fully transcribed into domestic institutional structures and policies. However, it may also represent the cynical use of norm affirmation to deflect political pressure and avoid concrete action. It is thus necessary to evaluate behavior as well as rhetoric to gauge the domestic salience of the emergent norm. Analyzing the connections among international and domestic forces in the development of climate policies touches upon a number of important domestic policy areas, including energy, transportation, commerce, taxation, and foreign policy. Analytically linking the large number of actors, policy areas, and multiple levels of analysis is a daunting task. However, in order to gauge domestic norm salience, it is essential to evaluate the incorporation of international norms into the domestic and foreign policy responses to climate change across the full range of these policy areas, and it is the ability to evaluate these complex relationships that provides the foundation for evaluating the forces affecting domestic norm salience.

Both foreign and domestic strategies are essential to effectively address the threat of climate change. International agreements create pressure on countries to fulfill their international commitments and provide a mechanism for coordinating domestic efforts. However, meaningful international agreements to reduce GHG emissions require effective domestic measures. The close connection between international commitments and domestic policy provides an opportunity to analyze the relationships among national rhetoric, international negotiating stances, and domestic policy. The focus of this study is on the climate policies pursued by the European Union, Germany, the United Kingdom, and the United States between 1985 and 2005. The four political entities and twenty year history of climate policy provide both comparative and longitudinal studies to evaluate variation in the domestic salience of international norms.

The foreign policy element of this study analyzes the development of international climate policy from its rise to the forefront of the international environmental agenda in the mid-1980s, through the negotiation of the Kyoto Protocol, the completion of the Kyoto implementation agreement at Marrakech, Morocco in November 2001, and the entry into force of the Kyoto Protocol in February 2005. The domestic policy analysis focuses on the national framing of the threat posed by climate change and the politics of reducing CO_2 emissions. Other GHGs will be discussed where they are relevant. To the extent that there is an identifiable domestic climate policy, governments pursue it through changes in related policy areas. Reducing CO_2 emissions requires adjustments in some combination of transportation, energy production, energy use, and taxation policies. The politics of these policy areas can be highly contentious and are intimately linked to issues of economic competitiveness, economic growth, and domestic standards of living. The contentious nature of the links highlights the forces shaping climate policy and offers insight into the domestic effects of international norms.

The analysis focuses on a series of climate policy "decision points." A "decision point" is the juncture at which a government must make a policy decision relevant to a particular issue. A decision point may not require a change in policy. The continuation of an existing policy reflects a decision. In fact, it is the most common type of decision, because altering the status quo typically requires the expenditure of more resources than the continuation of the existing policy. No change is thus the default outcome. Either domestic or international factors can produce a decision point. Each of the chapters explains the generation and outcome of decision points related to climate change and analyzes the role of international norms in the policy debates. For example, the United States and Germany both undertook reviews of their national energy strategies in 1990 and 1991. The trigger for these reviews was not climate change, but rather the Gulf War and concern for the security of oil supplies from the Middle East. The reviews created an opportunity to address the relationship between energy and climate change. Each government had to decide whether CO_2 emission reductions would be included as a primary goal of energy policy. The Kohl government addressed the issue, and the Bush administration made only passing reference to it. The energy policy reviews created a brief window of opportunity to link climate policy with energy policy. Why did Germany debate the relationship between climate change and energy while the United States did not? By 1991 an international norm requiring all developed states to accept a CO_2 emission reduction commitment and establish a domestic strategy to reduce national emissions was achieving prominence. This norm appeared to significantly affect the German debate, but not the American debate. What explains the variation in norm salience? This is the type of question that is of paramount interest to this study.

Domestic and international forces exert pressure for changes in national policies, but typically these forces are insufficient to trigger a decision point without a precipitating event. Domestically, national elections or legislative initiatives on issues related to climate policy may act as precipitating events. National elections force candidates to articulate positions on climate change, which may initiate a review of existing policies. Legislation on related issues also creates decision points. In the United Kingdom, the privatization of the electricity industry resulted in substantial reductions in CO_2 emissions and eventually stimulated a debate on the relationship between power generation and climate change. The German energy policy review forced a debate on the relationship between Germany's heavy reliance on coal and its commitment to reducing CO_2 emissions. Attempts to increase government revenue initiated discussions of the relationship between energy taxation and CO_2 emissions in the European Union, the United States, Germany, and the United Kingdom. The appearance of a crisis event can also produce decision points. The exceptionally hot summers of the late 1980s created a public perception of a crisis, which pushed climate change onto the domestic policy agenda in the United States.[5]

External forces also precipitate decision points. Pressure from other states forced all three countries to articulate policy positions or to reexamine existing ones. International organizations created decision points by forcing states to articulate policy positions in international forums. The Intergovernmental Panel on Climate Change (IPCC), the United Nations Environment Program (UNEP), the Intergovernmental Negotiating Committee on Climate Change (INC), and the European Union (EU) all forced states to articulate policy responses to initiatives put forward by these organizations. The long line of climate conferences and negotiating sessions forced states to continuously articulate and justify their positions in the face of critiques from international organizations, NGOs, and other states. As each decision point emerged, international norms were a part of the decision making environment that had the potential to influence the outcome of the policy debate. These decision points thus provide opportunities to gauge international norm salience in domestic political dialogue, policy choice, and implementation.

MEASURING THE DOMESTIC POLITICAL SALIENCE OF INTERNATIONAL NORMS

Constructivist and liberal international relations scholars have led the research into international norms; however, they have emphasized different types of norms.[6] Liberals have emphasized "regulative norms," and constructivists have tended to stress "constitutive norms." Regulative norms constrain national behavior and alter the incentive structures facing states. Constitutive norms are fundamental to the identities and interests of actors.[7] Constructivists argue that norms primarily affect behavior by becoming integrated into the actor's identity and altering the perception of the appropriate response to a given set of circumstances. The actor's identity and interests are reconstituted by acceptance of the norm. Liberals argue that prominent norms influence behavior by altering the actor's incentive structure, which affects the cost-benefit calculation of alternative strategic options. The norm constrains or regulates behavior.

Norms can have both effects. Whether a norm has a constraining or constituting effect on a particular actor depends in part on the process of norm affirmation and acceptance. An actor may be persuaded of the appropriateness of the norm and its behavioral imperatives, in which case the norm will likely be incorporated into the identity of the actor and structure the actor's behavior. Alternatively, an actor may affirm an emerging norm as a result of coercion. In this case the norm constrains the options available to the actor and may alter the actor's behavior, but it is not accepted as part of the actor's identity. The distinction between coercion and persuasion in the process of norm emergence has important consequences for the translation of the norm into the domestic political system.

The central mechanism in most constructivist accounts of norm emergence is social diffusion.[8] Constructivists emphasize the role of persuasive communication in altering the intersubjective understanding of the proper response to a given set of circumstances. In the process of norm building, actors attempt to "frame" normative ideas in a way that resonates with existing norms and with the interests of the target audience. Frames are "specific metaphors, symbolic representations, and cognitive cues used to render or cast behavior and events in an evaluative mode and to suggest alternative modes of action."[9] Frames are tools used to define a problem and mobilize support for a particular response. Actors utilize frames to persuade a target audience of the appropriateness of a proposed normative response. However, the emphasis on persuasion obscures the important role played by material factors.[10] Actors strategically use norms to pursue both ideational and material interests. Actors may apply material incentives and disincentives to influence norm acceptance and compliance without necessarily redefining the target's preferences. Thus, norms may emerge that do not reflect the beliefs and preferences of most actors but rather reveal calculated norm compliance to achieve benefits and avoid costs.

Coercion plays a prominent role in norm affirmation. This suggests that rhetoric and even behavior may not reflect true motivations. Rather, actors are responding to shifts in incentive structures caused by the emerging norm and supporters of the norm. This is an important distinction because if behavior is dictated by coercion a state will be more likely to alter its behavior when the consequences of compliance or noncompliance change. On the other hand, if norm acceptance is based primarily on persuasion that a norm is appropriate, then it is more likely to be transcribed into the domestic political dialogue, and compliance is probable regardless of changes in incentive structures. This issue is particularly important during the early phases of norm emergence. Once a norm becomes institutionalized domestically—even if it is the result of coercion—it is likely to continue to influence national behavior regardless of shifts in the underlying incentive structure.[11]

The focus on the effect of international norms on state behavior raises a larger question related to the target actors that must be persuaded or coerced to accept a norm. The constructivist literature has emphasized the role of national decision makers. The empirical literature on norms appears to highlight two primary forces shaping elite support for an emerging international norm.[12] First, norm entrepreneurs may mobilize international and domestic support for the norm in an attempt to coerce political leaders to affirm the norm either by threatening political consequences or by "shaming" through concerted efforts to condemn national leaders for their failure to accept the norm. Success does not necessarily reflect authentic persuasion; rather, the leader may affirm the norm in response to coercion. A second mechanism involves a process of learning on the part of national leaders, who internalize the norm and create an intersubjective understanding of the appropriateness of the behavioral imperatives contained in the norm. In this case, the norm is likely to have maximum effect on the definition of interests and their strategic pursuit. It is possible that both mechanisms can be at work. Some leaders may be persuaded of the correctness of the norm, and others may respond to coercion. It is also likely that a different combination of persuasion and coercion will be at work in different countries. Domestic institutions may also affect the ability of norm entrepreneurs to influence national leaders.[13]

Elite acceptance of an international norm is necessary but not sufficient for the norm to alter state behavior. Elite acceptance is particularly important in issue areas where decision makers have significant independence. For example, national leaders are fairly insulated in the process of choosing targets to bomb during a military operation. There are many norms that constrain targeting decisions, but the choice is ultimately up to the civilian and military leadership. It typically does not require the prior consent of other domestic actors. In this case, it is critical that national leaders either be persuaded of the appropriateness of relevant norms or perceive a sufficient incentive structure to enforce compliance for the norm to have an effect on behavior. However, many issue areas involve multiple linked issues and much larger groups of participants. The domestic implementation of a norm may require the support of national leaders and at least the passive support or ambivalence of a large number of other actors. Climate change is a good example of this type of situation. The executive has significant leeway to negotiate on behalf of the country; however, climate policy will require domestic policy changes that demand broad political support to enact them. For example, the norm requiring developed states to adopt a GHG emission reduction commitment will require changes in energy, industrial, taxation, and/or commercial policies. Numerous domestic actors will be involved in these policy debates. Persuasion of norm appropriateness or coerced acceptance of the norm among the political elite will be insufficient to achieve domestic compliance. The implementation of the behavioral imperatives contained in an emergent norm may require the persuasion or coercion of a broad set of domestic interests for the state to effectively implement the norm. This points to the problem of determining the domestic salience of international norms.

The domestic salience of an international norm is critical to evaluating the likelihood of a norm altering national behavior. How do you measure the domestic salience of international norms? Certainly, rhetoric is an important indicator of political salience. Rhetoric may indicate support for— or at least acknowledgement of—an emerging norm, but it does not necessarily provide evidence of persuasion of the appropriateness of the norm or evidence that national behavior will inevitably change. Rhetoric can be cynically manipulated to bolster a state's image or to postpone costly policy changes. The combination of national rhetoric and behavior provides stronger evidence of norm salience. Has the government justified national policy changes with reference to international norms? Are other policy initiatives consistent with the norm? Domestic norm salience can be arrayed along a continuum from domestic irrelevance to a "taken for granted" status where the norm is embedded in domestic institutions and policies.

To measure domestic norm salience, it is typically necessary to focus on several domestic actors. For an international norm to affect national behavior, it is critical that national leaders affirm the norm and commit to act on it. As discussed above, leaders may either be persuaded of the appropriateness of the norm or coerced to affirm it. Persuasion is likely to produce a greater commitment on the part of national leaders to fulfill the behavioral requirements of the norm. If leaders are not persuaded of the appropriateness of the norm, then coercion may become important, and the mobilization of domestic interest groups is critical to creating pressure on national leaders to affirm the norm. International norms may circumvent the national leadership and directly enter the domestic political debate. Domestic actors may become convinced of the appropriateness of the emergent international norm or calculate that it serves their interests. These domestic interest groups, combined with international supporters, may be able to coerce the political leadership to affirm the norm and perhaps act on it. However, persuasion or coercion of the political leadership may not be sufficient to achieve compliance with the behavioral requirements of the norm. If domestic policy changes are necessary or if domestic actors must alter their behavior, then the affected interest groups must be either persuaded to act or coerced. The eight-point scale included below provides a potential measure of domestic norm salience. The scale expands upon Andrew Cortell and James Davis' (2000) three-level scale of salience. Cortell and Davis focus on the domestic salience across "domestic actors."[14] The scale below attempts to differentiate between the salience of the norm for the domestic political leadership and broader public discourse. Norms may achieve salience through the promotion of the norm by public leaders, who seek to alter domestic political discourse and policy. However, it is also possible that an international norm may be rejected by the political leadership, but the norm may become embedded in domestic political discourse by resonating with important domestic actors, which may force the leadership to acknowledge the norm and act on it. It is thus necessary to differentiate among the political leadership and the broader political discourse as well as between norm affirmation as the result of persuasion of the appropriateness of the norm and norm affirmation resulting from coercion. The scale below attempts to capture the effects of these variables on norm affirmation.

1. *Irrelevance.* National leaders do not acknowledge the emergent international norm in any way, and it is not a part of the foreign or domestic policy dialogue. National leaders do not even feel compelled to justify actions that contravene the proposed norm.

2. *Rejection.* National leaders acknowledge a proposed norm but reject it. The state will likely support an alternative norm and engage in debate with supporters of the less desirable alternative. The dialogue is conducted primarily on the international stage, and the normative debate has not entered mainstream domestic political dialogue.

3. *Domestic Relevance.* National leaders continue to reject the proposed international norm, but it has entered the domestic political dialogue. At this point the government faces pressure from both international and domestic actors to affirm the emergent norm.

4. *Rhetorical Affirmation.* National leaders affirm the norm as a result of political pressure from within and/or internationally. The norm is now

a part of the domestic and foreign policy dialogue, but it has not been translated into foreign or domestic policy changes.

5. *Foreign Policy Impact.* National leaders adjust the state's foreign policy to affirm the norm and may support its inclusion in international agreements. The change in position may be the result of persuasion of the appropriateness of the emergent norm or through domestic and/or international coercion. However, national leaders continue to reject changes in domestic policy to implement the norm's behavioral imperatives, or domestic actors continue to reject the norm and block domestic changes required by the norm.

6. *Domestic Policy Impact.* National leaders and other actors begin to justify changes in domestic policy on the basis of the international norm. At this point, the policy changes typically serve other purposes as well, but the norm provides additional justification for the changes. The norm is fully embedded in the domestic political dialogue, but the onus is still on the supporters of the norm to justify policy changes that may adversely affect domestic interest groups.

7. *Norm Prominence.* Domestic interest groups that wish to continue policies or pursue new initiatives that contradict the norm must now justify the violation of the norm. The burden of proof has shifted and the norm is becoming embedded in the domestic institutional structures and policies of the state.

8. *Taken for Granted.* The norm has become embedded in the domestic institutional structure of the state, and compliance with the norm is nearly automatic.

Measuring norm salience raises a number of important questions. Was persuasion or coercion the primary mechanism shaping norm salience? How did international forces alter the domestic debate? Which domestic actors were central to determining the level of salience? To what extent did material considerations affect norm salience? Did differences in domestic institutions or political culture matter? The literature on international norms has articulated a series of hypotheses related to the variables that should influence the level of domestic political salience. The hypotheses are presented below and then evaluated in the substantive chapters.

HYPOTHESES: VARIABLES INFLUENCING THE DOMESTIC SALIENCE OF INTERNATIONAL NORMS

Hypothesis 1. The greater the congruence between an international norm and domestic political norms, the greater the potential for the norm to be integrated into domestic political dialogue and achieve a high degree of political salience.[15] When domestic actors perceive the norm to be an extension of preexisting domestic political norms, it is likely to face only limited opposition, and domestic actors are predisposed to acknowledge the norm and act on it. Conversely, when the international norm is perceived as alien or contradicting preexisting domestic political norms, it will face substantial opposition.[16] Such norms will likely require a reexamination of domestic political norms before the international norm can achieve substantial domestic salience.[17]

Hypothesis 2. The greater the congruence between the domestic policy implications of the international norm and the material interests of influential actors, the more likely that the norm will achieve political salience.[18] The debates over international norms should not be seen as distinct from the pursuit of material interests. States will seek to promote norms that minimize adjustment costs. International norms that do not entail substantial domestic redistributive consequences should face significantly less opposition than norms that will adversely affect the material interests of influential domestic actors. Actors facing adverse material consequences will attempt to block the domestic incorporation of international norms that will harm their interests. However, in cases in which the international norms are consistent with domestic norms, such actors will likely face substantial opposition to their efforts unless they can justify their opposition on the basis of something other than the effects on their material interests.

Hypothesis 3. The stronger the perception that a norm serves the "general interests" of humanity and environmental protection, the more likely that it will be perceived as legitimate by a broad coalition of interested actors. Important normative debates typically occur within the public sphere, which will include political leaders as well as domestic interest groups, NGOs, and the broader public. This larger audience will look suspiciously upon a state or other actor that they perceive to be promoting a norm that merely serves narrow self-interests. The influence of NGOs is closely linked with the public perception that they are concerned with a broader general interest.[19] As Thomas Risse notes, "actors who can legitimately claim authoritative knowledge or moral authority (or both) should be more able to convince a skeptical audience than actors who are suspected of promoting 'private' interests."[20] However, states whose interests happen to be consistent with an emergent norm may also utilize the norm to provide "cheap legitimacy" to their preferred policies.[21] Frank Schimmelfennig has called this strategic use of norm-based arguments "rhetorical action"—"rhetorical action changes the structure of bargaining power in favor of those actors that possess and pursue preferences in line with, though not necessarily inspired by, the standard of legitimacy."[22] The broader perception of the legitimacy of a norm in providing for the "public good" will be a critical force shaping the salience of the nascent norm.

Hypothesis 4. Normative debates that are more public in nature and require domestic policy changes expand the number of relevant actors and create greater potential for private actors to create an incentive structure to force political actors to accept the norm regardless of their conviction related to the appropriateness of the norm. The extent to which normative debates are conducted in the public sphere will affect the influence of private actors on public officials. Normative debates that are primarily held among official actors without significant public input limit the range of actors that must be convinced of the appropriateness of the nascent norm. It is sufficient for political actors to be persuaded of the appropriateness of the norm for it to achieve salience. This situation also limits the potential for coercion by other interested actors to force political leaders to affirm the norm.

The greater the access and influence of norm entrepreneurs in the political process, the more likely that their norm will achieve significant salience. The domestic political structures of the states, the representative mechanisms for interest groups, and the number and significance of political access points will influence the domestic salience of international norms.[23] The extent to which norm entrepreneurs have opportunities to engage political leaders and persuade them of the appropriateness of their preferred norm or shame them into affirmation of the norm will significantly influence the potential for the norm to achieve domestic political salience.

Based on these hypotheses, it is possible to identify the conditions, which should provide the strongest foundation for a nascent international norm to achieve domestic political salience as well as those conditions that will reduce the level of salience. International norms that resonate with existing domestic political norms and which are also consistent with the material interests of significant domestic actors should rapidly achieve domestic norm salience. Obviously, cases in which the international norm does not resonate with existing domestic political norms and which would adversely affect significant domestic economic actors will be least likely to achieve domestic norm salience. The potential domestic salience of international norms in cases in which either the norm resonates with existing domestic norms but negatively affects domestic economic actors or in which the norm does not resonate with existing domestic norms but positively affects the material interests of domestic economic actors is much more difficult to predict. The level of salience should be significantly affected by the domestic political structure and the relative influence of important domestic actors in such cases. The broader perception of the legitimacy of the norm will also be critical in determining whether it will achieve domestic salience. These hypotheses will be evaluated in the case studies of climate policy.

WHY STUDY BRITISH, GERMAN, AND AMERICAN CLIMATE POLICY?

Greenhouse gases such as water vapor, carbon dioxide (CO_2), methane, and nitrous oxide make up less than 1 percent of the Earth's atmosphere, but they are responsible for maintaining the Earth's temperature at levels capable of supporting life. Without the greenhouse effect, the Earth's average temperature would be –18 C (–.5 F). With the greenhouse effect, the surface temperature averages +15 C (59 F). The concentrations of all GHGs, with the possible exception of water vapor, are increasing in the atmosphere as a result of human activity. Scientists have concluded that the Earth's average temperature has increased by approximately one degree over the past one hundred years, and at present trends the average temperature will increase between 2.5 and 10.4 degrees Fahrenheit (1.4 and 5.8 degrees centigrade) between 1990 and 2100.[24]

The warming of the atmosphere poses a number of potential problems. It will cause thermal expansion of the oceans and a net loss of ice at the poles and contained in glaciers, leading to an increase in the average sea level of between 3.5 and 34.6 inches (.09 and .88 meters) by 2100.[25] Such increases could engulf small island states and submerge large tracts of low-lying coastal areas in countries around the world. Scientists predict that the higher ocean temperatures will produce more frequent and more powerful storms leading to higher costs from storm damage. Regional weather patterns are also likely to change. Some regions may benefit from greater amounts of rainfall while others will suffer from drought. Changing weather patterns could have significant effects on agriculture, urban water supplies, as well as forcing changes in ecosystems. The higher temperatures could also affect human health through the northern migration of tropical disease and the adverse effects of prolonged heat waves. The impact and costs of these changes are highly uncertain. Much of the effect will depend on the speed and regional variation of the predicted effects. The slower the warming, the easier it is to adapt. Depending on the specific local effects, it is possible that some countries could be net beneficiaries from longer growing seasons, increased water supplies, and reduced energy use for heating. Some scientists have suggested that dramatic climate changes are also possible due to shifts in ocean currents that could have catastrophic effects on weather patterns. The potential costs of climate change remain highly speculative.

Carbon dioxide is responsible for roughly 60 percent of the "enhanced greenhouse effect," or the additional warming above preindustrial levels.

The burning of fossil fuels is the primary source of carbon dioxide emissions. Methane is responsible for approximately 15 to 20 percent of the enhanced greenhouse effect. The major sources of methane emissions include rice paddies, cattle, waste dumps, leaks from coal mines, and natural gas production. Nitrogen oxides, CFCs, and ozone contribute most of the remaining portion of the enhanced greenhouse effect. It does not matter where the GHGs originate. They have the same effect on the atmosphere. Any solution to the problem of climate change necessarily requires multilateral action, and, if it is to be meaningful, a solution entails changes in domestic policies.

Domestic climate policies must inevitably address carbon dioxide emissions and/or removal from the atmosphere, because CO_2 is the most important of the GHGs. To reduce CO_2 emissions, states must decrease the burning of fossil fuels, but these fuels lie at the heart of every state's economy. Managing CO_2 emissions presents risks to a state's competitive position by increasing costs of production, and it threatens to alter domestic lifestyles and standards of living. In addition to reducing emissions of CO_2, it is also possible to remove CO_2 from the atmosphere. Plant life acts as a "sink" for CO_2 by removing vast quantities of the gas through photosynthesis. It is thus possible to partially offset emissions of CO_2 with better land management and the expansion of forested areas. There are also a number of other technologies that could potentially remove CO_2 from the atmosphere and sequester it in the deep ocean, below the surface of the Earth, or chemically convert it into a solid form. At this point, these options remain impractical, and the reduction of CO_2 emissions and the use of sinks to remove CO_2 dominate the climate policy debate. While political debates and international negotiations over the reduction of all GHGs will be addressed in this book, the primary focus will be on attempts to regulate CO_2 emissions as the most important GHG and the most politically charged gas to regulate.

The United States, Germany, and the United Kingdom offer several advantages for analyzing the role of international norms in the evolution of climate policy. They have been critical actors in the climate negotiations. They interacted within the same international institutions (with the important exception of German and British membership in the European Union) and had significant influence within those structures. They also share a number of common traits which hold important domestic variables constant. They are democratic states with close economic and political ties. They have been active in pursuing international environmental interests and have played major roles in environmental negotiations. Conservative governments led each country during the formative years of climate policy, and liberal governments eventually assumed power in all three countries after the signing of the Framework Convention on Climate Change (FCCC). Additionally, they are all advanced industrial states with similar patterns of CO_2 emissions, though the overall scale of emissions from the United States dwarfs those of Germany and the United Kingdom. In 1990, over 60 percent of CO_2 emissions in all three countries emanated from the energy transformation industry and mobile sources (i.e., cars, trucks, and trains). The bulk of the remaining emissions were from industry. Thus, each government would have to address the same sectors to reduce CO_2 emissions.[26]

While these similarities hold many variables constant, differences in domestic institutional structures have the potential to affect whether and how international norms are translated into domestic policy. For example, Germany's hybrid single member district and proportional representation electoral system for the Bundestag has created an opening for the Green Party to have a much larger effect on German policy than such parties could achieve in the British and American political systems. The dominant position of the prime minister in British politics permits the government to act more expeditiously to change domestic policies than either the German or American governments. The German chancellor can typically push policy changes through the lower house, but he must contend with an influential upper house of parliament (the Bundesrat) that is often controlled by the opposition. The American president faces a much more independent House of Representatives and Senate even if the bodies are controlled by the president's party. The adversarial legalism of American regulatory politics also creates obstacles to policy implementation. The domestic institutional structure of each state affects the strength and influence of domestic actors in the policy process, shapes actor strategies, and affects the ability of the executive branch to formulate and successfully pursue domestic and foreign environmental policies. These variables have their greatest effect upon domestic environmental policy, but they also impinge on the foreign policy process. A full discussion of the effects of institutional variation on climate policy is beyond the scope of this study. However, these may be important intervening variables affecting the domestic salience of international norms; therefore, they will be discussed when relevant to the incorporation of the norms into the domestic policy process.

Each state also possesses a unique approach to state-sponsored environmental action that influences the national response to new environmental problems. This approach is a product of the state's institutional framework, domestic environmental policy norms, cultural differences, and historically contingent choices made in both the domestic and international policy processes.[27] The state's approach to environmental action is not static. It will change incrementally over time, and in times of crisis it may change very rapidly.[28] As a new environmental problem emerges, the domestic approach to environmental policy structures the national response. Environmental policy norms dictate the types of evidence required to induce action. They influence the institutional path through which the issue will be addressed as well as which actors will shape the national response. Proposals to change national policies to address the problem must also be consistent with existing environmental policy norms.

The national response to the new environmental problem will thus emerge from a contested process of political interaction structured by the national approach to environmental policy. Altering policies to address the problem will require domestic actors to overcome the status quo bias in environmental policy. Domestic actors who would be adversely affected by the proposed policy changes will attempt to obstruct the changes. However, they cannot openly and vigorously attack the state's environmental philosophy without facing public pressure to submit to national environmental norms. There will also be individuals and groups with more extreme environmental positions. The influence of these groups is also constrained by the national approach to environmental policy, which reflects a generally accepted balancing of societal interests. Once regulations are enacted, the various domestic actors respond to the incentives and strategic opportunities created by those regulations. Any proposal that threatens the domestic status quo must overcome the inertia of established policies. The effect is that previous policy decisions constrain the range of acceptable international policy initiatives as well as the ability to alter domestic policy. Therefore, two states with similar economies and even geographic circumstances may produce divergent responses to a new environmental challenge.

Several scholars have explored the variations in national approaches to state-sponsored environmental action.[29] Two major differences in the norms governing environmental policy in the United States, United Kingdom, and Germany have arguably had important effects on the emergence of international climate norms and the translation of those norms into domestic policy: the application of the "precautionary principle" and the perception of the role of the market in environmental protection. One of the core principles of German environmental policy is the precautionary principle.[30] The precautionary principle requires the government to address potential environmental threats even before scientific evidence provides substantial confirmation of the hazard. The application of the precautionary principle predisposed the German political system to address climate change even before there was conclusive scientific evidence linking GHG emissions to climate change. The British and American political systems, on the other hand, have tended to require significant scientific evidence before taking regulatory action to address a potential problem. In the American case, the frequent need for regulators to defend their actions before the judiciary has reinforced the requirement to justify regulations on the basis of concrete scientific evidence. The result has been a politicization of environmental science. Advocates of various policy responses seek to support their positions with scientific evidence and challenge the research of political opponents, which has undermined the formation of a national consensus that a policy response to climate change is necessary.

The role of market mechanisms in environmental protection was also an important element in the response to climate change. The success of the American sulfur emission market colored the American debate surrounding the principles that should guide the policy response to climate change. The antiregulatory legacy of the Ronald Reagan and George Herbert Walker Bush administrations was also important. Both administrations emphasized the need for cost-benefit analyses to justify regulatory action. The uncertainties surrounding both the science and economics of climate change made meaningful cost-benefit analysis nearly impossible, which complicated the American debate. Both Germany and the United Kingdom were experimenting with economic incentives to address environmental problems, but neither had gone as far as the United States in requiring cost-benefit analyses to justify regulatory action.

Differences in domestic institutional structures and environmental policy norms should affect the domestic salience of international norms. Each of the chapters seeks to trace the concurrent evolution of German, British, American, and EU (the inclusion of the EU is necessary to understand German and British policies) policy responses to climate change and the emergence of related international norms. The objective is to measure the salience of the international norms and evaluate the forces influencing the level of domestic political salience.

This book focuses primarily on two normative debates that were critical to the development of international and domestic climate policy. First, who should bear primary responsibility for reducing global GHG emissions? Should developed states be forced to act first because they are historically responsible for the vast majority of GHG emissions, or should all states bear a common responsibility to reduce emissions? This debate involved issues of justice and fairness as well as economic costs and efficiency. If developing and developed states faced similar obligations then this would limit the competitive effects of emission reduction policies as well as reducing the costs of emission reductions globally since there were more cost effective emission reductions available in developing countries. The second primary normative debate focused on the principles that would guide global emission reductions. Should individual states be held to a principle of national accountability, which would require every state to reduce its domestic GHG emissions, or should the principle of economic efficiency guide global emission reductions? Most environmental NGOs, developing countries, as well as most European states argued for a norm requiring national responsibility. The United States, Japan, and Australia (among others) argued that the important point was to reduce global emissions, and that these emission reductions should be achieved wherever they were most cost effective. The resolution of these normative debates and the degree to which their related norms achieved domestic political salience would significantly shape the development of both international and domestic climate policies.

The chapters are organized chronologically. Chapter 2 focuses on the early identification and framing of climate change in the mid-1980s through the establishment of the Intergovernmental Negotiating Committee on Climate Change (INC) at the end of 1990. This was a period when climate change was primarily a foreign policy issue and not a significant domestic political issue. Chapter 3 analyzes the Framework Convention on Climate Change negotiations (1991–1992) and the early domestic political debates in Germany, the United Kingdom, and the United States. The early protocol negotiations after the completion of the FCCC through the Berlin Mandate agreement (1992–1995) are discussed in chapter 4. The focus shifted in this period from international negotiations to domestic policy debates. Chapter 5 focuses on the Kyoto Protocol negotiations (1995–1997), and finally chapter 6 analyzes the failure of the Hague negotiations to complete the Kyoto Protocol, the subsequent decisions by the United States to pull out of the Kyoto Protocol and the German, British, and EU decisions to ratify the Kyoto Protocol without the United States (1997–2001), and the Protocol's entry into force in February 2005.

Each chapter traces the evolution of the domestic and foreign policy responses to climate change adopted by the three states within the context of the larger normative debates surrounding climate policy. To what extent were international norms incorporated into the domestic political dialogue? Were domestic and foreign policies consistent with the national rhetorical positions and with the emerging international norms? If there were discrepancies, what explains the inconsistency? An evaluation of these questions provides the foundation for making judgments about the salience of international norms to the domestic political process as well as evaluating the hypotheses related to the forces affecting norm salience.

CHAPTER TWO

Issue Framing, Norm Emergence, and the Politicization of Climate Change

(Villach to Geneva)

This chapter analyzes the issue definition and agenda setting stages of climate policy. The scientific community initiated the research and scientific discussion that created the foundation for the ensuing political debates. The growing scientific evidence of a human impact on the atmosphere compelled each country's political institutions to define the problem, determine appropriate domestic policy responses, and develop an initial foreign policy position on the desirability and character of an international response. During this initial stage, the relationship between climate policy and domestic policy responses was more speculative than concrete. The level of involvement of domestic interests was much lower than in the ensuing phases of international negotiation and domestic policy development. In this first phase, the primary actors were scientists, environmental groups, and international organizations such as the World Meteorological Organization (WMO) and the United Nations Environment Program (UNEP). In addition, each state's foreign policy establishment worked to develop an initial diplomatic response to the potential problem of climate change.

The international normative debates that would form the foundation for climate policy emerged during this period. By the mid-1980s, scientists were framing climate change as a human-induced problem that required a coordinated multilateral response. Germany and the United Kingdom accepted this framing of the problem, but the United States was reluctant to accept climate change as human-induced and demanded additional scientific study. Once climate change moved onto the political agenda, norm entrepreneurs began to promote a norm that would require states to accept responsibility for past GHG emissions and adopt a domestic quantitative CO_2 emission reduction targets. Germany was one of the primary proponents of obligatory domestic CO_2 emission reduction targets. The United

States argued that an alternative normative framework based on the efficient reduction of global emissions rather than domestic emission reduction commitments was more appropriate. The United Kingdom was sympathetic to this alternative approach, but it eventually accepted a binding emission reduction target, while the United States continued to reject the norm. The differences in national positions provide opportunities to analyze the forces shaping the domestic framing of the problem, the international normative debates, as well as the domestic salience of the international norms.

The domestic political and economic situations in the three countries during this time period help to control for a number of important domestic variables. Conservative governments won elections in all three countries during this period. All three countries also experienced economic growth up until 1989 when the British and American economies began to lose momentum. Both countries slipped into recession in 1991; however, reunification sustained German economic growth. The economic situations affected climate policy. Both the American and British governments became more sensitive to the costs of climate policy, while economic cost was not as significant for German leaders.

The positions of all three countries were also influenced by the ease of CO_2 emission reductions. American emissions rose rapidly during the late 1980s, and there was little expectation of emissions declining significantly without additional domestic policy measures. British emissions remained reasonably constant and there was initially little expectation that emissions would fall in the near future. The British calculations began to change after the electricity industry initiated a shift from coal to natural gas. West German emissions remained reasonably constant as well. However, a unified Germany experienced a rapid decline in emissions resulting from the economic restructuring of the former East and the closing of inefficient factories and power plants. The expectation of future emission trends played an important role in shaping the willingness of all three countries to support international commitments to reduce CO_2 emissions.

Domestic institutional constraints and the unique political setting in each of the countries affected the salience of climate change as a domestic political issue, but climate policy during this period was primarily oriented toward international debates over the nature of the problem and the norms that would govern the international response. The relationship to domestic policy reform emerged slowly as the international negotiations approached in 1992. This chapter begins with a brief discussion of the politicization of climate change and then traces the initial policy responses of the United States, the United Kingdom, and Germany.

ISSUE FRAMING AND THE POLITICIZATION OF CLIMATE CHANGE (1979–1990)

Scientists had been aware of the role of greenhouse gases and the potential for human impacts on climate since 1895.[1] However, it was only in 1979 that climate change emerged as a significant issue on the international scientific agenda. In February, the WMO convened the First World Climate Conference. It received scant political notice, but the delegates set in motion the process that would eventually raise climate change to the international diplomatic agenda. To continue the work of the conference, the participants established the World Climate Program (WCP) with a mandate to study the links between human activity and climate change. The WCP created a mechanism for pursuing the climate change research agenda and provided a place for climatologists to interact and promote their work. The WCP also initiated a series of conferences that publicized the issue and effectively raised political and public consciousness of it.

The first conference held under the WCP was in November of 1980 in Villach, Austria. The report of the Villach conference, "The Assessment of the Role of Carbon Dioxide and Other Greenhouse Gases in Climate Variations and Associated Impacts," provided a stark warning that the growth in atmospheric levels of greenhouse gases (GHGs) posed a grave threat to the Earth's natural equilibrium and should be urgently addressed. The Villach conference indicated an emerging consensus among climate scientists that human-induced climate change was a serious phenomenon that required urgent scientific attention to determine the likely long-term consequences. By 1985, WCP scientists had concluded that the evidence suggested that human-induced climate change was occurring and required a public policy response to forestall potentially cataclysmic changes. The October 1985 Villach, Austria WCP conference report noted that since "the understanding of the greenhouse question is sufficiently developed, scientists and policy makers should begin an active collaboration to explore the effectiveness of alternative policies and adjustments."[2] The 1985 Villach conference marks the transition of climate change from a principally scientific issue to an international political issue as well.

The work of the WCP led UNEP to include the negotiation of a climate convention as one of its goals in its 1985 long-term planning document. Following up on suggestions made at the Villach meeting, UNEP Executive Director, Mostafa Tolba sent a letter to Secretary of State George Schultz suggesting that the United States initiate the process to introduce a global response to the threat of climate change. Tolba's request stimulated an American decision to support an intergovernmental scientific panel to study the issue.[3] At the tenth WMO congress in May 1987, the United States proposed that the WMO organize a panel to explore the scientific issues surrounding climate change. In July, the WMO's Executive Council called for the creation of the Inter-governmental Panel on Climate Change (IPCC) to assess the scientific understanding of global warming to provide a foundation for an appropriate policy response.

The extreme heat wave that hit North America during the summer of 1988 led to greater public awareness of the potential threat from climate change. In the midst of the heat wave, the Canadian government-sponsored the Toronto Conference on the Changing Atmosphere. The conference brought together scientists, government officials, businessmen, and environmentalists. It differed from its predecessors because it was government-sponsored, which conferred greater significance in the international political arena. The Toronto Conference was the first major conference to call for specific policy responses to the threat of climate change. The conference report called for a 20 percent reduction in CO_2 emissions by the year 2005, the negotiation of a comprehensive global framework convention to protect the atmosphere, and the creation of a "World Atmosphere Fund" to be financed in part by a tax on fossil fuel consumption in industrial countries. The call for states to accept a quantitative emission reduction target marked the introduction of a normative debate related to how states *should* respond to the threat of climate change.

The Toronto Conference served to effectively raise the political profile of climate change and created pressure for states to address the issue in both their domestic and foreign policies. Climate change received a further boost from United Nation resolution 43/53, "Protection of Global Climate for Present and Future Generations of Mankind." The resolution called on UN agencies to fully support the work of the IPCC and urged "governments, intergovernmental and non-governmental organizations and scientific institutions to treat climate change as a priority issue."[4] Between December 1988 and November 1990, there were a series of major international meetings where climate change was an important issue on the agenda. The growing international attention compelled Germany, the United Kingdom, and the United States to articulate national positions on climate change. The international pressure is critical to understanding the development of the initial national positions discussed in the sections below.

Just prior to the May 1989 UNEP ministerial meeting in Nairobi, the United Kingdom put forward the first official proposal for a climate convention. The proposal split the participants between those who argued that international negotiations were premature because the IPCC had not finished its assessment (United States, Japan, Australia, New Zealand, and a number of developing countries), and those who argued that negotiations should begin immediately (Canada, Germany, and most of the European Community members). A compromise was reached in Nairobi that allowed discussion of policies to be included in a convention, while putting off the negotiation of a convention until after the IPCC produced its report in 1990.[5] Supporters of climate policy took every opportunity to point out the laggards in the process and succeeded in whittling the number of countries vocally opposing international action on climate change down to the United States, the Soviet Union, the OPEC states, and a few developing countries.

During this period, the rhetorical positions of Germany and the United Kingdom changed dramatically. Between December 1988 and November 1990, the German position was transformed from one of apathy to primary promoter of action on global climate policy. The United Kingdom moved from activist to laggard, as other countries pressed beyond the British position. American opposition to international action on climate change hardened, which increasingly isolated the United States. The United States grudgingly accepted the inevitability of a climate convention, but it lobbied vigorously to assure that it would possess no teeth. International organizations played a significant role in maintaining pressure for national action on climate change. In particular, the ongoing nature of the IPCC process created a momentum for international negotiations. UNEP also played an important role in pushing the participants forward by providing a forum for the proposed convention to take root and by focusing attention on climate change through the Second World Climate Conference. Additionally, a number of crucial states, such as the United Kingdom (early on), Germany, the Netherlands, Norway, and Canada, stepped forward to provide diplomatic pressure for action. International pressure forced states to articulate national positions on how the problem should be addressed. Each state sought to shape the norms that would govern the international response to climate change to minimize the domestic adjustment costs and limit the changes required in domestic policies.

INITIAL CLIMATE DEBATES IN THE UNITED KINGDOM

It is appropriate to begin with the United Kingdom because it was one of the initial leaders of international efforts to address climate change. It was a primary proponent of the IPCC and the initial promoter of an international climate convention. British policy also evolved significantly during this period. The British government shifted from an international leadership position to become a laggard and then to more of a follower. It thus provides an interesting case of apparent evolution in the government's understanding of its interests or a shift in the cost-benefit calculation of addressing climate change.

As climate change emerged as a significant political issue in the mid-1980s, the British response was heavily influenced by its recent experience with international environmental policy. The UK had been pilloried over its role in the acid rain problems of Europe. The Thatcher government's emphasis on deregulation and privatization had pushed environmental policy toward the bottom of the policy agenda. Environmental organizations castigated Britain as the "dirty man of Europe," and public pressure was building for the government to more aggressively address environmental issues. Prime Minister Thatcher shifted the Conservative Party stance on environmental issues in the fall of 1988. As a sign of its new interest in environmental affairs, the government adopted climate change as its highest priority environmental issue. The government became a strong advocate for international negotiations on climate change, but it aggressively sought to control their evolution.

The Conservatives had a number of reasons for pursuing a leadership position on climate change. It was a new and "sexy" issue. It provided an opportunity to assume a high profile leadership position that could help to improve the government's green credentials. It also had very low short-term costs. The climate negotiations were likely to be a long process. As a result, short-term changes in government policy would be unnecessary. The government also perceived climate change to be the next major international environmental issue. By assuming an early leadership role, it could shape the development of the issue. The government had learned a number of lessons from its recent experiences with ozone depletion and acid rain. In the case of acid rain, the European Community had assumed regulatory responsibility through its Large Combustion Plant Directive (LCPD). The negotiation of the LCPD had been an extremely arduous task for the Thatcher government and was proving to be both politically and economically costly. The ozone case on the other hand was initially handled through UNEP, where the UK was in a much stronger position to protect its interests and minimize the costs of policies to address ozone depletion. The Thatcher government sought to keep climate change in a broader international forum, rather than allow the EC to dictate policy.

Britain's political role in international climate policy commenced with the 1988 creation of the IPCC. The United Kingdom actively sought a prominent role in the IPCC process. British scientist, Sir John Houghton, became the chair of Working Group I on the science of climate change. The United Kingdom had a long history of research on atmospheric pollution issues stemming from its examination of the effects of its industrial emissions on continental Europe. This prior research had created a core of respected atmospheric scientists. Climate change provided an opportunity for the government to build on its existing research strengths.

Prime Minister Thatcher sought to seize the initiative on climate change and assure that it would be addressed in an international forum where British sovereignty would be protected, and the United States would be present to counter the influence of the EC. This motive was apparent in the prime minister's response to the proposed Hague Summit on the Atmosphere in March 1989. France, the Netherlands, and Norway had called the summit to prepare a convention on the atmosphere that would create a new world environment organization to be backed by the International Court of Justice. The United Kingdom forced the EC to withdraw from the conference, and Prime Minister Thatcher refused to attend, even though seventeen heads of government participated.[6] The United Kingdom emphasized that it would not accept a body with supranational powers that could supersede national sovereignty on environmental issues. The Thatcher government repeatedly rejected proposals for an "international ecology authority" and instead was able to guide the conference toward an affirmation of the existing UN structures.[7]

In April 1989, the British Foreign Office began actively promoting a climate convention as the most appropriate response to climate change.[8] The British attempted to preempt EC unilateral action and guide the negotiations into a broader intergovernmental forum. At a meeting of the UN General Assembly in May, the British permanent representative to the UN, Sir Crispin Tickell, called for the negotiation of a framework convention on climate change laying out principles for "good climatic behavior." He argued that the convention should be completed as soon as possible with protocols to be negotiated later "as scientific evidence requires and permits."[9] He then called for a strengthening of UNEP and suggested that it be made a specialized agency with improved funding. He contended that the climate negotiations had to be handled at a high level of diplomatic involvement. The British proposal put the UK at the forefront of climate policy, established its preference for negotiations to be conducted in an intergovernmental forum, and because it was only proposing a framework convention with no concrete commitments, no immediate policy changes were necessary. The government supported a multilateral response to climate change, but it was unwilling to take specific domestic actions or accept emission reduction commitments at that time.

The Thatcher government followed up on the proposal to the UN with a similar proposal before the governing council of UNEP in Nairobi in May. It called for the development of a framework convention on climate change to be negotiated within UNEP with any protocols to be developed after completion of the convention. However British representatives also sought to slow the negotiation process. At the Nairobi meeting, a group of countries, including West Germany, called for an immediate start to negotiations. The United States rejected negotiations as premature. The British representatives played an important role in drafting a compromise on the issue that delayed the start of negotiations until after the IPCC produced its report.[10] The United Kingdom's action illustrated the limits to its support for action on climate change. Encouraging early negotiations would have damaged relations with the United States and conceded the initiative to more aggressive supporters of international climate policy.

The spring of 1989 was a period of intense environmental interest in the United Kingdom. The prospect of the June European elections and the strength of the British Green Party in contesting those elections created further pressure on the Conservative Party to improve its environmental image. The Green Party did not win any seats in the election, but it succeeded in polling nearly 15 percent of the vote. As a result, the Conservative Party moved environmental policy much more to the forefront of its priorities. The Thatcher cabinet sought to recast the domestic environmental debate by extending its market-based philosophy to environmental affairs. The Conservatives argued that there did not need to be any trade-off between economic growth and environmental protection. The newly appointed Environment Minister, Christopher Patten, noted that the choice "is not between higher or lower rates of growth but between different ways of growth in the economy."[11] The Conservatives were considering "green taxes" and market mechanisms to fundamentally change the United Kingdom's approach to environmental policy.

The Labour Party rejected the government's market-based approach and called for strong government regulation and intervention in environmental matters. The Labour Party leadership emphasized the application of the precautionary principle to environmental issues.[12] Environmentalists criticized the Conservative government for its reactionary stance to environmental problems. Contrary to the German philosophy of environmental action, the Conservative government tended to address the consequences of environmental policy and to seek clear scientific evidence of a threat before acting.

In the midst of the domestic debate, the Conservatives continued to point to climate policy as an example of strong British environmental leadership. Patten promised a vigorous British role in immediately pushing forward a climate convention with "binding agreements on subjects like energy efficiency and forestry, as the science and political will come into balance."[13] The Conservative's domestic environmental policy, on the other hand, was primarily comprised of promises for future action. The newfound Conservative interest in the environment was met with skepticism from environmentalists. They noted that even as it talked of environmental action, the government was undertaking a twelve billion pound road program, as well as cutting funding for energy efficiency and fuel conservation.[14] The government faced a widening gap between its rhetorical support for international action to address climate change and the lack of domestic policies to address GHG emissions.

The Dilemmas of British Climate Policy

The dilemmas facing the Thatcher government's climate policy became apparent at the November 1989 Noordwijk ministerial conference on climate change. An international norm requiring states to adopt domestic CO_2 emission reduction commitments was gaining international acceptance. Several European countries, including Germany, had established domestic targets. The draft declaration called for countries to commit themselves to the stabilization of CO_2 emissions by the year 2000. It also called for research into the possibility of reducing emissions by 20 percent by the year 2005. The United Kingdom was reluctant to go along with specific targets, both because it was wary of the costs to its economy and because of opposition from the United States. However, it also did not wish to be perceived to be undermining the international negotiations. Junior Environment Minister, David Trippier, noted that any specific agreement would be "premature." "All countries should commit themselves to the work of the IPCC and not allow that work to be diverted at this stage by arbitrary and unsubstantiated targets. In any case, we have no basis for setting a target of 20 percent reductions when so many other figures have been cited elsewhere."[15] Trippier called for all nations to support a framework convention with specific goals to be negotiated after the IPCC provided a scientific basis for action.

British negotiators attempted to find a compromise solution. Under the British proposal, the signatories would commit to stabilize CO_2 emissions by the year 2000 with the levels of stabilization left undefined.[16] However, even this compromise was unacceptable to the United States, the USSR, and Japan, and the final statement only asserted that "in the view of many industrialized nations . . . stabilization of (carbon dioxide) emissions should be achieved as a first step at the latest by the year 2000."[17] The other states in attendance committed themselves to a nonbinding goal of stabilizing CO_2 emissions by the year 2000. Labour leaders lambasted the government for undermining the possibility of a meaningful international agreement. "While other European countries are prepared to accept targets for reductions, our government and the U.S.A. are refusing to join them. Doesn't this show the government's claim to be at the forefront in tackling global warming to be a bogus one?"[18]

In the midst of the Noordwijk conference, Prime Minister Thatcher addressed the United Nations General Assembly. She was put in the uncomfortable position of attempting to stress the importance of international environmental policy while at the same time justifying the United Kingdom's refusal to accept firm commitments to reduce CO_2 emissions. She stressed the active role that Britain had played in climate policy and promised to continue to play a prominent role. She announced the establishment of a Centre for the Prediction of Climate Change within the Meteorological Office, and she promised an additional £100 million of bilateral assistance for the preservation of tropical forests. She also attempted to deflect criticism of the United Kingdom's position in Noordwijk by noting that solutions to climate change had to involve "sound scientific analysis" before targets for reductions could be negotiated.[19]

While Britain was attempting to sustain its climate image, it was already facing the prospect of another climate conference with another proposal for CO_2 emissions limits and another battle with its continental partners. Preparations for a follow-up conference to the 1987 publication of the Brundtland Report were under way in December 1989. Germany, along with the Nordic countries and The Netherlands, were promoting the establishment of quantitative emission reduction targets. Britain supported the American position and opposed targets until after the completion of the IPCC report, but such a policy was becoming increasingly untenable due to the United Kingdom's desire to be considered a leader in climate policy. The government also faced the possibility that agreements to reduce CO_2 emissions could impair the planned privatization of the state-owned electricity industry. A meaningful international agreement would require reductions in CO_2 emissions. One of the primary groups of emitters was the electricity generation industry. The government had already experienced the heavy costs to the industry in addressing sulfur emissions. The need to cut CO_2 emissions would likely create uncertainty surrounding the costs to the industry and undermine the proceeds from privatization. While the government had accepted that climate change was an important issue, it was unwilling to internalize the domestic policy implications of its international commitment to addressing climate change. The government continued to reject the quantitative commitment norm.

Conceding British Leadership on Climate Change

The United Kingdom continued to balk at European climate initiatives. At an EC Environment Council meeting in March 1990, the United Kingdom accepted that the Commission should coordinate the EC negotiating position. The Commission proposed that the EC countries agree to an emissions freeze by 2000 and significant cuts by 2010. The Netherlands, Denmark, and Germany criticized the Commission proposal as too weak. British Environment Minister Patten rejected the emissions targets and called for stricter emissions limits on trucks and the deregulation of the transportation and energy sectors. These were reforms that the British were already pursuing at the EC level. He argued that action on these issues would go a long way toward reducing carbon emissions and would reduce inefficiencies in the EU marketplace. He asserted that the British proposals could reduce carbon emissions by 100 million tons a year and would be more effective than "simplistic political formulas."[20] The Thatcher government was attempting to recast the normative debate. Rather than focusing on quantitative targets, governments should focus on economically efficient policies to reduce GHG emissions. The British government was engaged in a debate over how the response to climate change should be framed. Would symbolic commitments to cut emissions be the benchmark for acceptance as a supporter of climate policy, or would specific policy initiatives be required? The government was loathe to accept quantitative emission reduction commitments when it was not clear how such targets could be achieved or how much it would cost to meet the commitments.

A series of climate conferences in 1990 heightened international pressure to act. In particular, the impending release of the IPCC report created pressure to accept a commitment to reduce GHG emissions. Britain had consistently argued that it would act when the IPCC had finished its work. Rather than attempt to undermine the IPCC's findings, the United Kingdom again sought to take the offensive on climate policy. The Prime Minister announced that the United Kingdom would conditionally accept a quantitative commitment. "Provided others are ready to take their full share, Britain is prepared to set itself the demanding target of a reduction of up to 30 percent in presently projected levels of carbon dioxide emissions by the year 2005. This would mean returning emissions to their 1990 levels by that date."[21] This was five years later than the other European countries had agreed and would only occur if other countries (presumably the United States) acted as well. The United Kingdom finally gave in to pressure to affirm the international norm requiring a quantitative emission reduction commitment, though it rejected the specific target date.

The advantage of 2005 for the British government was that most of the actions necessary to bring the United Kingdom in line with the EC's Large Combustion Plant Directive (LCPD) would take place between 1990 and 2003 with the majority occurring after 1998. Though directed at SO_2 and NO_x emissions, the LCPD created incentives for British electricity generators to switch from coal to natural gas for power generation to avoid expensive retrofitting of existing plants with flue gas desulfurization equipment. Natural gas plants were also cheaper to build and run. As older coal burning plants closed, and newer, cleaner natural gas plants came on line, British emissions of CO_2 would naturally fall. An earlier target would have required a renegotiation of the Environmental Protection Act of 1990.

Though the British policy shift appeared to be well considered on the economic side, it engendered a great deal of opposition from domestic environmentalists and other EC states who argued that the British were moving too slowly. The United Kingdom's new commitment to stabilize CO_2 emissions by the year 2005 clashed with the broader EC commitments. The EC Environment Council met in September 1990 to finalize a proposal to stabilize emissions by the year 2000. Prior to the meeting, Junior Environment Minister Trippier called attempts to act by the year 2000 "ludicrous" and said that Britain would not budge from its target.[22] An EC Commission study bolstered British opposition to the early date. The report asserted that a carbon tax would be necessary to achieve the desired level of CO_2 emission reductions. The study also concluded that the carbon tax would likely raise British fuel prices by as much as 300 percent.[23] In October the Thatcher government relented, and the Environment and Energy Councils jointly declared that the EC as a whole would stabilize CO_2 emissions at 1990 levels by the year 2000. However, the declaration acknowledged that not all member countries were willing to meet that target, thus noting the British rejection of 2000.

Conclusions from the British Case

The Thatcher government framed climate change as a human-induced problem, and it promoted the negotiation of an international agreement to address the threat. The British public was broadly supportive of international action, and growing public interest made climate change a significant political issue. The government integrated support for an international agreement into its foreign policy and it sought to aggressively shape the international norms to minimize its domestic adjustment costs. The foreign policy position allowed the government to deflect criticism of its environmental policies, but it became increasingly untenable as momentum grew for concrete action. As an international norm requiring quantitative CO_2 emission reduction commitments emerged, the Thatcher government stepped back and aligned itself more closely with the United States. In finally adopting a specific target for CO_2 emission reductions, the government embraced a target that would likely be met as a result of policies already in place to achieve other objectives. The British government also effectively stymied EC attempts to capture climate policy and successfully maintained the climate negotiations in a multilateral setting where the United Kingdom would not be isolated and where the United States would thwart costly initiatives. The Thatcher government was thus willing to affirm the emergent norm, but it refused to incorporate the behavioral imperatives into domestic policy.

While it appears that British leaders were persuaded that climate change was an issue that should be addressed internationally, the government was not acting out of an immediate commitment to alleviate the threat. Rather, it seemed to respond to the coercive pressure of international censure and domestic public opinion. Domestic political requirements and international economic imperatives drove British climate policy during this initial stage, but the emerging international norm requiring domestic emission reduction targets constrained British climate policy. The Thatcher government utilized climate policy as a tool to improve its electoral position on environmental issues and as a justification for its broader policy goals, such as expansion of nuclear energy and its EC reform initiatives. However, it was unwilling to pursue a policy that could harm its competitive position in the world economy. British climate commitments were dictated by the ability of existing measures to reduce CO_2 emissions. The government supported the American attempts to slow the international process to assure that the international response did not proceed more quickly than domestic constraints would allow.

On the scale of norm salience discussed in chapter 1, the norm requiring the acceptance of a quantitative emission reduction commitment had a foreign policy impact during this period. The government and the public were persuaded that climate change was a serious problem requiring international action. Facing significant political pressure, the government altered its foreign policy position to accept a quantitative emission reduction commitment. However, this international norm was not yet of sufficient salience to translate into significant changes in domestic policy. The salience of the international norm was heavily conditioned by the domestic economic implications of reducing CO_2 emissions.

INITIAL CLIMATE DEBATES IN THE UNITED STATES

By the mid-1980s, climate change had not yet been framed as an issue for political debate in the United States. International forces provided the impetus for the first articulation of an American position on climate change. In 1987, UNEP Executive Director Tolba sent a letter to Secretary of State George Schultz proposing that the United States initiate an international process to address climate change, which launched an internal conflict over how to frame the issue. The Commerce and Energy departments in particular emphasized that climate policy could not be addressed merely as an environmental issue.[24] Commitments to reduce GHG emissions had the potential to adversely affect the American economy. The early and active involvement of the Commerce and Energy departments created an immediate check on more activist sentiments within the State Department and the EPA, which was largely absent in the early policy debates in Germany and the United Kingdom. The product of the administration's deliberation was the promotion of an intergovernmental scientific review of climate change, which eventually became the IPCC. For opponents of initiatives to address climate change, the proposal was a delaying tactic designed to provide the appearance of American leadership, which would allow the United States to shape the evolution of the international debate. The supporters of a more active policy accepted the delaying tactic, but they recognized that the IPCC process would force a reevaluation of American climate policy in the future.[25]

As the administration began to articulate a position on climate change, the issue had not captured the attention of the American public; thus, domestic pressure to act was limited. However, public awareness increased rapidly during the 1980s. A number of policy entrepreneurs seized upon climate change as a potentially useful issue—particularly in Congress. Senator John Chafee called hearings in 1986 on the potential effects of climate change. Ongoing negotiations regarding ozone depletion and its predicted effects on the health of the American people generated additional interest in the relationship between human activity and the atmosphere. In addition, a harsh drought in the upper Midwest and Canada combined with record high temperatures throughout the summer of 1988 combined to raise the public profile of climate change. In hearings before the Senate Energy Committee, Dr. James Hansen of NASA dramatically announced that he was 99 percent certain that the current warming trend was due to global warming and was not a mere chance occurrence.[26] Dr. Hansen's testimony was broadly debated in the scientific community, with most scientists arguing that there was insufficient evidence to conclude that the heat wave was a result of climate change. However, the testimony, combined with heat waves, droughts, and a dramatic fire in Yellowstone National Park, raised the media attention accorded to the problem.

In response to the growing interest, the Reagan administration advocated the continued study of climate change, but it consistently rejected calls for a policy response as premature. During fiscal year 1988, the United States spent almost $200 million on climate activities, and President Reagan's proposed fiscal 1989 budget included $232 million for climate research.[27] This increase was proposed, even as the overall EPA budget was being reduced by $600 million or 11 percent of its 1988 funding.[28] The administration's views on climate change were spelled out by Acting Assistant Secretary of State, Richard J. Smith, in testimony before a House committee in 1988. He asserted that it would be "premature" to seek an international convention on climate change. "We believe it is time for governments to take a hard look at what we know and what we need to know about climate change and its potential for impacts in order to provide governments with a sound consensus of scientific evidence from which policy options can be developed."[29] The administration developed a "wait and see" attitude toward climate policy. If scientific evidence eventually demonstrated that climate change was a significant danger to the United States, then the government would initiate appropriate responses. The Reagan administration framed climate change as a scientifically uncertain problem that required additional study. It portrayed policy initiatives to reduce GHG emissions as excessively costly and scientifically unjustified in the short term. Advocates of immediate action faced an uphill battle to reframe the issue in the American political debate.

The United States launched its diplomatic strategy to avert international action on climate change at the 1988 organizational meeting of the Intergovernmental Panel on Climate Change (IPCC). Frederick Bernthal, the head of the American delegation, articulated the American position. "We do not know yet whether or when a substantial increase in greenhouse gases will lead to an irreversible warming of the earth or what the consequences of such an increase might be. . . . But the potential consequences of such a warming are so great that we cannot ignore the possibility."[30] This would be a constant refrain of American climate policy until the IPCC released its first report in 1990. The science was uncertain, and thus further study was necessary before policy actions would be justified. The priority that the United States placed on shaping the international response to climate change was apparent at the IPCC organizational meeting. As the heads of the various working groups were assigned, the administration pursued the chairmanship of the policy response group rather than the more prestigious science group. This was consistent with the importance placed on shaping the international debate on the appropriate response to climate change to avoid costly domestic policy changes.

The Bush Administration and Growing International Pressure

The growing public interest in climate change inserted the issue into the 1988 presidential election. Republican presidential candidate George Herbert Walker Bush split with the Reagan administration on climate change. He declared in a September 1988 speech in Boston that "those who think we're powerless to do anything about the greenhouse effect are forgetting about the White House effect. As President, I intend to do something about it."[31] Candidate Bush's rhetoric gave renewed hope to those advocating stronger international action.

The inauguration of George H. W. Bush in 1989 appeared to bode well for a shift in American climate policy. Secretary of State James Baker chose the meeting of the US-led IPCC working group on policy responses as the venue to make his first formal appearance as secretary of state. Echoing the Reagan administration's position on climate change, Baker said that scientists must still "refine the state of our knowledge," but he went on to say that "we can probably not afford to wait until all of the uncertainties have been resolved before we do act."[32] He particularly emphasized the pursuit of "no-regrets" policy measures that could be justified on other grounds such as energy efficiency or reduction in ozone depleting chemicals. However, the apparent shift in tone did not represent a change in policy. The United States proposed a time-consuming process of data collection while avoiding concrete policies to reduce GHG emissions.

The IPCC address was the only major speech Secretary Baker would make on climate policy. He was persuaded that climate change was a major threat to US interests, and during the campaign he had been a staunch advocate of an international response. However, following the speech, he recused himself from further involvement based on a potential conflict of interest related to his prior work in the oil industry. Baker's recusal was broadly perceived to be a response to Chief of Staff John Sununu's skepticism of climate science and his vehement opposition to actions to reduce GHG emissions.[33] It is interesting to consider whether American climate policy would have been significantly different without Sununu's influence. Sununu and a number of presidential advisors gave voice to important economic actors that would have been adversely affected by efforts to reduce domestic GHG emissions. It is likely that the American international rhetorical position would have been more positive with Secretary Baker leading the climate initiative, but domestic action would have continued to be extremely difficult to initiate.

The rising level of international and domestic political attention paid to climate change created increased tension within the Bush White House. In March 1989, a draft of the EPA's report, "Policy Options for Stabilizing Global Climate" was leaked to the press.[34] The report contained the first specific policy recommendations to address climate change, including a steep rise in automobile fuel efficiency, more energy efficient homes, and fees on the use of coal and natural gas. The policies proposed in the report added to the ongoing debate within the administration over the proper response to climate change, but the administration continued to argue that that there was no international consensus on the appropriate response to climate change and that additional research would be essential to justify expensive domestic actions.

The American position that climate science did not yet justify international action was an increasingly untenable position in international negotiations and was becoming divisive within the administration. A May 1989 dispute over the testimony of NASA scientist James Hansen provided insight into the growing conflict within the Bush administration. Following Hansen's testimony before a Senate committee, it was revealed that the Office of Management and Budget had changed his testimony to make the prospects of climate change appear more uncertain.[35] The revelation of OMB altering a scientist's testimony created a public outcry. In the midst of the controversy, US representatives were attending a climate change meeting in Geneva where the United States continued to argue that existing climate science did not justify the negotiation of a climate treaty. The Bush administration's position changed significantly following the dispute over Hansen's testimony. Sununu sent a telegram to the American delegation in Geneva instructing them to press for a global warming workshop to be held in Washington in the fall. The workshop was intended to provide a foundation for a "full international consensus on necessary steps to prepare for a formal treaty negotiating process."[36] The administration's shift in position followed intense criticism from Congress and environmental groups. In particular criticism from prominent Republican Senator John Chafee created a significant level of pressure on the president. EPA Administrator William Reilly denied that the administration had shifted its position due to political pressure. Rather, he argued that the "issue had ripened" and that the time to move forward was at hand.[37] Reilly stressed that the administration was committed to beginning negotiations on a framework convention, but it was unwilling to endorse specific elements of a convention at that time. However, privately, the White House acknowledged that the overwhelming criticism emanating from Congress and the public at large forced the administration to act.[38]

As international momentum for a climate convention began to build, the Bush administration found it increasingly difficult to thwart international attempts to launch negotiations. At a May 1989 UNEP meeting in Nairobi, the United Kingdom proposed the negotiation of a framework convention on climate change, and Germany along with Canada and several European countries argued that negotiations should begin immediately. The United States, with support from Japan, Australia, New Zealand, and a number of developing countries, argued that negotiations should wait until after the IPCC produced its final report in 1990. The United States would continue to use the IPCC to delay concrete measures to address climate change. The repeated affirmation of the role of the IPCC gradually established it as the primary source of policy relevant science for the negotiations.

In an attempt to deflect the growing pressure, the United States sought to recast the international environmental agenda. Leading up to the July 1989 Paris G–7 summit, the Bush administration advertised the fact that it would be pushing a broad agenda of environmental issues at the meeting, which included a redeployment of international development agency spending to address environmental issues, the possibility of debt-for-nature swaps, and tropical forest preservation. In the area of climate change, the administration negotiated a final statement that called for the establishment of an "umbrella convention" to set out general principles for protecting the atmosphere.

It also affirmed the need to limit the emissions of carbon dioxide and other greenhouse gases, but the United States avoided specific commitments in the final communiqué.

The November 1989 Noordwijk Conference on Global Climate Change provided a test of American openness to a climate convention. The conference, hosted by the Dutch and the United Nations, was structured as a stepping-stone toward the negotiation of a climate convention. The United States faced significant pressure to accept a goal of freezing CO_2 emissions at their existing levels by the year 2000. Prior to the conference, EPA administrator Reilly, with the support of the State Department, had recommended that the United States agree to the stabilization of CO_2 emissions at their existing levels at some point in the future. However, the White House Policy Council overruled Reilly with strong opposition from Sununu and OMB.[39]

The goal of stabilizing CO_2 emissions was broadly accepted at Noordwijk with only the United States, Japan, and the Soviet Union actively opposing it, and Britain was balanced between the European and American positions. The United States, along with Britain and Japan, argued that Noordwijk was not the appropriate forum for negotiations on climate change. The American delegation suggested that the United States might eventually agree to a stabilization goal, but "[w]e would like to have a better understanding of the economic consequences."[40] The United States was one of the few countries raising concerns about the potential costs of climate policy. The American delegation rejected the proposed goal, but it did accept a statement calling for the completion of a climate change convention no later than the 1992 Rio Conference. The remaining states attending the conference committed themselves to a nonbinding goal of stabilizing emissions by the year 2000, though the level at which they should be stabilized was left undefined.

The increasing international pressure for the United States to fall in line and affirm the norm of freezing CO_2 emissions created a growing split within the administration. In February 1990, the IPCC was to meet in Washington, DC, and President Bush was scheduled to speak to the meeting. Just prior to the meeting, White House Chief of Staff John Sununu laid out the views of one part of the administration in a television interview. He asserted that "faceless bureaucrats on the environmental side" were advocating policies that would cut off the use of coal, oil, and natural gas.[41] Sununu continued to rail against what he and many other conservative Republicans saw as the exaggerated claims of environmentalists bent upon slowing economic growth. On the other side, Secretary of State James Baker, Energy Secretary James Watkins, and EPA Administrator William Reilly argued that President Bush should use the opportunity of the IPCC meeting to seize a leadership role in climate policy.[42]

President Bush chose an intermediate course. He acknowledged that "human activities are changing the atmosphere in unexpected and unprecedented ways."[43] This represented a shift in American rhetoric. Up to that point, the administration had consistently emphasized the uncertainty involved in climate science. He also renewed his commitment and argued that research was essential to reduce uncertainty, develop hard data, create accurate models, and find new ways to address the challenges posed by climate change. He called for an "international bargain, a convergence between global environmental policy and global economic policy, where both perspectives benefit and neither is compromised. . . . Wherever possible, we believe that market mechanisms should be applied and that our policies must be consistent with economic growth and free-market principles in all countries."[44] The president also pointedly avoided endorsing any limits on GHG emissions.

A Council of Economic Advisor's Report in February substantiated many of the administration's claims regarding the costs of climate policy. The report predicted that a 20 percent cut in American emissions would cost between $800 billion and 3.6 trillion.[45] The lack of enthusiasm for the policies necessary to reduce GHG emissions was apparent in a number of policy actions in the weeks leading up to the IPCC meeting. The administration sought to weaken provisions in the 1990 Clean Air Act Amendments. It rejected measures that would have imposed a forty mile per gallon fuel efficiency standard for automobiles. Given that the average fuel efficiency for American cars was eighteen miles per gallon, such a standard would have provided a significant stimulus toward reductions in carbon emissions. The administration also proposed cutting funding for the Department of Energy's energy efficiency programs by almost 50 percent. The only policy proposal to reduce atmospheric GHGs was a plan to plant a billion trees a year.[46] The administration had shifted its rhetoric to support the eventual negotiation of a framework convention, but it rejected domestic policies to reduce GHG emissions.

In April 1990, the Bush administration sought to reframe the terms of the climate debate. The White House sponsored the Conference on Science and Economic Research Related to Global Change. The conference was intended to refocus the climate debate onto the uncertain costs of addressing climate change. The conference was a fiasco for the administration. The European delegates complained that the United States was using the conference to push through its point of view while limiting the participation of others. The conference agenda called for only one non-American to speak.[47] Many of the representatives expressed the opinion that the United States used its conference to preempt a conference proposed by several Northern European countries. The American meeting, they argued, was intended to give the impression of action without producing any substantive progress. President Bush's address to the group did nothing to dispel these concerns.

He focused again on the need to undertake additional research before specific policies could be agreed.

German Environment Minister Klaus Toepfer assailed the American position. "Worldwide action against the climatic threat is urgently required, even if the complicated scientific interrelationships of climatic change have not been fully understood. . . . Gaps in knowledge must not be used as an excuse for worldwide inaction."[48] President Bush in his closing remarks to the conference responded to the storm of protest.

> We have never considered research a substitute for action. . . . To those who suggest that we're only trying to balance economic growth and environmental protection, I say they miss the point. We are calling for an entirely new way of thinking, to achieve both while compromising neither, by applying the power of the marketplace in the service of the environment.[49]

The administration's problems at the conference persisted with the leaking to reporters of a document containing the administration's conference "talking points." The document listed several points under the heading "debates to avoid." One of the points noted that it was "not beneficial to discuss whether there is or is not [global warming]. . . . In the eyes of the public we will lose this debate. A better approach is to raise the many uncertainties that need to be better understood on this issue."[50] In the eyes of European governments and environmentalists, the document confirmed the view that the administration was committed to delaying and obstructing progress on an international climate treaty.

The pressure on the American position continued unabated, but the administration was also on the offensive. In May 1990, the IPCC working groups completed their draft reports. The United States successfully managed the work of its group on response strategies to limit proposals for concrete policy responses. The report merely listed the kinds of responses that were possible without any discussion of costs or recommendations for action. The only policy prescription in the report was a call for states to undertake policies to reduce CO_2 emissions that are "already economically and socially justified in their own right and which also provide benefits from a climate change standpoint."[51] The report also called for an international treaty to address global warming but with no obligations for specific actions. The Response Strategies report was at odds with the other reports in emphasizing the uncertainty of climate science. The other two reports presented a consensus that significant climate change would occur.

The US obstructionist policy on climate change continued at the IPCC meeting in Sundsvall, Sweden that was to approve the IPCC's report. The United States, often with the support of OPEC countries and the Soviet

Union, attempted to weaken the final report. The American delegation sought to insert language claiming that the forecasts of global warming were still highly uncertain. The initiative failed, but the United States was successful in weakening other sections of the report. At one point, the United States inserted language stating that the information available for policy analysis was inadequate. The United States was also able to maintain the response strategies report as an inventory of possible policy responses without advocating any concrete measures.[52]

Following the release of the IPCC report, the United States attempted to limit any mandatory actions on climate change. In an October speech to the Press Club, EPA Administrator Reilly responded to criticisms that the United States was the only major industrial country to not have a plan to reduce CO_2 emissions. He chided reporters and suggested that "[t]he next time you feel the urge to write about climate change, you might consider the question: 'How many other countries can point to real action on this issue— and back it up? . . . How many others have laid before the public the details—if these even exist—of how they plan to cut greenhouse gas emissions while maintaining economic growth?" He then went on to defend the Bush administration's position on global warming. "And while others talk about ambitious—and perhaps unattainable—carbon dioxide emissions reductions in the future, the United States has been spending hundreds of millions of dollars a year—growing to more than $1 billion in the coming fiscal year— to learn more about the scope, causes, effects, and responses to the problem." Finally, reviving the Bush administration's skeptical tone regarding climate change, he suggested that the United States was taking some policy actions that will "yield benefits should climate change prove to be, as some have suggested, a problem of serious consequence."[53]

The United States continued its attempts to reframe the climate debate at the Second World Climate Conference in Geneva, Switzerland. The American delegation once again emphasized the need to undertake a cost-benefit analysis before undertaking new climate initiatives. Richard Schmalensee of the President's Council of Economic Advisors argued that "[l]ittle is known about the economic and other costs of changing the rates of emissions and changing the rate of global climate change." He argued that CO_2 forecasts were "flaky" because they were based on assumptions about technology, population, and emissions over "extraordinary time horizons."[54] The American delegation brought thirty pages of amendments to the statement that was being prepared at the conference. Among the amendments was the deletion of a statement declaring that the "ultimate global objective should be to stabilize and reduce greenhouse gas concentrations," as well as the replacement of a statement calling for the stabilization of greenhouse gases by industrialized countries by the year 2000.[55] The United

States again was assailed for its obstruction of international efforts to deal with climate change. The United Kingdom had recently accepted a goal of stabilizing greenhouse gas emissions by the year 2005, which further affirmed the norm of states accepting binding emission reduction commitments. Nevertheless, the US position prevailed in the conference statement. The final declaration urged governments to set targets, national programs or strategies to reduce GHGs, but there were no firm commitments or timelines.

The climate conference represented the last major international meeting before the climate negotiations began in Washington, DC in February 1991. The administration had achieved some success in reframing the international debate to include economic as well as environmental considerations. It was also aggressively promoting an international norm that would require any international response to be cost effective and rely on market mechanisms to achieve emission reductions rather than adopting "arbitrary" emission reduction commitments.

Conclusions from the American Case

The United States was the most intransigent of the three countries in its response to climate change. American climate policy developed under different domestic conditions than German or British policy. First, there was no political consensus that an immediate domestic policy response was necessary. In Germany, the Enquete Commission would create a consensus among the political leadership and the public that climate change was a significant threat that had to be addressed (see next section). There was no similar political consensus in the American debate. The administration was divided with the skeptics holding the most influence, and the public was largely apathetic. The relationship between science and policy in the United States is extremely open and competitive. Scientific ideas, no matter how marginal, compete for attention in the policy process. The existence of numerous private centers of scientific research also leads to the politicization of science to advance the agendas of interest groups. The result is that environmental research is well funded and is typically at the cutting edge, but interest groups are also able to utilize research supporting their positions to bolster their lobbying efforts.[56] The open competition of scientific claims makes it difficult to achieve a consensus for political action. In this case, industrial interests sponsored research that raised questions about the science of climate change and thus undermined the consensus to act. The Reagan and Bush administrations both used the uncertainty created by the scientific conflicts to justify delays in the negotiating process.

Second, American policy makers from the beginning framed climate change as an issue with significant economic consequences. In Germany and the United Kingdom, the environment ministries took the lead on climate policy. Other ministries became more involved after the initial positions had been formulated. The Commerce and Energy Departments were major actors in formulating the initial American position and continued to be involved throughout the process. Their emphasis on the economic consequences of policies to reduce CO_2 emissions created a significant obstacle to American action.

It is an interesting counterfactual exercise to consider how American policy would have developed under a Democratic administration. American rhetoric might have been much more positive, but the policy content would likely have been very similar. The scientific debates would have been similar and economic interests would have had significant influence in a Democratic administration. The effects of partisan politics will be explored in greater detail in chapter 4. The transition in climate policy from the hostility of the Bush administration to the enthusiastic rhetorical support of the Clinton administration provides an interesting case study in the structural constraints shaping the freedom of the executive branch to pursue policy changes in the American political system.

The United States operated from a position of strength internationally. As the largest producer of GHG emissions, American participation was essential to achieve meaningful emission reductions. Thus, the Reagan and Bush administrations had a veto over most aspects of the international negotiations and successfully used that veto to protect American interests. International institutions and norm entrepreneurs did play a role in raising awareness and concern about climate change in the American political system, but they had a marginal effect on policy. UNEP and the WMO helped to create pressure on the Reagan and Bush administrations to conform to the emerging international norms governing climate policy. The ongoing process of international climate conferences obliged the American government to repeatedly justify its position and block international action, but the overall effect on American policy was marginal. The Bush administration eventually accepted the need for some international response, but it carefully controlled the process to ensure that an international response would have a limited effect on domestic policy.

Though some members of the Bush administration were convinced that climate change was a legitimate threat requiring international action, the administration obstructed efforts to initiate international negotiations until 1990. The administration also continued to reject the norm requiring a domestic GHG emission reduction commitment on the grounds that there was insufficient scientific evidence to justify costly GHG emission reduction policies. The administration used the IPCC scientific review as an excuse to delay international action. However, the repeated affirmation of the IPCC as the primary arbiter of climate science eventually would require the United States to act on its findings. Though much of the administration remained unconvinced of the threat of climate change, it nonetheless accepted the IPCC report as the basis for the negotiation of a climate convention. The administration eventually adjusted its foreign policy rhetoric and dropped its opposition to the negotiation of a convention. However, fundamentally, American policy remained unchanged. The United States would not undertake domestic initiatives to reduce GHG emissions, and it would continue to oppose international efforts to negotiate binding emission reduction targets.

GERMANY

Climate change was a particularly difficult issue for German politicians in the 1980s. The SPD had traditionally been more pro-environment than the CDU/CSU, but climate change split the party among anti-nuclear, environmental, and pro-coal factions. While addressing climate change fit well with the CDU's desire to promote nuclear energy, it also had the potential to adversely affect members of its core business constituency. Prior to 1985, the German government, like its British counterpart, had not undertaken a serious government study of climate change, and public opinion remained focused elsewhere. German climate policy was further complicated by the delegation of environmental responsibilities. The Federal Ministry for the Environment (BMU) was created in 1986, following the Chernobyl accident. Prior to its creation, environmental policy was split among various ministries. Climate policy fell under the purview of the Transport Ministry, which made an aggressive response to climate change unlikely. The splits among the parties and the lack of a ministerial champion allowed climate policy to languish as a political issue.

As climate change emerged in the United States and United Kingdom as a significant political issue, it was largely overshadowed in Germany by the debate over nuclear energy. Following on the heels of the 1986 Chernobyl disaster, the January 1987 elections produced a significant triumph for the Green Party, which received 8.3 percent of the national vote—up from 5.6 percent in the 1983 elections. The Greens, along with the SPD, advocated the dismantling of Germany's nuclear energy program. The SPD also promoted the expanded use of coal as an alternative to nuclear power. These positions ran counter to meaningful action to reduce CO_2 emissions. All of the parties recognized that climate change was becoming a significant international issue, but no party was willing to adopt climate change as a high priority issue. The result was the creation of the Inquiry Commission on

Preventive Measures to Protect the Atmosphere (Enquete Commission) in December 1987.[57] With the void in the political process, the commission stepped in to address the scientific and policy implications of climate change.

The formation of the inquiry commission offers an interesting comparison with the initial framing of the climate debate in the United States and the United Kingdom. The inquiry commission was composed of an equal number of experts and politicians. It was intended to provide an unbiased review of the relevant scientific evidence and nonpartisan policy advice to parliament. In the United States, the Reagan administration asserted that there was insufficient scientific evidence to support policies to address climate change and decided upon a policy of scientific study coupled with a wait and see attitude. Governed by Germany's precautionary principle, the Commission reviewed the existing scientific evidence and decided that there was credible evidence that climate change was occurring and advocated preventative action to address a potentially serious threat. The Commission publicized its first report, "Protecting the Earth's Atmosphere; An International Challenge" in October 1988. The Commission called for a 30 percent CO_2 emission reduction target by 2005 (using a 1987 base year). It also argued that with current state of the art technology, Germany could reduce its CO_2 emissions by 35 to 45 percent.[58]

The lack of political leadership on climate policy created an opening for the Enquete Commission to frame the domestic context for the policy debate. Had either of the major parties taken the initiative, German climate policy might have developed very differently. The Enquete Commission framed the problem of climate change as a serious threat that demanded both an international and a domestic response. However, it was also a problem that could be addressed at minimal economic cost by using existing technologies. The framing of the issue made it more difficult for the government and opponents of GHG emission reductions to effectively argue against taking action.

Germany Seizes International Leadership

The Kohl government's response to climate change had been uninspiring up until mid-1989. The Transportation Ministry, which had responsibility for climate policy, had neglected to send a high level delegation to the IPCC organizational meeting, and thus Germany failed to secure a leadership position within the IPCC. The Kohl government subsequently shifted the responsibility for coordinating climate policy to the Federal Ministry for the Environment, Nature Conservation, and Nuclear Safety (BMU) where it would receive a higher priority.[59] Germany lagged behind the climate initiatives of its EC partners. The Netherlands, France, and Norway spearheaded the Hague

Conference on the Atmosphere in March 1989. The United Kingdom seized the initiative by calling for a framework climate convention early in 1989. The release of the Enquete Commission's report, public criticism of Germany's mediocre climate policy, and the growing strength of the Green Party and environmental issues in German politics created significant incentives for the Kohl government to pursue a more aggressive policy.

The government attempted to seize the initiative on climate policy during the second half of 1989. It pursued an aggressive strategy of promoting climate issues within the EC, UNEP, and the Group of Seven. Leading up to federal elections in 1990, the government utilized climate change to bolster its green credentials by adopting an impressive CO_2 emission reduction target and identifying a series of domestic policies to achieve the target. The Kohl government shared motivations similar to those of the Thatcher government. Climate change provided a valuable opportunity to secure a leadership position on an important international environmental issue and deflect domestic criticism. The electoral system allowed the Green Party to constantly challenge the major parties on environmental issues. Chancellor Kohl had to protect the party's Green flank, and climate change provided a tool to enhance the CDU's environmental image.

The government pursued an aggressive foreign policy response to climate change. At the May 1989 Nairobi UNEP Governing Council meeting, the United Kingdom repeated its call for the negotiation of a framework convention. Germany attempted to steal the initiative from the British and called for negotiations to begin immediately. The proposal placed the United States on the defensive and challenged the United Kingdom's leadership position. American and British opposition forced Germany to settle for a call for negotiations to begin after the IPCC report was released. From this point forward, Germany was at the forefront of efforts to launch the climate negotiations. Germany, along with the Netherlands and France, successfully raised climate change as an EC policy issue and requested that the Commission develop a common EC position. At the June 1989 meeting of the EC Environment Ministers, the Council announced that the member states would seek to act collectively and individually to combat the threat of climate change. This represented the first attempt to coordinate Europe's response to climate change.

The Kohl government argued consistently that climate change was a serious problem, that it had to be addressed at the international level, and that reductions in GHG emissions would be necessary to mitigate its adverse effects. It also became the foremost national champion of the norm requiring states to accept domestic CO_2 emission reduction commitments. In late 1989, Germany pushed at the Noordwijk climate conference for an agreement to freeze CO_2 emissions at 1989 levels by the year 2000. The United States, the USSR, and Japan opposed the German and European proposals; and Germany and its continental European partners were forced to accept a weakened statement noting that "in the view of many industrialized nations . . . stabilization of [CO_2] emissions should be achieved as a first step at the latest by the year 2000."[60] The statement represented growing acceptance of the emission reduction commitment norm.

Germany's international initiatives added to the sense of urgency surrounding climate change, but the United States, Russia, and Japan were not prepared to move as quickly. Germany worked successfully with other EC member states to launch an EC discussion of climate issues, though the United Kingdom attempted to minimize the EC role. Germany had assumed a leadership role, and it emerged as a primary advocate of an aggressive international response to climate change.

German Domestic Commitments

Following the February 1990 IPCC meeting, Germany began to raise the prospect of introducing domestic policies to reduce GHG emissions. At a closed meeting of government representatives to the IPCC meeting, the German delegation presented a report demonstrating that Germany could reduce its emissions of GHGs by 7 percent in twenty years without major changes to its domestic policies. The German estimates included a carbon tax that would raise fossil fuel energy costs by 20 percent by the year 2010. The German government was considering the tax, and it had been raised within the EC as well. However, its passage was not the foregone conclusion that the German CO_2 predictions implied it to be. These German estimates should be contrasted with a concurrent British estimate of an increase of 38 percent in CO_2 emissions and Japanese estimates of an increase of 23 to 44 percent.[61]

Germany's ability to significantly cut its CO_2 emissions was given a boost with reunification. The electricity industry released a report in 1990 on the costs of reducing emissions from electricity generation. The report noted that Germany could reduce its CO_2 emissions from energy production by 12 percent by 2005 and 20 percent by 2014 with existing technologies. In addition the report said that East German CO_2 emissions from lignite fired power plants could be reduced by 30 percent at a cost of approximately 60 billion deutsche marks (DM). Power plant efficiency in the East was two-thirds lower than in the West.[62] The ease with which Germany could apparently cut its CO_2 emissions minimized the opposition from industrial interests and emboldened Germany's foreign policy position. Tough international targets would appear to require little domestic policy reform, but they could force other states to undertake potentially expensive policy changes.

The German government's activity on climate change also included a renewed emphasis on research and development of alternative energies. In February 1990, the cabinet released its "Third Energy Research Program."

The program focused largely on renewable energy sources and energy efficiency research. Nuclear energy made up the bulk of the renewables research, but wind and solar energy also received increased funding. Climate change had become much more integrated into the German political agenda than in either the British or American cases. The Enquete Commission's conclusions that climate change was a serious threat and that domestic policies could sharply reduce GHG emissions at little additional cost marginalized arguments that the costs of GHG reductions were prohibitive.

Germany continued to press the United States on climate change. At the April 1990 Washington conference on global warming, Germany's Environment Minister, Klaus Toepfer, chastised President Bush for his cautious approach to climate change. He challenged the American position noting that "[g]aps in knowledge must not be used as an excuse for worldwide inaction."[63] During the conference, Toepfer announced that Germany fully supported the conclusion of a world climate convention for signature at the Rio Conference in 1992. He also suggested that a CO_2 emission reduction protocol should also be agreed at that time. The German position reflected the influence of the precautionary principle. Once the public and government accepted that an environmental threat might exist, the government was obliged to act, rather than wait for scientific confirmation. Such an approach contrasted with the British and American approaches that typically looked for significant scientific proof of a threat before deciding upon a policy response.

Following the conference, Toepfer announced that the cabinet would act in June 1990 on a plan to reduce Germany's CO_2 emissions by at least 25 percent by the year 2005. Toepfer argued that "ecological necessities" must take precedence over long-term economic development. Toepfer's willingness to concede that CO_2 reductions could be expensive and that they were still necessary sharply contrasted with the American position that only "no-regrets" policies were justified given the existing state of scientific knowledge.[64] In June 1990, the cabinet backed up its rhetoric on climate change with the announcement that Germany would reduce its CO_2 emissions by 25 percent relative to 1987 levels by the year 2005. The cabinet had been engaged in an extended debate over the workability and desirability of a firm commitment to reduce CO_2 emissions. Minister of Trade and Commerce, Helmut Haussman, championed the German business interests and argued that any unilateral commitment would put German industry at a competitive disadvantage. He argued that a common international agreement was crucial to protecting German industry.[65] With one eye to the upcoming elections, Chancellor Kohl sided with the environmental interests in the cabinet and approved of the commitment. The cabinet announcement lacked any specific policy information, but it included the creation of an interministerial working group to formulate proposals to meet the target. German officials emphasized that the 25 percent reduction would occur in West Germany alone, which excluded the huge reductions that would accompany reunification with the East. This was the first of a number of skirmishes in the cabinet over the nature of the German CO_2 emission reduction commitment.

German pressure on climate change was again an issue at the July 1990 Houston G–7 Summit. Prior to the summit, German Chancellor Kohl sent a letter to the other heads of state calling on them to join in a stronger response to environmental threats. He called for "internationally binding regulations with radical measures to limit" greenhouse gas emissions.[66] At the summit, Chancellor Kohl proposed language in the final communiqué calling for mandatory reductions in CO_2 emissions to be agreed in time for the Rio Conference, but President Bush again blocked the German initiative. Kohl emphasized the need for a precautionary approach to climate change in the proposed communiqué language. "Industrialized countries . . . have an obligation to be leaders. In the face of threats of serious or irreversible environmental damage, lack of full scientific certainty should not be used as an excuse to postpone action."[67] The Bush administration held firm in its opposition, and the final communiqué reflected the American position. The communiqué stated that "[w]e strongly advocate common efforts to limit emissions of carbon dioxide and other greenhouse gases, which threaten to induce climate change, endangering the environment and ultimately the economy."[68]

Germany took its climate policy to the EC in the fall of 1990 and sought to secure an EC commitment to stabilize CO_2 emissions at 1990 levels by the year 2000 and a 25 percent reduction "target" by 2005. However, the United Kingdom and southern member states blocked the German initiative at the September 1990 meeting of Council officials. Instead, a joint energy and environment working group was created to negotiate an agreement to put before the joint Environment and Energy Council meeting in October. The German delegation refused to allow the October meeting to break up without an agreement to stabilize emissions at their existing levels. In a compromise developed by German Environment Minister Toepfer, the declaration noted that not all countries were prepared to meet the 2000 goal, but that the EC as a whole would meet it jointly.[69] The declaration was part of a European strategy to create pressure on the United States prior to the Second World Climate Conference in Geneva, which would be the final international climate event before negotiations on a climate convention began in February 1991.

Just prior to the Geneva Conference, Germany took the additional step of adopting a national CO_2 reduction program. The Kohl government announced that it had adopted a resolution containing sixty measures to reduce CO_2 emissions. The measures included promoting combined heat and power generation, energy efficiency, improved coal combustion technology, renewable energy development, a carbon tax, and increased vehicle efficiency. Environment Minster Klaus Toepfer announced that "with this decision, we have clearly supported the leading position in the climate discussion worldwide."[70] The program was ambitious, but the measures were largely commitments to future action, and there was almost no discussion of reducing the country's reliance on coal for energy, which would have offered significant opportunities for reducing CO_2 emissions.

The climate program was shrewdly aimed at the domestic environmental vote going into the 1990 election, but it had the added advantage of providing legitimacy to Germany's international negotiating position. The Greens had included climate change as a prominent element of their election platform. By promising action on climate change and producing a set of policy proposals, the Kohl government co-opted one of the Greens' primary issues. The difficult economic and social problems created by reunification had reduced the importance of climate change to the electorate, but the government left little room for challenges to its green credentials. It effectively focused the elections on reunification and simultaneously undermined Green support by stealing their primary issue. The West German Greens polled less than the 5 percent necessary to be seated in Parliament.[71]

At the Geneva Conference, Germany and its continental partners took the lead in advocating specific cuts in CO_2 emissions, and again the United States prevailed in blocking the European attempts. The final document adopted by the conference included only a plea for individual countries to pursue CO_2 reductions. The Kohl government had failed to generate an American commitment to reducing GHG emissions. However, it had secured a leadership position on climate change both within the EC and internationally. It had also successfully capitalized on the issue to improve its domestic green credentials and undermine political support for the Greens.

Conclusions from the German Case

The Kohl government quickly became an essential international catalyst in the climate debate. It pressed the EC to act and created momentum toward international negotiations. German policy was initially driven almost exclusively by domestic political variables. The German electoral system created a fertile ground for environmental issues to assume political salience. The 1990 elections and the Greens' focus on climate policy compelled the Kohl administration to address the issue. The emphasis on the precautionary principal and public support for environmental issues also obligated the government to act. The Kohl government had the additional advantage of facing limited costs to its early climate policies. The international focus allowed the government to be very aggressive and forced other countries to block the proposals. There was little chance that any short-term GHG emissions reduction commitments would be achieved, and even if such an agreement was possible, Germany was well placed to cut its emissions following reunification.

Unlike the American or British cases, scientists, policy experts, and norm entrepreneurs played a significant role in shaping the German climate debate through the Enquete Commission. The Commission's nonpartisan consensus on the serious nature of the problem, combined with the assertions that climate policy would not entail significant costs, made it difficult to argue that action should be delayed or to oppose emission reduction commitments on economic grounds. Once the Enquete Commission had framed the climate debate it would have been difficult to alter the terms of debate. Climate change was a significant issue that the government had to address. The policy debate was thus over the content of the response, as opposed to whether the government should act.

It is difficult to judge the underlying strength of the Kohl government's commitment to climate policy. It took no significant unilateral actions to reduce CO_2 emissions during this period. It did set an ambitious emissions reduction target and committed itself to reasonably specific policy proposals prior to the December 1990 elections. The government had demonstrated an ability to act quickly to implement environmental policies in the past. During the five years between 1983 and 1988, Germany completed a larger program of flue gas desulphurization retrofitting than the United Kingdom was able/willing to commit to over a fifteen year period. Thus, Germany had the capacity to pursue aggressive environmental policies, but the Kohl government had not yet demonstrated a willingness to act domestically to reduce CO_2 emissions. The strength of the Kohl government's resolve and the domestic salience of the norm requiring emission reduction commitments would be tested during the INC negotiations, when dilemmas created by the costs of climate policy and an economic downturn would force a reevaluation of Germany's domestic commitments.

CONCLUSION

The links between international and domestic climate policy were not fully developed during this first period so there is limited capacity to examine these connections. The focus in this period was primarily on international issue definition, agenda setting, and the development of initial foreign policy positions. The primary catalyst for the formulation of domestic responses to climate change emerged on the international level. The international scientific community, IGOs, and NGOs framed the early climate debate and played important roles in persuading governments and mobilizing domestic constituencies to recognize the threat posed by climate change. They framed climate change as a major human-induced environmental problem that required multilateral action to address it. The regular cycle of UNEP and WMO meetings forced governments to establish national positions on the problem, which enhanced the political salience of climate change both internationally and domestically.

The subsequent domestic framing of the issue critically shaped the initial national responses. Governments initially responded to international persuasion in accepting climate change as a political problem. However, domestic political concerns largely dictated national responses. In particular, economic competitiveness concerns placed limits on how far each state was willing to go to address climate change. However, an exclusive focus on material interests does not fully explain the evolution of international climate norms or the effects they had on national policies. This period illustrates the important interactions between international and domestic forces in framing international environmental problems. International institutions facilitated a socialization process that built momentum toward international negotiations to mitigate the threat of climate change. At first glance, this approach might appear to be an obvious response. However, the United States initially disputed the threat posed by climate change and rejected international negotiations, and American opposition stalled the international process until domestic political pressure forced the administration to affirm the need for an international response. The international framing of the problem provided a tool for domestic advocates to influence the Bush administration. Faced with rising domestic political pressure to address climate change, acceptance of international negotiations was the easiest way to relieve the pressure. Once it accepted that the problem required international cooperation, it was then committed to negotiate an international agreement, and it would have been politically costly to go back on that commitment.

Once it was agreed that a multilateral response was necessary, the norm requiring states to accept domestic emission reduction commitments emerged as the most important nascent norm during this period. The origins of the norm were in the work of NGOs and scientists. However, it was primarily Germany and its EC partners that placed the issue on the international agenda. Any international commitment that could gain sufficient international support would be easily achievable through reductions in former East German emissions. It is thus difficult to gauge whether the German proposal reflected true commitment to action, or whether it was primarily an opportunity to reap significant political benefits by establishing a progressive international position.

Regardless of the reasons for action, German support for the norm established a benchmark against which support for climate policy would be judged. The British and Americans attempted to recast the debate by focusing on economic efficiency and specific policy commitments to reduce GHG emissions as opposed to "arbitrary quantitative commitments." However, quantitative commitments offered a clear indicator of support for addressing climate change, and NGOs used them effectively to shame states that rejected such commitments. Over time, the vast majority of developed states accepted a commitment, though the sincerity of the commitments was suspect. Most states made few meaningful domestic policy changes to reduce their emissions. Even the United Kingdom eventually accepted the norm, though only when it became apparent that it was achievable with existing policies. The United States, however, refused to accept this norm. The international power position of the United States and the lower domestic political salience of climate change provided American leaders with the latitude to withstand international pressure and avoid what they regarded as an economically devastating international commitment.

This period offers a number of insights into the early emergence of international norms and their translation into domestic political debates. First, the focus on norms and their effects on state interests and behavior must not overlook the importance of material interests. Material considerations established limits upon the range of viable policy options. None of the states were willing to undertake policy commitments that would entail significant competitive effects. Material interests constrained the range of acceptable policies, but within that range norms play a prominent role in shaping state strategies. Second, domestic institutions, norms, and the political environment were critical intervening variables influencing domestic norm salience. Germany's emphasis on the precautionary principle, its electoral system that created openings for the Greens, and the ability of the Enquete Commission to provide a scientific consensus for action created a fertile ground for supporters of efforts to address climate change. On the other hand, the fragmented American political system, the lack of scientific consensus, and the strong influence of economic interests created numerous obstacles to action in the American case.

Third, the country studies suggest that persuasion was not the primary mechanism inducing norm affirmation. States may rhetorically affirm a norm. They may agree to the institutionalization of the norm in an international agreement. However, if state commitments do not reflect persuasion that a norm is appropriate and just, compliance is unlikely—unless there are significant penalties for noncompliance. The commitment by developed countries to achieve specific emission reduction targets appears to provide a good example of the effects of coerced acceptance on norm compliance.

Many states affirmed the norm because rejecting it would produce significant domestic and international political costs. However, the norm did not achieve significant domestic salience. Most states affirmed it rhetorically, but they did little to reduce their emissions. In this case the overwhelming focus on establishing a norm, requiring a commitment to quantitative emission reductions, distracted attention from the problems associated with meeting those targets. This problem would continue to bedevil international climate negotiations. The headline normative debates masked the complexity of implementation. Norm affirmation under political pressure did not ensure compliance because there were insufficient incentives to force compliance.

By the end of the period, the emission reduction commitment norm had achieved a foreign policy impact (level five on the index of salience) in both Germany and the United Kingdom. In the German case the norm was on the verge of achieving a domestic policy impact (level six) as the government began to consider domestic policy changes to meet the norm's requirements. In the British case, the government affirmed the norm, but it was not actively pursuing the domestic emission reductions that the norm required. In the United States, the norm had achieved domestic relevance (level three). The Bush administration continued to reject the norm and argued for an alternative normative framework emphasizing economic efficiency and global emission reductions rather than national commitments. However, the norm had entered the domestic political dialogue, and the government faced growing pressure domestically and internationally to affirm the norm. The United States would continue to try to alter the normative context of the climate negotiations. The resolution of the normative debate had critical implications for how states would be expected to respond to climate change. This ongoing debate and its effect on domestic climate policy will be explored in the subsequent chapters.

_____

CHAPTER THREE

International Norms and the Politics of Emission Reduction Commitments

(Chantilly to Rio)

The initiation of the Intergovernmental Negotiating Committee on Climate Change (INC) in February 1991 marked the beginning of the second stage of climate negotiations. The international diplomatic focus began to shift from problem definition to the negotiation of an international policy response. Consequently, the nature of the negotiations and the power positions of important domestic and international actors began to shift as well. During the problem definition phase, the primary actors were scientists, nongovernmental organizations, government departments with responsibility for environmental affairs, and intergovernmental organizations such as UNEP, WMO, and the IPCC. Other interest groups attempted to influence the process, but their role in the first period was relatively limited.

Governments must ratify and implement international agreements, and domestic actors bear the associated costs and benefits. The manner in which the domestic groups are organized and represented through the domestic political process will affect the definition of national preferences and the choice of strategies. Governments faced a range of options as they developed both domestic and international positions on climate change. What would be the costs and benefits of achieving an international agreement and pursuing domestic emission reductions? Governments could attempt to negotiate international agreements that were broadly compatible with existing domestic policies, which would either produce a weak international agreement or force other countries to undertake more substantial emission reductions. Alternatively, they could undertake a range of domestic policy changes to reduce domestic GHG emissions to comply with commitments contained in the international agreement. In essence, one of the most important policy decisions to be made was where policy adjustments would be made—internationally or domestically. International norms played a critical role in establishing the boundaries for the international and domestic responses to climate change.

Because of the intimate connection between climate change and fossil fuel consumption, the fossil fuel industry, the manufacturing sector (particularly energy intensive industries), the transportation sector, and the electricity generation industry expended significant resources to affect the definition and pursuit of national preferences. In addition, government ministries with responsibility for these sectors also inserted themselves more forcefully into the debate. The expanded interest and involvement of actors, who were largely mobilized to protect economic interests, set up a clear conflict between the actors that were primarily responsible for identifying and defining climate change as a problem and the actors that would be directly affected by the solutions. This is consistent with the hypotheses discussed in the first chapter.

During, the pre-INC period most states had accepted that an international response to climate change was necessary, and a norm requiring domestic GHG reduction commitments had achieved prominence internationally, though the United States continued to oppose it. Three primary issues dominated the international negotiations leading up to the signing of the Framework Convention on Climate Change in 1992. First, which GHGs would the treaty regulate? Carbon dioxide was the most significant GHG, and it was also the easiest to monitor. Environmental groups in particular pressed for a norm that would require all industrial states to accept a specific CO_2 emission reduction commitment. The CO_2 commitment was tied to broader environmental objectives to reduce fossil fuel dependence and improve energy efficiency. Other GHGs such as methane, NO_X, and some ozone depleting substances and their substitutes were also significant contributors to global warming, but they were also much more difficult to monitor. Second, what would be the nature of the reduction target and the timetable for achieving the reductions? Would the target be binding or voluntary, differentiated among countries or standardized? Would the target be calculated based on per capita or total emissions, gross or net (total emissions minus sinks) emissions? This debate was couched in normative terms. Should developing countries be required to reduce GHG emissions, when the developed countries were responsible for the vast majority of CO_2 emissions released since the Industrial Revolution? Was it fair for Japan and France to be forced to reduce their CO_2 emissions when their per capita emissions were dramatically lower than American or Canadian emissions?

Third, would the treaty require the domestic implementation of specific policies to achieve reductions, or would each state have the flexibility to achieve emission reductions by utilizing a domestically determined mix of policies? There was a broad range of domestic policies capable of reducing GHG emissions: automobile fuel efficiency regulation, automotive emission taxes, carbon/energy taxes, energy efficiency regulation, promotion of alternative fuels, and so forth. These policies varied widely in their effects on economic growth and employment, on the distribution of costs and benefits across sectors of society, and on their potential for reducing GHG emissions. The United States and its partners sought to frame this debate in terms of economic efficiency and the harnessing of market forces to achieve environmental objectives without sacrificing economic growth. The Europeans and environmental NGOs attempted to frame the debate as one of national obligation. Governments had an ethical obligation to cut domestic emissions to safeguard the global environment.

There were several parallels in the political setting for the climate debates in the United States, Germany, and the United Kingdom. Conservative governments led each of the countries. Chancellor Kohl was reelected in December 1990. Prime Minister Major faced reelection in April 1992 just prior to the Rio Conference, and President Bush faced reelection in the fall of 1992. Both Chancellor Kohl and Prime Minister Major made commitments to address climate policy in their election campaigns. President Bush had supported international action to address climate change in his 1988 campaign. However, in his 1992 campaign, he placed a much greater emphasis on improving economic growth and creating jobs, and he argued that climate policy should not be permitted to adversely affect the American economy. All three countries and the European Union had strong environment ministers committed to an aggressive climate policy during this period. However, the relative influence of these ministers varied greatly. German Environment Minister Klaus Toepfer had the most influence over his country's climate policy and American EPA Director William Reilly the least, but all three worked tirelessly to promote an international agreement on climate change. Each state's foreign ministry also supported international cooperation in the climate negotiations. Sharp divisions between the environment ministries and the commerce and energy ministries characterized the climate policy debates within all three governments and within the European Commission. The commerce and energy ministries typically argued for a minimal policy response on the grounds that industrial competitiveness would be harmed.

Power generation produced the largest portion of each country's CO_2 emissions. Strategies to reduce carbon emissions had to address the energy sector. Both the United States and Germany completed comprehensive national energy strategy reviews between 1990 and 1992. The United Kingdom undertook the privatization of the electricity industry and began the privatization of the coal industry during the negotiations. The combination of the energy policy reviews and the climate policy debate created a window of opportunity to address the fundamental relationship between energy and climate policy.

The economic situation in all three countries was also similar during this period. The United States and the United Kingdom dipped into recession during 1990 and maintained either negative or minimal economic growth leading up to the Rio Conference. Germany did not slip into recession until 1992, but the Kohl government faced a number of economic problems related to reunification. In all three countries, economic growth was a major political concern, and it acted as a restraint on policies to reduce GHG emissions.

A brief review of the origins and structure of the Intergovernmental Negotiating Committee on Climate Change provides an international institutional context for the pursuit of national climate policies. The release of the IPCC report in the fall of 1990 made the Framework Convention on Climate Change negotiations a foregone conclusion. First, the report noted that there was significant evidence that climate change was occurring, and second, it appeared that it was being influenced by human activities. On December 21, 1990, in response to the IPCC report, the UN General Assembly adopted UN Resolution 45/212, which established the Intergovernmental Negotiating Committee (INC) for Climate Change with the task of completing a climate convention for signature at the 1992 Rio Conference. The most important effect of the INC process on the positions of the member states was the truncated timetable it established for concluding the negotiations. The Rio deadline made it difficult for states to delay or obstruct the negotiations, but it also created leverage for those seeking to weaken the treaty. If there were no agreement by Rio, the negotiations would be perceived to have failed.

Between February 1991 and May 1992, the INC held five negotiating sessions. As the Rio Conference approached, even those countries hoping for a breakdown in the negotiations were unable—or unwilling to be held responsible for—killing the negotiations. The negotiating process moved extremely slowly with little momentum prior to the final three months. The negotiations split the participating countries along several fault lines. There was a North-South divide over responsibility for causing climate change and obligations to remedy the situation, as well as disputes over technological flows and financial transfers to developing countries. There was also a South-South divide between those countries adversely affected by climate change (i.e. Pacific island states and states with low-lying coastal areas) and those adversely affected by policies to remedy climate change (i.e., OPEC) with most countries somewhere along the continuum between the two groups. There was also a North-North divide between those favoring an activist policy to slow climate change (i.e., the EC and Germany) and those seeking to minimize the domestic costs of addressing climate change (i.e., the United States), with the remainder on a continuum between the two extremes.

The chapter is divided into six sections. The first section provides an overview of the negotiations. It identifies the principal issues for the developed states and offers an introduction to the most important compromises made in the FCCC negotiations. The subsequent four sections focus on the development of domestic and international climate policies in the United States, the United Kingdom, Germany, and the European Community. The European Community is addressed in a separate section because German and British climate policies are incomprehensible without reference to the EC. The EC also emerged as a major actor in the international negotiations, and the coordination of the EC negotiating position through the Commission created a more formidable negotiating partner for the United States. Each section analyzes the salience of international norms in the development of both domestic policies to reduce GHG emissions and the negotiating positions adopted by each of the states. Finally, the concluding section of the chapter provides an analysis of the interrelated development of domestic climate policy and international norms during this period.

NEGOTIATING THE FCCC

While there were any number of important institutional issues that had to be negotiated to create the Framework Convention on Climate Change, the primary point of conflict among the developed states was whether the convention would contain binding emission reduction targets and timetables. The first meeting of the INC was held in February 1991 in Chantilly, VA. It concluded with the adoption of guidelines for the negotiations and a deadline of June 1992 for completion of an agreement. The treaty should address GHG emissions, transfer of technology and resources to developing countries, and international scientific and technological cooperation. The outcome of the talks also included an "agreement to focus future negotiations on 'appropriate commitments,' " which was purportedly inserted at the insistence of the United States to weaken the call for "concrete" commitments and timetables in the convention.[1] The chasm between the United States and the European Community member states over targets and timetables was apparent from the beginning. The completion of the negotiations would require some mechanism to bridge the gap.

The Geneva INC II meeting began with the introduction of at least sixteen "non-papers," or informal position papers seeking to clarify national or regional positions. The British delegation, with Japanese, Norwegian, and Australian support, proposed a system of "pledge and review." Under the system, states would make individual commitments to cut GHG emissions, which would then be binding on the country and would be evaluated by an independent body for compliance. The Convention itself would be a framework with no specific targets or timetables. The British proposal represented an attempt to alter the normative debate by focusing on specific policies and variation in national circumstances rather than common GHG emission reduction commitments as the benchmark for support of climate policy. The EC proposed a common commitment to stabilize CO_2 emissions at 1990 levels by the year 2000. The United States rejected any concrete targets or timetables.

The INC III meeting in Nairobi proved to be largely a rehash of the Geneva proposals. The EC member states and environmental NGOs condemned the "pledge and review" proposal as "hedge and retreat," and Japan and the United Kingdom were forced to back away from the initiative. The United States continued to reject any binding emission reduction targets. The split between the United States and the Europeans produced deadlock in the negotiations. With no definitive agreement reached at the "final" negotiating session in December 1991, the negotiations were extended to an additional meeting to begin in late April 1992. The United States faced strong international and domestic pressure to affirm the norm requiring the adoption of domestic timetables and targets for CO_2 emission reductions. As the only industrial country publicly rejecting the norm, the United States withstood a barrage of charges from nearly all of its negotiating partners. Nevertheless, the Bush administration adamantly rejected any proposals for timetables or targets. On May 1, 1992, INC Chairman Jean Ripert offered a draft text to the INC meeting that contained no targets or timetables. The text essentially contained compromise language agreed in late April in meetings between British and American negotiators.[2] Environmental groups lambasted the proposal, and the German government initially refused to accept the text. However, it became apparent that American participation at Rio was dependent upon an acceptance of the chairman's text, and on May 9 the draft text was approved. The next four sections explore the interplay between the international negotiations and domestic climate policy debates.

GERMANY

The outline of Germany's position in the climate negotiations had been set during the climate conference period. The Kohl government accepted that climate change was a serious environmental threat and acknowledged that the industrial countries should bear primary responsibility for addressing climate change. The focus of domestic climate policy was achieving the goal of cutting carbon emissions by 25 percent by the year 2005. Internationally, the government supported a minimum goal of stabilizing CO_2 emissions at 1990 levels by 2000 for the developed countries. The primary area of dispute was how to meet the domestic goal. Should the goal be met solely in the former West as it had been originally formulated, or should it apply to Germany as a whole? If the goal applied to the West alone, it would be necessary to enact a number of ambitious and potentially costly domestic policies to reduce carbon emissions. On the other hand, the target could potentially be met without significant new policies if the large carbon emission reductions from the East could be counted.

The German negotiating position was in flux leading up to the first INC meeting. Chancellor Kohl had won a resounding victory at the polls in December 1990. Prior to the elections, the Kohl government had proposed a number of domestic initiatives to address Germany's CO_2 emissions. With the reunification of Germany, the government had the possibility of relying on cuts in CO_2 emissions in the East to meet its reduction target. The Environment Ministry pushed for a significant increase in the CO_2 emission reduction target and argued that reductions would be easy and cheap in the former East. Following a contentious debate, the cabinet settled upon the rather vague formulation of decreasing CO_2 emissions by more than 25 percent in the country as a whole by 2005.[3] This new formulation represented a significant retreat from the earlier pledges to meet the 25 percent reduction in the West alone. Climate change remained an important part of German domestic and foreign policy, but initiatives to cut CO_2 emissions became much more conservative as the debate shifted from reduction commitments to concrete policies to achieve the emission reductions. The emission reduction commitment norm had achieved a domestic policy impact (level six). The policies were debated within the context of Germany's international responsibilities, but the norm was not yet sufficiently embedded in the domestic political debate to achieve norm prominence (level seven) and overcome the opposition of important interest groups.

The Kohl government continued to be a leader in pressing for international action to reduce GHG emissions. It promoted an aggressive EC climate policy to pressure the United States and Japan to accept a climate treaty containing legally binding commitments to reduce GHG emissions. The government worked within the EC to develop common EC targets and timetables, a carbon tax, and energy efficiency measures. The Kohl government effectively used the EC to deflect criticism of the paucity of specific domestic measures to reduce GHG emissions and to avoid potentially harmful competitive effects from undertaking unilateral emission reduction measures. A coordinated EC position had the additional advantage of undermining American attempts to divide EC member states in the negotiations, which would put greater pressure on the Americans to compromise.

Leading up to the FCCC, the German domestic climate debate focused on three policy areas. First, domestic coal consumption was a major source of German carbon emissions, but it was also a source of intense political conflict. Ongoing discussions with the EC over the subsidization of the coal industry created an opportunity for Germany to address both the inefficient system of coal subsidies and the effects of coal consumption on

CO_2 emissions. Related to the issue of coal production and consumption, the German government had a further opportunity to address the relationship between energy production and the environment through the 1991 review of Germany's national energy strategy, which created an opportunity to fundamentally alter the relationship between energy and climate policy.

The second area of domestic and EC climate policy related to proposals for a carbon and/or energy tax. The carbon/energy tax offered significant potential for CO_2 emission reductions. Tax proposals circulated both at the German and EC levels throughout the INC process. Finally, Germany debated a combination of additional policies directed at climate change. Some of these policies included proposals for a graduated tax on vehicles based on their emissions, a national speed limit, phasing out of HCFCs (a replacement for ozone depleting CFCs but also a potent GHG), and a voluntary program directed at manufacturers to improve the energy efficiency of consumer goods. The domestic debates surrounding these proposals provide insight into the level of salience of the emission reduction commitment.

Before the FCCC negotiations began, there was a consensus among German politicians and bureaucrats that climate change was occurring, that it was caused by human activity, and that aggressive reductions in GHG emissions were necessary to address the threat. In addition, the Enquete Commission's analysis of German energy use suggested that West Germany could improve its total energy efficiency between 35 and 45 percent by utilizing state of the art technologies. Renovation of existing buildings could provide 70 to 90 percent efficiency gains over existing levels. Reform of new building standards could save 70 to 80 percent. Higher efficiency standards for electrical appliances could save 30 to 70 percent, and improvements in automobile and aircraft fuel efficiency could contribute 50 to 60 percent. These improvements were possible with existing technologies, if utilized fully.[4]

The Enquete Commission also concluded that consumers could achieve an additional 20 percent reduction in energy use through more energy conscious behavior, such as reducing room temperature in winter and temperatures for home water heating. In addition automobile use held significant potential for cutting energy consumption. Based on the analysis of potential energy savings, the Enquete Commission endorsed a 30 percent binding national reduction goal for CO_2 emissions by 2005 based on a 1987 baseline. The Enquete Commission also recommended that by the year 2020 Germany should achieve emission reductions of 70 percent in nitrogen oxide, 75 percent in carbon monoxide, 50 percent in methane, and 90 percent in volatile organic compound emissions.[5] A 1990 study by the EC supported the Enquete Commission's findings. According to the study, Germany could cut its CO_2 emissions by up to 25 percent without net negative costs to the economy.[6]

The German industrial and energy sectors remained skeptical of the low cost predictions and opposed some of the policy proposals, but they did not dispute the conclusion that carbon emission reductions were necessary and achievable. German policy makers apparently did not accept the analysis or were unable to act upon the recommendations, because they did not adopt the most significant of the recommendations. In particular, the government was unwilling to significantly cut coal use, nor was it able to enact a carbon/energy tax. The decision not to implement these policies made stabilization in the West nearly impossible to achieve. These decisions are discussed in greater detail below.

German Energy Policy

The Kohl government initiated a review of its national energy policy in 1991. It conducted its review concurrently with the American National Energy Strategy (NES), which provides an important parallel to the development of the NES. The German program was remarkable for the emphasis it placed on environmental concerns. In announcing the energy policy revisions in the fall of 1991, Economic Minister Juergen Moellemann and Environment Minister Klaus Toepfer put forth a set of principles that were intended to guide German energy policy. Energy policy should assure the long-term availability and security of supply and provide the foundation for economic growth. German policy should be guided by the conservation of energy and should fully incorporate environmental concerns. In particular, the environmental and health costs resulting from the production of energy must be fully reflected in the price of energy. Finally, market mechanisms should be used to push for conservation and environmentally sound consumption and production.[7] The program directly addressed the problem of climate change. The new energy policy called for an expansion of nuclear energy. The emphasis on nuclear power was not new, but the need to meet emission reduction commitments provided an additional rationale for expanding nuclear power production at a time when the nuclear industry was under attack. The revised policy also took the politically unpopular position of calling for significant cuts in coal production and consumption. It is difficult to gauge the earnestness of this call because the specific policy proposals were to be filled in later, and the revised energy policy continued to emphasize domestic coal as a significant part of Germany's long-term energy plan. The plan projected that the lignite coal industry would lose 27 percent of its one hundred thousand man workforce by the end of 1991, but these cuts were largely due to the closure of inefficient East German pits.[8]

The German government also successfully pursued a number of energy efficiency measures. It convinced the domestic appliance industry to adopt a voluntary program of energy efficiency improvement targets for its products. Targets ranged from improvements of 3 to 5 percent for electric cookers, 10 percent for washing machines, 10 to 15 percent for dishwashers, and 15 to 20 percent for refrigerators. All of the targets were met by the industry, and most were beaten by wide margins.[9] The government revised ordinances on thermal insulation, new building codes, and furnace efficiency to improve energy efficiency, which had the potential for significant energy savings.[10] In addition, the government instituted an ambitious program of grants and loans to raise energy efficiency in the former East.

Finally, the government also stressed the role of renewable energy in its long-term plan. As part of the new renewable energies program, households installing solar energy would receive 70 percent of the cost in reimbursements from the government. The most important program to the development of the renewable energy industry was the passage of the 1991 *Stromeinspeisungsgesetz*. Under the program electricity producers were required to purchase wind, solar, and hydro power at rates fixed at approximately 75 to 90 percent of the mean electricity rate paid by end consumers. The law was passed even over the strong objections of the utility industry. However, the promotion of renewable energy was popular with the public, and it reinforced the government's image as a leader in addressing climate change.

The Kohl government's reform of energy policy provided a unique opportunity to combine energy and environmental goals in a more constructive manner. The emphasis on renewable energy sources, nuclear power, and conservation fit well both with Germany's need for energy security and its goal of reducing CO_2 emissions, but the continued emphasis on coal limited the ability to achieve dramatic emission reductions. The government was also unwilling to adopt the carbon tax that it had been promoting as the key to reducing carbon emissions. Though the appliance and building standard policies would provide energy savings, they would be insufficient to achieve a 25 percent reduction in CO_2 emissions without additional measures to address coal consumption and/or a carbon/energy tax. Germany's climate commitments were beginning to have an effect on domestic policy, though powerful domestic interests limited the adoption of the policies that would produce the largest emission reductions.

German Coal

One of the primary problems that the German government faced in cutting CO_2 emissions was that nearly 45 percent of its emissions came from the energy transformation sector. Germany relied on the burning of coal for 36 percent of its primary energy supply.[11] Unfortunately, German coal reserves were composed primarily of lignite or "soft coal," which produces relatively higher amounts of CO_2 and other waste gases when it is burned than "hard" coal. Fuel switching from soft to hard coal or more significantly from coal to natural gas for energy production offered the greatest potential for near term CO_2 emission reductions.

While German lignite production was financially sustainable, the German bituminous coal industry was unable to compete in world coal markets without significant subsidies and aid from the federal and state governments. The International Energy Agency estimated that the cost of producing West German hard coal was three times the world market delivery price.[12] This cost of production was only sustainable because electric utilities and the iron and steel industries were contractually bound to purchase minimum annual volumes of domestically produced coal. In addition, electricity customers paid an 8.5 percent surcharge to support coal production through the *Kohlepfennig* system, and the federal and state governments provided an additional $15 billion a year in subsidies.[13] Removing the subsidies would lead to the closure of a number of coal mines. From the government's perspective it would also save the high costs of subsidizing the industry and open the way for substantial reductions in carbon emissions and other noxious gases if power plants switched from coal to natural gas.

The issue of coal fired power generation was fraught with political land mines for the Kohl government. The European Commission was pressing Germany to cut its coal subsidies on the grounds that they represented an illegal form of state aid. Domestically the coal industry and coal states lobbied aggressively to maintain the subsidies. The government faced the difficult task of negotiating with the Commission to find a compromise solution to reduce the subsidies without devastating the coal industry. The dispute with the Commission provided a potential opening for the government to jointly address the costly coal subsidy program and to achieve significant cuts in CO_2 emissions. The Kohl government recognized the inefficiency of the subsidization of the coal industry and attempted to support its rationalization by encouraging the closure of the most inefficient mines. Amendments to the Third Power Generation Act in 1989 limited the amount of coal to be supplied for electricity generation. The *Kohlepfennig* surcharge was also to be gradually reduced to 7.5 percent by 1993. All of these measures reduced the financial support for the industry, but they were not intended to dramatically reduce total coal production. The government continued to view coal as an essential component of Germany's long-term energy strategy. Talks among the coal industry, the federal and state governments, and labor organizations produced an agreement in November 1991 to substantially cut subsidized coal production by 2000 and to sustain that level until 2005.

After 1990, the government also faced the daunting task of addressing East Germany's coal industry, which relied heavily on lignite coal to power its economy. Many of the coal mines were inefficient and unable to compete, and pollutant emissions from coal fired power stations were well above West German standards. Most of the East's coal and power production industries were closed or modernized following reunification. Coal production and carbon emissions from the combustion of coal fell sharply in the unified Germany as a result of economic restructuring in the East but these reductions did not help the German government with its commitment to reduce emissions in the West. The sacrosanct nature of the West German coal industry placed significant limits on the ability of the government to significantly reduce CO_2 emissions in the West. The government's emission reduction commitment proved to be insufficiently salient to overcome coal industry opposition.

The German Carbon Tax Debate

Next to reform of the coal industry, a carbon tax offered the greatest potential for reducing German CO_2 emissions. Environment Minister Toepfer was a champion of a carbon tax that would spur additional emission reductions by using the tax revenue to fund emission reduction projects. He also supported the unilateral adoption of the tax as a sign of international leadership on climate change. The Energy and Industry Ministries opposed the tax, but they argued that if one was to be implemented, it should only be adopted as part of an EC wide carbon tax, and the tax had to be revenue neutral to preserve the competitiveness of German industry.

A Rheinisch-Westfaelisches Institut (RWI) study reinforced the Industry Ministry's argument. The Institute analyzed the effects of several variations of carbon/energy taxes and their effects on emissions and economic performance. It concluded that a small tax would have little effect on emissions because structural constraints would not allow power companies to respond to the economic stimulus of the tax. A relatively small levy would have a minor consumption effect, but it would not promote fuel substitution, which would provide the largest emissions reductions. Only a substantial levy would have the desired effect on CO_2 emissions, but such a levy would have dire consequences for industrial competitiveness according to the RWI.[14] German industrial groups concurred and argued that only an OECD wide adoption of the tax could prevent substantial competitive effects on German industry and avoid giving American and Japanese manufacturers significant advantages.

Following the December 1990 elections, the coalition agreement among the CDU, CSU, and FDP called for a carbon tax to be implemented—contingent upon the adoption of a similar tax at the EC level. By mid-1991, support for a carbon tax was weakening in Germany. The slowing of the

German economy and the need for increases in other taxes to fund reunification diminished support for a carbon tax, but the government astutely shifted the controversial and politically risky issue to the EC level. At the presentation of the second report of the interministerial working group on climate change, it was decided that "for reasons of effectiveness and the competitiveness of German industry, an effective climate protection strategy requires international agreement. . . . The Federal Government therefore supports the introduction of an EC-wide combination CO_2/energy tax."[15] The EC would later take a similar strategy when it would shift responsibility for the tax to the OECD level. A properly implemented carbon tax theoretically had the potential to produce significant cuts in carbon emissions. The Kohl government refused to pursue the tax and thus further limited Germany's ability to achieve significant near-term emission reductions.

Other German Climate Related Policies

Outside of energy policy, the German government was attempting to create a broader consensus for climate action. The government held meetings with consumer, labor, and industry groups to try to create a consensus on the actions necessary to meet Germany's CO_2 emission target. The release of the second report of the interministerial committee on climate change revealed an aggressive program to meet the challenge of reducing CO_2 emissions. Despite divisions within the cabinet, the Kohl government was moving ahead with a number of new climate initiatives. In the sensitive transportation sector, the government was developing a new automobile tax that would operate on a sliding scale with owners of large, inefficient vehicles being forced to pay a higher tax than those with smaller, more fuel efficient vehicles. The government was also exploring an increase in the gasoline tax.

The Kohl government undertook a high profile approach to addressing climate change. The policies actually enacted at this time were relatively minor, but they were occasionally adopted over the opposition of industrial interests. There was also the potential for longer term reductions if all of the proposed policies were enacted. The Kohl government displayed a willingness to pursue policies directed at climate change that was largely missing among the other states studied here. These specific policy proposals provided German negotiators with some legitimacy in pressing other states to adopt more proactive approaches to reducing carbon emissions. The Kohl government was reluctant to take actions that would have broad competitive effects on German industry. However, it also demonstrated a clear commitment to reducing national GHG emissions. The international norm requiring commitments to cut emissions was emerging as a significant force in German domestic policy debates. The norm had reached the sixth level of salience,

"Domestic Political Impact." The government and other domestic actors began to justify policy changes on the grounds that they were necessary to meet the norm, but the onus was still on the supporters of the norm to justify changes that harmed the economic interests of domestic actors. Appeals to economic competitiveness were sufficient to block many of the most important policy changes.

German Foreign Policy

Though the German government had the most ambitious target for reducing carbon emissions, its influence in the climate negotiations was quite limited. The United States and/or the United Kingdom stymied German proposals at every turn. In many ways, the German role in the international climate negotiations is the least interesting of the three countries. The government was not forced to make any difficult domestic policy tradeoffs. It was free to push other states to make the maximum cuts in carbon emissions because the cuts would create economic costs for other countries that the German economy would not have to bear.

German policy focused heavily on shaping EC internal and foreign climate policy. The German/EC position paper, presented at the INC II meeting in Geneva, sought to define the parameters of the climate treaty to fit German domestic interests. The focus of the position paper was the negotiation of a legally binding commitment to reduce CO_2 emissions. The EC and Germany called for a common goal for all industrial countries of stabilizing carbon emissions at 1990 levels by the year 2000. The United States rejected the German/EC position, and the Kohl government had little leverage, other than public condemnation, with which to influence the American position. Environment Minister Klaus Toepfer was an outspoken critic of the American position and frequently attacked American intransigence in the climate negotiations. Though Germany was publicly critical of the American position, there was no suggestion of linking climate policy to other issues. The Kohl government was left to promote its preferred norms and to try to shame the United States into accepting the agreement.

The slow pace of the early INC negotiations shifted Germany's attention to the EC and attempts to conclude an agreement on the European carbon tax. Germany and the Commission perceived action at the EC level to be imperative for pressuring the United States to accept a concrete CO_2 emission target and timetable. However, the EC carbon tax debate languished in the face of stiff resistance from the United Kingdom and southern member states. The German government approached the Rio Conference from a position of weakness. The United States was threatening to reject the climate treaty. The EC had failed to achieve a common climate policy. The United

Kingdom and the United States had negotiated a text containing no concrete targets or timetables, and INC Chairman presented the British/American text at the final INC meeting. Germany was presented with a fait accompli. Initially, the government rejected the text. However, faced with a potential failure of the negotiations, the German delegation accepted the text.

In a last ditch effort to force the United States to accept a binding carbon emission reduction target, several European states organized a declaration of FCCC signatories. The declaration called for the stabilization of CO_2 emissions and criticized the United States for failing to accept the commitment and sabotaging the FCCC. German negotiators offered a less confrontational alternative declaration that called on developed states to fulfill their commitment to stabilize CO_2 emission by the year 2000, but the German alternative offered no criticism of the United States. In the end, the EC member states adopted the German statement setting out their intent to stabilize emissions at 1990 levels by the year 2000, which established the international normative benchmark against which national support for addressing climate change would be measured.

Conclusions from the German Case

German climate policy developed within a domestic context shared by no other Western developed country. German policy makers had the advantage of built-in carbon reductions following reunification. The goal of reducing emissions by 25 percent could potentially be met through the restructuring of the East German industrial and energy sectors. It would thus be easy to argue that the aggressive international negotiating position is explained by the fact that the policy was essentially cost free. However, the timing is not that simple. The government established the goal of reducing CO_2 emissions by 25 percent by the year 2005 prior to reunification. Important institutional factors created an environment receptive to the international norm requiring a national emissions reduction commitment. Germany's emphasis on the precautionary principle meant that the government would be expected to act when there was credible evidence of an environmental threat. The Enquete Commission's reputation for nonpartisanship and integrity led to the broad acceptance of its conclusions that climate change was occurring and that Germany could reduce its carbon emission by more than 30 percent at minimal cost to the economy. The German electoral system also facilitated the high visibility accorded to climate change as a political issue. The Green Party seized upon climate change as a major electoral issue in the 1990 elections. The ability of the CDU/CSU to co-opt the Greens' primary environmental issue not only undermined electoral support for the Greens, but it also raised the profile of climate change and forced the Kohl government to undertake policy actions to address it. It is clear that Germany's domestic institutional structure facilitated the increasing salience of its international commitment in the domestic policy process.

EUROPEAN COMMUNITY

Prior to the INC negotiations, the EC had played a relatively minor international role in the development of climate policy. Once the negotiations began, the Commission adopted an aggressive strategy to manage the EC's negotiating position and coordinate member state domestic policy responses. The Commission sought a more significant foreign policy role, and the climate negotiations provided a vehicle for it to take a high profile international leadership position. Additionally, the need to reduce CO_2 emissions created an opening for the EC to expand its influence over energy and taxation policy, which many member states had resisted.

German support for a common EC policy facilitated the Commission's ambitions. Germany was responsible for one third of the EC's emissions. If the EC was to achieve its goal of stabilizing carbon emissions at 1990 levels by 2000, Germany would have to make significant cuts. In 1990, it was estimated that EC emissions (excluding East Germany) would increase by 15 percent by the year 2000.[16] If each member state achieved its individual CO_2 reduction target, the EC as a whole would be close to its aggregate target. However, the member states were not legally bound by their targets, and most had not enacted any policies to achieve them. The emission reductions associated with reunification would be critical. In addition, common policy measures at the European level would be essential.

The Commission published its first communication on measures to reduce GHG emissions in October 1991. It assumed in its communication that European carbon emissions would have to be reduced by 11 percent to achieve stabilization at 1990 levels by 2000.[17] The Commission's climate strategy was tentatively agreed at an informal meeting of environment ministers in Amsterdam. The tentative agreement included a carbon/energy tax, which was still controversial among member governments. The Commission estimated that the carbon/energy tax could reduce CO_2 emissions by 6.5 percent. The other elements of the plan included a number of conservation and alternative energy measures as part of the EC's SAVE (3.0 percent reductions in CO_2), THERMIE (1.5 percent reduction), and ALTENER programs (1.0 percent).[18] The agreement was to be adopted in December with subsequent directives developed and in effect by January 1993. While informally the environment ministers were able to achieve an agreement on a CO_2 strategy, formal agreement proved to be more difficult.

The European debates are crucial to understanding German and British climate policies. Germany utilized the EC both as a means to move controversial decisions surrounding carbon taxes out of the domestic policy realm and as a tool to force other states to accept the German approach to combating climate change. Aspects of British climate policy can be explained as attempts to limit EC competence over energy, environmental, and taxation issues. The intense conflict surrounding energy and taxation policy eventually forced the Commission to abandon the most ambitious of the common policy proposals. In lieu of a common set of policies, the Commission was forced to accept a "monitoring mechanism" to measure member state, and thus indirectly, EC progress toward achieving the stabilization target. The Commission's role in coordinating EC climate policy would be extremely limited by member state opposition.

European Energy Policy

In 1989, the Commission set up a joint working group between its environment and energy directorates to explore the potential for integrating energy and environmental policies. The Commission approved a communication to the Council in February 1990, which stressed the importance of improving energy efficiency and conservation to achieve many of the EC's environmental and energy goals. The result was the Commission's proposal for a "Special Action Programme for Vigorous Energy Efficiency" (SAVE). The SAVE program was intended to provide a framework for developing energy efficiency measures to be implemented by the member states. SAVE was included as a part of the EC's internal climate policy in 1991. However, the only significant measure passed under SAVE during this period was a 1991 directive on boiler efficiency. Even in this case the UK watered down the directive by negotiating an exclusion for the production of less efficient British boilers for domestic consumption. The Commission faced significant opposition from member states to a number of its SAVE proposals. In June 1992, just prior to the Rio Convention, the Commission intended to publish a list of directives to be adopted under SAVE, but intense lobbying by member states and industry groups forced it to drop the list of common measures. Instead, the Commission deferred to the principle of subsidiarity and offered a list of policy areas within which member states should adopt domestic legislation. Ostensibly, the revision was intended to speed member state action, but in effect the bickering among the member states crippled the SAVE program.

The other components of the Commission strategy for addressing climate change were the ALTENER, THERMIE, and the energy/carbon tax proposals. The ALTENER program was designed to support the expanded use of renewable energies, but the program's budget was very small. The THERMIE program was intended to support the development of new energy technologies. Again the budget was small, and its effectiveness in reducing carbon emissions over the near-term was questionable. For the EC to have any hope of meeting its target, the carbon/energy tax proposal was imperative.

The Commission's climate strategy (particularly SAVE and the energy/carbon tax) represented an attempt to centralize the European policy response. The alternative approach was to allow the member states to formulate their own policy responses to achieve the common goal. The Commission sought to build on the EC experience with acid rain and ozone depletion. In both cases, the Commission coordinated the EC negotiating position and successfully expanded its control over related policy areas. The Commission saw climate change as an opportunity to further extend its reach into taxation and energy policy. It appealed to the emerging international climate norms to justify its actions, but it faced significant opposition from member states.

European Carbon Taxes and International Climate Policy

The most important component of the EC's climate policy was the proposal for a carbon/energy tax. The EC desperately needed to adopt the carbon tax to demonstrate its commitment to achieving its emission reduction target and to fend off accusations by the United States that the EC was being hypocritical. As early as 1990, the EC's Environment and Energy Commissioners (with the support of the German government) were preparing a plan for EC-wide energy and carbon taxes to cut Community CO_2 emissions. The Environment Council took up the initiative in December 1990. The official statement following the Council meeting failed to include proposals for environmental taxes. Instead, the focus was on conservation and research into new technologies. Environmental taxes were to be studied further.

The difficulty of achieving a common position on energy/carbon taxes did not lessen the Commission's enthusiasm for the tax. The Commission presented its energy/carbon tax proposal in September. The early drafts of the proposal called for a combined energy and carbon emission tax with 75 percent of the value of the tax related to energy consumption and 25 percent on CO_2 emissions. However, the final proposal altered the ratio to make each component worth 50 percent of the tax. The Environment Commissioner and environmental groups argued for a smaller portion of the tax to fall on CO_2 emissions, because it gave nuclear energy a significant advantage over other power sources. However, the Energy Commissioner, with support from most member governments, argued that the primary objective of the tax was to reduce carbon emissions, and nuclear energy had to play a significant role if those emissions were to be cut. The tax would add ten dollars to the price of a barrel of oil by the year 2000. The equivalent tax on coal would be fourteen dollars but a mere five dollars on nuclear energy.[19]

The Commission proposal contained exemptions for industries where energy costs represented 5 to 10 percent of total production costs. The industries included steel, chemicals, nonferrous metals, cement, glass, and paper. The exemptions would be dropped after other non-European industrial countries adopted their own energy taxes. The exemptions were an attempt to reduce the competitive effects of the tax and make it more palatable to industry. Industrial interests opposed the tax and argued that its implementation should be made contingent upon all OECD countries adopting a comparable tax.

While the Commission was able to put forward the taxation proposal, the proposal did not have the support of all commissioners. Following the tax announcement, EC Taxation Commissioner Christiane Scrivener took offense at the characterization of the Commission communication as an official proposal. "I am afraid that it has not been well explained that this is an initiative of reflection on several points. . . . The College [of Commissioners] is not unanimously in favor of the tax. We agree with studying the possibility of a tax alongside other instruments."[20] The split within the Commission reflected the larger split among the member states. Germany along with Denmark and the Netherlands strongly favored the adoption of the tax, but the United Kingdom and the southern member states opposed it. Britain, on principle, questioned the increased role of the EC in fiscal matters. It was also cautious about the effects of a carbon tax on the British economy and European competitiveness. The British argued that a tax was only acceptable if it was implemented internationally. Environment Minister David Trippier forcefully expressed the British position on the tax, "[w]e have set our face against taking that kind of action unilaterally because it would be disastrous for British industry."[21] He suggested that two-thirds of the Member States opposed the tax.

The December 1991 joint meeting of the Environment and Energy Councils provided an important test of the member states' support for the carbon tax. During the joint meeting, supporters of the tax were able to sway undecided countries to support a request to the Commission to develop a formal tax proposal. EC Energy Commissioner Antonio Cardoso e Cunha argued that the EC action would put pressure on the United States and Japan to alter their negotiating positions. "Very clearly the message today was that we are progressing, and if they [the United States and Japan] had any ideas that confusion within the EC would be an excuse to do nothing, they were wrong."[22] The Commission and tax supporters trumpeted the success of their efforts, but the prospects for imposing the tax were poor. Supporters were able to put together enough votes to request a formal proposal, but passage of the tax over the opposition of a significant number of member states would be impossible, because taxation measures required a unanimous vote of the Council for passage.

In the face of opposition to the carbon tax and other EC emission reduction policies, the member states agreed at the December Council meeting to hold individual member states accountable for meeting their domestic targets. The Council established an EC deadline of April 1992 for producing national plans to achieve CO_2 reduction targets. Should the member states fail to produce national plans capable of meeting the 2000 stabilization goal, the Commission and the carbon tax supporters would be in a stronger position to argue that a carbon/energy tax was essential to meeting the obligations of the EC. The deadline would place a great deal of pressure on the member states to accept the tax and make it difficult for them to further delay action.

By April 1992 only five countries were willing and/or able to submit specific policy proposals to achieve their carbon reduction targets (Germany, Denmark, the Netherlands, Luxembourg, and France). The failure of the other member states to submit their plans lent credence to American claims that the European countries were engaged in a disingenuous campaign to force the United States to agree to targets that the Europeans themselves would be unable to achieve. EC Environment Commissioner Ripa di Meana attempted to use the Rio Conference deadline as leverage within the EC on the carbon tax issue. He argued that the tax proposal was critical to the EC's position in Rio and to the EC's ability to meet its stabilization target. He threatened to boycott the Rio meeting if the Council did not officially accept a proposal for a carbon tax.[23] The tax supporters failed. The prospects for an EC carbon/energy tax were diminishing as the Commission took up the debate on the tax proposal. Environment Commissioner Ripa di Meana had been pushing for a vote on the tax prior to Rio, but on April 29 the Commission failed to adopt a final proposal after a contentious meeting.[24]

In an effort to meet the criticisms of several member states and to bridge disputes among commissioners, the Commission agreed to make any tax contingent upon the introduction of similar taxes in the United States and Japan. In the end, the Portuguese President of the EC (over the strong objections of the German delegation) refused to put forward the carbon/energy tax proposal for approval by the Council. Officially, the reason was that the final proposal was not ready for debate, but unofficially, Commission officials noted that a tax proposal was unlikely to pass in any form.[25] The tax was deferred to avoid a split in the European front prior to Rio, but the consequence was that the EC did not have any significant policies in place to counter the American charge that the Europeans were not serious about meeting their commitments.

Following the failure of the Council to provide any support for the carbon tax proposal, Commissioner Ripa di Meana announced that he would not attend the Rio conference. "I believe in environmental policy based on facts, binding obligations, and precise undertakings and not on mere words. I have decided not to go to a conference where everything has already been arranged." He denounced the treaty, which he said "contains exceptions which verge on the unacceptable."[26] As the Rio negotiations approached a climax, Germany and the EC became increasingly marginalized. The British and Americans stole the initiative and presented the Europeans with what amounted to a fait accompli. Germany and the EC had the choice of torpedoing the agreement and calling the American bluff or accepting the weak compromise text that the Americans and British had negotiated. At the May 5 joint meeting of the Environment and Development Councils, the member states officially endorsed the compromise text.

Conclusions from the European Case

The Commission's attempts to coordinate member state climate policies and to introduce a common carbon/energy tax were stymied by reluctant member states and divisions within the Commission itself. These internal difficulties had the effect of broadening the range of international policy outcomes that would be acceptable to the EC. The internal disputes weakened the EC's negotiating position and exposed it to charges of hypocrisy. Had the Commission succeeded in achieving agreement on a carbon/energy tax or at least realistic member state plans to reach the EC goal, the United States would have been under greater pressure to accept the binding targets and timetables supported by the EC. Unfortunately for the Commission, it faced internal conflicts similar to those experienced by the United States, Germany, and the United Kingdom. Disputes over the competitive effects of climate policy and taxation issues weakened Commission cohesion. The Commission demonstrated the same reluctance to impose economic costs on industry that the United States, United Kingdom, and Germany displayed. The international emission reduction norm had not achieved sufficient salience within the EC and the majority of the member states to force changes in EC policy.

UNITED STATES

As the climate negotiation began, there was the potential for a fundamental reevaluation of American climate policy. The Bush administration launched a review of energy policy in 1989, which created an opening to reexamine the relationship between energy and environmental policy. Interest groups promoted a wide-ranging debate of American climate policy, and the congressional and presidential elections in the fall of 1992 created an opportunity to debate American policy. However, the American economy weakened between 1990 and 1991. Job creation and economic growth dominated the 1992 elections. While German climate policy shifted to the specific policies and international agreements that were necessary to reduce GHG emissions, the American debate remained embedded in conflicts over the science and economics of climate change. American concerns over the costs of reducing GHG emissions, particularly CO_2, undermined support for emission reductions. Beyond the energy strategy discussions, there was very little substantive debate of domestic measures to reduce GHG emissions during this period. Instead, the United States focused on achieving an international agreement that would be consistent with broader American preferences.

The framing of the domestic climate policy debate was very different in the United States than in its European counterparts. European governments tended to characterize climate change as a significant environmental threat that could be addressed in a cost-effective manner. In 1988, Congress attempted to establish a similar foundation for domestic action. Congress requested that the National Academy of Sciences study the scientific and technical issues surrounding policy responses to climate change. The NAS appointed a forty-six member panel consisting of scientists, economists, and public policy analysts. The NAS panel reported its findings in its April 1991 report, "Policy Implications of Greenhouse Warming."[27] According to the NAS study, the United States could reduce its emissions of GHGs by 10 to 40 percent below 1990 levels over thirty years at little or no economic cost. Specifically, the panel recommended that the United States should raise energy prices to reflect the environmental costs of energy, improve the efficiency of automobiles through regulation and tax incentives, increase mass transit support, improve efficiency standards for electrical appliances, and slow deforestation.

The Bush administration's response to the report was less than enthusiastic. Presidential Science Advisor D. Allan Bromley called the NAS recommendations "reasonable goals" but rejected any policies based on new taxes or "command and control" regulation such as federally mandated efficiency standards. According to Bromley, "the goals we [the Bush administration] have in mind are going to be achieved more effectively by people who believe they are doing it for their own benefit or the nation's benefit, rather than being forced by some centralized control mechanism."[28] Even in the face of recommendations from the most respected scientific body in the United States, the Bush administration refused to alter its opposition to policies to reduce GHG emissions. The administration relied on Energy Department studies, which suggested that reducing CO_2 emissions by 20 percent would cost $95 billion per year and harm American competitiveness.[29] However, between 1991 and 1992 several private studies produced analyses consistent with the NAS findings. A Union of Concerned Scientists report estimated that aggressive action to cut CO_2 emissions by 70 percent over forty years could cost $2.7 trillion, but it could also save consumers and industry $5 trillion in fuel and electricity bills, a net savings of $2.3 trillion.

EPA studies also suggested that GNP would rise over the next twenty years if a carbon tax were imposed on fossil fuels and the money was recycled back to industry through investment tax credits.[30] The contested nature of the policy analyses made it much more difficult for a consensus on climate policy to form.

The economic debate largely revolved around four assumptions about the future of the American economy. First, how fast would the economy grow? The higher the growth rate, the higher the emissions of CO_2 would likely be. The Energy Department estimated annual growth of 3 percent, while most private studies typically assumed growth closer to 2 percent. Second, how efficiently was the economy utilizing energy (the less efficiently, the greater the potential gains from conservation measures)? The Energy Department assumed that industry had already undertaken the most profitable conservation investments. Most private studies assumed that there were significant unrealized opportunities for energy savings. Third, how quickly and efficiently could industry respond to economic incentives? The Energy Department argued that expensive command and control measures would be necessary to achieve marginal energy savings. Most private studies assumed that minimal economic incentives would be required to induce the desired behavior. Fourth, would the American economy continue to move toward less polluting service industries, or would manufacturing remain a significant part of the American economy? Private studies typically assumed a continuing trend toward the service sector, while the Energy Department assumed a leveling of the relative proportion of the economy devoted to services and manufacturing. Depending on the assumptions used, researchers could come to vastly different projections of the economic effects of climate policies.[31]

In Germany, the Enquete Commission played a crucial role in shaping the political consensus on both the science of climate change and the feasibility of policy responses to cut carbon emissions. The United States lacked a central body capable of shaping a similar consensus. American economic studies broadly supported the German conclusions that carbon emission reductions were possible at minimal economic cost; yet, Energy Department and industry studies suggested that costs would be high. Opponents of action on climate change argued that the conflicts among the studies illustrated the need for further research and highlighted the potential danger to the economy from rash policy actions. The debate undermined the foundation for aggressive domestic action.

While opponents of addressing GHG reductions mobilized, the American public was becoming increasing concerned about the threat of climate change. A poll conducted at the end of 1990 revealed that 69 percent of Americans believed that the United States should join other countries in limiting emissions from fossil fuels. Seventy-three percent of the respondents said they would be willing to spend more on fossil fuels to prevent serious effects from climate change.[32] A small, but vocal, bipartisan group in Congress was also advocating a more ambitious climate policy. However, American opponents of climate action initiated a much more active campaign to alter public opinion in the spring of 1991. The American National Coal Association funded a series of test marketing programs for an advertising campaign to try to convince Americans that climate change was not occurring. The campaign enlisted the services of scientists from respectable institutions to put forth material questioning the validity of climate science through television, print, and radio ads.[33]

While American public opinion supported action on climate change, it was not an issue that motivated significant political participation. The recession and job creation dominated the 1992 presidential campaign, and environmental issues largely dropped off the political agenda. Senator Gore's "Leadership Forum on Global Warming" demonstrated the ebbing interest in climate policy. Senator Gore invited all of the presidential candidates to attend the forum and put forth their views on climate policy. Only one Democratic candidate attended. Four candidates made statements via satellite, and President Bush refused to participate. Only Democratic candidate Paul Tsongas ran ads on the environment, and President Bush did not even utter the word "environment" in his 1992 State of the Union Address. Climate change did not resonate domestically, and public opinion put few restraints on the conduct of American climate policy.

The American National Energy Strategy

If the United States was going to significantly reduce its CO_2 emissions, it had to reduce emissions from the energy and transportation sectors. As preparations for INC I began, the administration was in the midst of producing its National Energy Strategy (NES). Presumably, the American position in the climate negotiations would be heavily influenced by the NES. After eighteen months of intense debate within the administration, there was still significant disagreement over the policies to be included in the NES. The DOE prepared a draft strategy that placed a heavy emphasis on the relationship between the environment and energy production. In particular, the DOE advocated the use of tax credits or subsidies to promote the use of alternative fuels as well as policies mandating energy conservation. However, the White House, led by Chief of Staff Sununu, Budget Director Richard Darman, and Economic Advisor Michael Boskin, rejected the use of "command and control" policies. They emphasized the importance of market mechanisms in energy policy. In Congress, Democrats formulated their own NES, which called for higher fuel efficiency requirements for cars, increased funding for mass transit, support for renewable energy research, and incentives for conservation of energy.[34]

The NES created a window of opportunity to fundamentally alter the American approach to energy production and use and in turn to reduce CO_2 emissions sufficiently to accede to targets and timetables in the climate treaty. However, the White House rejected proposals to set federal efficiency standards for electric lights, to create tax credits for renewable energy production, and to develop a self-financing federal fund to make loans for efficiency projects. Other conservation measures had been eliminated earlier in the policy debate including an increase in automobile fuel efficiency standards and higher energy taxes. In the end, the NES included calls for opening the Arctic National Refuge to oil drilling, restructuring the electric utility industry, requiring business vehicle fleets to use alternative fuels, deregulation of interstate oil and gas pipelines, and deregulation of the import of natural gas. According to administration officials, consumers would save $750 billion in fuel costs and $126 billion in electricity bills between 1991 and 2010 if the NES were fully implemented.[35] The focus of the NES was increasing supply, as opposed to reducing demand, which would inevitably translate into higher emissions.

Congressional hearings and debate took place throughout the FCCC negotiations. Much of the president's plan for improving energy supply and lowering prices was included in the "Energy Policy Act," but Congress added a number of additional measures that the White House had rejected. The congressional revisions had the potential to reduce national CO_2 emissions. Of particular importance were new tax incentives for renewable energy sources and alternative fuels, measures to promote energy efficiency, and reforms to encourage nuclear power plant construction. However, Congress failed to include increased automobile fuel efficiency standards that could have provided significant reductions in energy use and carbon emissions.

The American experience with the NES provides an interesting comparison to the German energy policy review. German policy, as expressed by the Kohl government, included a number of major and minor policy initiatives focusing on alternative energy production, improving energy conservation, and implementing carbon taxes to reduce energy use and carbon emissions. The German government ultimately enacted a number of minor programs to promote energy conservation and alternative fuels, though it failed to enact any of the major policy changes, such as the carbon tax, which would have had the greatest effect on carbon emissions. The failure to address CO_2 emissions in the NES put significant constraints on the Bush administration's ability to accept a CO_2 emission reduction commitment.

Following the failure to address climate change in the NES, the Bush administration felt obliged to offer two face saving programs to address

GHG emissions. First, the EPA announced a new "Green Lights" program, which created incentives for companies to replace existing lights with new, more efficient lighting. The program was voluntary and focused on a few large corporations. The second program was President Bush's plan to plant a billion trees. Both programs would have limited effects on net CO_2 emissions, but they represented an affirmation of the emerging norm that industrial states had an obligation to undertake domestic actions to reduce GHG emissions—though the administration rejected a quantitative commitment.

American Foreign Policy

American international climate policy was complicated by the fact that it was the only major industrial country openly seeking to block binding GHG emission reduction targets and timetables. The German and EC positions were much simpler. They supported targets and timetables for the reduction of CO_2 emissions as the foundation of a climate treaty. Their position was supported by the UN agencies, most of the developed countries, most developing countries, and generally by environmental NGOs. The Bush administration was in the position of challenging an emergent international norm that required countries to accept CO_2 emission reduction commitments as the first step toward addressing climate change.

The Bush administration sent mixed signals about its climate policy prior to the first INC meeting in February 1991. The EPA released a study in February that asserted that policies already in place would be sufficient to stabilize total greenhouse gas emissions at their existing levels.[36] This report was the foundation for the American position paper, "America's Climate Change Strategy: An Action Agenda," which was a glossy document presented at INC I that outlined American climate policy. The document represented a significant shift in tone by the Bush administration, but there was little concurrent shift in policy. The American "Comprehensive Approach to Climate Change" sought to include all GHGs (CO_2, methane, nitric oxides, carbon monoxide, volatile organic compounds, and most significantly CFCs) as one aggregate unit in the negotiations. The administration argued that it would be able to stabilize total GHG emissions at 1987 levels by the year 2000. CO_2 emissions would continue to grow, but the increases would be offset by reductions in CFC emissions required under the Montreal Protocol and reductions in pollutant emissions required under the recently passed Clean Air Act Amendments. The only new policy proposals directed at CO_2 were the program to plant a billion trees a year and the "Green Lights" initiative to promote energy efficiency. European delegates, developing country representatives, and environmentalists lambasted the American plan for "double counting" emission reductions required by other agreements. Environmental organizations noted that if Germany counted emissions reductions as the Americans did, Germany would cut its emissions by 40 percent by 2005.[37]

The Bush administration entered INC II with an unequivocal position of rejecting targets and timetables for GHG emission reductions. The American "non-paper" submitted to the INC stated emphatically "specific commitments for emissions reductions should not be included in a framework convention."[38] The United States, at least publicly, had become completely isolated in the negotiations. Every OECD country except the United States and Turkey had agreed to a target and timetable for stabilizing or cutting emissions. Yet, the Bush administration would not waver in its opposition. In the days leading up to the Nairobi INC III meeting, Japan, the United Kingdom, Germany, and the EC all publicly chastised the United States for its stand in the climate negotiations. Even within the United States, the Bush administration faced strong opposition. In July 1991, forty-four senators signed a letter pressing President Bush to provide stronger leadership on environmental matters. The administration refused to relent. It apparently calculated that if it rejected any treaty commitments beyond a framework convention, then the other countries would give in to American demands. The administration did achieve some preliminary success in its strategy. Japan and the United Kingdom put forward a plan for a "pledge and review" mechanism that would have opened up a number of loopholes to allow the United States to accept the plan. However, immediate and strident criticism of the proposal by environmentalists and other countries doomed the initiative.

During 1991, seven major points emerged as the foundation of the American negotiating position. First, the costs of reducing CO_2 emissions were high and largely unstudied. Second, given the high price of cutting emissions, more research was needed to understand the true nature of the problem and the appropriate solutions. The administration argued that there was no scientific basis for the proposed targets and timetables. Third, developing countries would play an ever-increasing role in CO_2 emissions, and eventually they would bypass the developed world in total emissions. Any agreement to reduce CO_2 emissions must thus include the developing countries. This was a direct challenge to an emerging norm, which would require developed states to accept responsibility for their past and reduce current emissions before developing countries would be obliged to do so. Fourth, the American energy profile was significantly different from most countries and required a different strategy to reduce GHG emissions. Any agreement must include the flexibility for countries to meet their total GHG emission reductions according to the requirements of their domestic situations. Fifth, although other countries were making pledges to stabilize GHG emissions, the United States was acting to cut emissions. The Bush administration argued that the United States would stabilize its GHG emissions by 2000. However, the United States would not tie its hands. Once a carbon reduction commitment became part of American law, it would be extremely difficult to change if circumstances changed. Sixth, any agreement should be based upon net emissions (i.e., sources minus sinks). Finally, the United States would not provide any new funding for developing nations to implement climate policies. The American position represented a rejection of the dominant norms that were emerging as the foundation of the new climate regime as well as an attempt to recast the normative debate in a framework more amenable to American preferences.

As the final scheduled negotiations in New York approached in February 1992, the Bush administration continued to reject concrete targets and timetables. In the place of quantitative commitments, the United States pushed for a framework convention containing commitments to policy action to be taken according to the particular circumstances of individual countries. The international negotiations became intertwined with the upcoming presidential elections, which made it increasingly difficult for the Bush administration to compromise after taking a hard line. The administration risked the president's reputation and significant political capital on achieving a convention consistent with the American negotiating position. On April 2, Representative Henry Waxman introduced an amendment to the House Energy Bill that would have forced the United States to stabilize CO_2 emissions by the year 2000. The "Global Climate Protection Act" had the bipartisan support of a substantial minority of House members. Nevertheless, it received relatively little public or media interest, and it failed to force a change in the American position.

Even in the face of growing international and domestic condemnation, the administration maintained its opposition to specific targets and timetables. The decision was interesting in light of an administration working group report (developed by representatives of the State Department, Energy Department, Office of Management and Budget, and the EPA) that had recently determined that the United States could cut its CO_2 emissions by 7 to 11 percent through initiatives already in place or under consideration.[39] These cuts would have put the United States within realistic reach of the European and Japanese reduction targets. The administration, by its own estimates, was capable of meeting the proposed international targets, yet it was unwilling to risk constraining its economic growth.

The administration's decision to maintain its opposition to targets and timetables led to a strategy of holding President Bush's attendance at the Rio Conference hostage to a convention acceptable to the United States. Foreign leaders condemned this tactic. Within the United States, both the

House and Senate passed bipartisan resolutions urging the president to participate actively in the Rio proceedings. The Bush administration sought a compromise that would secure American interests and allow President Bush to attend the Rio Conference. The British government acted as the primary bridge to the European states. In April, negotiations between American and British representatives achieved a rather convoluted compromise text based upon American proposals that the Bush administration had floated at the final INC meeting in New York. The proposed language was sufficiently vague that the Bush administration could interpret it to mean that it was not legally required to meet a carbon reduction target or timetable. The shift in the American stance resulted from two domestic political calculations that both favored American participation in the climate treaty. First, the climate change treaty would be the centerpiece of the Rio Summit. If the agreement failed, the United States would be blamed for the failure, which would have significant international and domestic ramifications. Additionally, Congress was debating energy legislation that would have mandated specific carbon dioxide emission reduction targets. At an April 27, 1992 meeting between President Bush and his closest advisors, there was significant debate over how to head off the congressional targets. While White House Counsel C. Boyden Gray argued that a compromise in the climate negotiations would fuel efforts in Congress, EPA Director Reilly countered that flexibility internationally would head off congressional action. The result was convoluted language accepting the need for GHG emission cuts without any binding targets or timetables, but with the "goal" of returning GHG emissions to 1990 levels.[40]

On May 1, INC Chairman Jean Ripert offered a draft text to the INC meeting that contained no targets and no timetables. The text essentially contained the compromise language agreed to in meetings between British and American negotiators. Despite widespread condemnation of the text, it was approved on May 9. On May 12, President Bush announced that he would attend the Rio Conference. The United States achieved its goals in the climate negotiations. The final text could be interpreted as requiring no targets and no timetables for reducing carbon emissions, and no domestic policy measures would be necessary to fulfill the commitments under the treaty.

Conclusions from the American Case

Perceived domestic obstacles to reducing carbon emissions and an apathetic public limited the domestic salience of climate change and the associated international norms. The failure of the NES and the Energy Policy Act to meaningfully address GHG emissions limited the United States' capacity to accept binding international agreements. Instead, the Bush administration forced the international community to adjust to American domestic policy requirements. There was limited domestic pressure for action on climate change, and the international community was unable to pressure the United States to alter its position.

It is an open question whether a Democratic administration would have pursued a significantly different approach. The transition from President Bush to President Clinton during the next period of the climate negotiations provides some insight into the role of party politics, but independent of party there were some clear domestic institutional obstacles to an activist climate policy. First, there was no official body to frame the climate debate and shape a political consensus on the threat posed by climate change or on the need for a policy response. The EPA, OTA, NAS, Union of Concerned Scientists, a multitude of environmental organizations, and internationally the IPCC and the German Enquete Commission provided evidence of the threat posed by climate change and the feasibility of policies to address it. Yet the White House, the Energy Department, and industrial interests were able to portray the evidence as controversial and unsubstantiated. Public and political opinion never galvanized behind aggressive climate policy action. New regulations were politically difficult to support. Domestic institutional constraints reinforced the bias toward protecting the economy at the cost of the environment.

UNITED KINGDOM

The United Kingdom entered the climate negotiations in 1991 straddling the positions of its European partners and the United States. The Thatcher government had conceded its international leadership position by refusing to accept the norm of stabilizing CO_2 emissions at 1990 levels by 2000. However, the British public and most political leaders continued to view climate change as a significant threat and sought a meaningful international agreement to address the problem. Following Thatcher's 1990 resignation, the new Major government faced several difficult decisions about the future of British climate policy. The United Kingdom had accepted a target of stabilizing carbon emissions at 1990 levels by the year 2005. Regulations adopted under the Long-Range Transboundary Air Pollution Treaty combined with electricity privatization were facilitating a shift from coal to natural gas for electricity generation, which had the fortuitous effect of reducing CO_2 emissions. However, it appeared in 1990 and 1991 that this conversion would not take place quickly enough to meet a 2000 stabilization target. The British Department of Energy projected in 1989 that British CO_2 emissions would be 29 to 34 percent above 1985 levels by 2005. [41] However, at least five studies produced in 1989 predicted that the United Kingdom could cut carbon emissions by 20 percent by 2005 if the government undertook a policy of promoting fuel switching from coal to gas and developed an energy conservation program. Studies undertaken jointly by the EC and the Department of Energy concluded that the United Kingdom could cut emissions by as much as 30 percent without net negative costs to the economy.[42] The various reports helped shape a consensus among politicians and the public that climate change was occurring and needed to be addressed and that the government could dramatically reduce British emissions at little cost by merely facilitating the rapid shift from coal to natural gas.

Domestically, the Major government attempted to capitalize on climate change to further its policy agenda. It linked the promotion of nuclear energy to its GHG reduction commitments. The government also desperately needed to increase government revenue to reduce the growing budget deficit. Climate change provided a justification for substantially increasing gasoline taxes. However, there were also significant limits to the policies that it was willing to implement. The Major government sought to slow the conversion from coal to natural gas for power generation to protect the remnants of British Coal for privatization. It also continued to object to the proposed European carbon tax. The government faced a growing tension between its desire to address climate change and the potential adverse effects of reducing CO_2 emissions on domestic economic interests.

Despite the economic concerns, the new Major government adopted a novel strategy to increase public and business support for climate policy. In May 1991, Environment Secretary Heseltine and Industry Secretary Peter Lilley set up a twenty-four member "Advisory Committee on Business and the Environment" (ACBE), which was composed of the chief executives and directors of some of Britain's largest companies and chaired by Shell Oil chief executive John Collins. The committee was created to provide a framework for dialogue between industry and the government on environmental policy. The committee's first task was to recommend a set of policies to reduce British GHG emissions. The committee issued its first report in September 1991. The report called on car companies to voluntarily improve gas mileage. It recommended higher gasoline taxes and taxes on less efficient automobiles. It also promoted more energy efficient consumer products through improved product standards and tax incentives. The group did not recommend any type of carbon or energy taxes; nor did it promote energy efficiency programs for industry. The report provided a foundation for the government's push for higher gas taxes.[43] It also helped to build business support for measures to reduce GHG emissions.

The British government also took the unusual step of putting forth a $17 million advertising campaign to convince consumers to use less electricity and heating fuels. The campaign focused directly on the link between energy use and global warming and sought to inform consumers about the relationship.[44] From a cynical perspective, the media campaign provided a relatively cheap way for the government to look like it was acting on climate change without incurring the wrath of major business supporters. However, it also raised public awareness of climate change and created the expectation of additional government action to address the problem. Eventually, the Major government would be forced to make some difficult decisions about its domestic climate policy.

Public interest in climate change was further piqued by a report published by the Energy Ministry in early 1991.[45] The report was the first output of the "British Climate Change Impacts Review Group." Though created by the DoE, the group of fifteen climatologists and other scientists operated as an independent body to assess the potential impact of climate change. The report's predictions of extreme droughts, powerful storms, reduced quality and quantity of potable water, damaged ecosystems, coastal erosion, and degradation of wetlands painted a stark picture of the effects of climate change on the United Kingdom. British meteorologists also announced just prior to INC I that 1990 had been the warmest year on record, and six of the seven warmest years since 1850 had occurred after 1980.[46] The British public and its leaders appeared to be persuaded that action was necessary to address climate change. The question was what types of action would be politically feasible.

British Energy Policy

The greatest potential for reducing British CO_2 emissions was in the energy sector. Three issued dominated British energy policy during this period. First, the government faced the impending privatization of the electricity generation and distribution sectors. This privatization program, when combined with the deregulation of the energy sector, had the potential to dramatically reduce CO_2 emissions. Second, as part of the energy sector reform, the government created a substantial program to support renewable energy production, which created the potential for significant future carbon emission reductions. Finally, the pending privatization of the coal industry had two primary effects on climate policy. The rationalization of British Coal led to the closure of uncompetitive mines and a reduction in production, but the pending privatization meant that the Major government was also seeking to assure the long-term viability of the coal industry to maximize income from privatization. The government was thus acting to slow emission reductions through the conversion to gas and assure a prominent role for coal in the British power generation sector. In total, the energy sector reforms laid the foundation for substantial reductions in carbon emissions.

Privatization of the electricity generation and distribution sectors was part of the Thatcher government's plans to bring market forces to bear in improving British competitiveness. The Thatcher government saw privatization as a means to lower electricity rates and improve economic competitiveness. Prior to 1990, the government had structured the electricity generation sector to support other policy goals, primarily the preservation of British Coal. To ensure the use of domestic coal, the government severely restricted the import of cheaper coal, virtually banned the use of natural gas, and allowed very limited use of fuel oil for electricity generation. Government regulation ensured the use of coal for electricity generation at the price of higher electricity rates. By 1988, 80 percent of British Coal's sales were to electricity generators. Contracts between British Coal and the state owned Central Electricity Generating Board guaranteed the volume of sales until 1993.[47]

As part of the privatization plan, generators would be allowed to utilize the most cost-effective fuels, which in the early 1990s appeared to be natural gas. It was unclear how quickly the shift to natural gas would occur, but the combination of lower fuel costs and the ability to avoid expensive retrofitting of existing coal plants with flue-gas desulphurization equipment led to a rapid conversion to natural gas. Privatization had the unintended, but fortuitous, effect of significantly reducing carbon emissions without extensive government intervention. However, the pace of these CO_2 emission reductions would largely dictate the GHG emission reduction commitments that the government could accept.

Though the coal industry's future looked bleak, the Major government wanted to assure the long-term presence of coal in the national energy mix to maintain the viability of the coal industry for privatization. In preparation for privatization, British Coal announced in October 1992 that it would close thirty-one of its fifty deep mines with the loss of thirty thousand jobs.[48] British Coal made it clear that the closures were necessitated by the anticipated decline in coal consumption in the newly privatized electricity industry. The public outcry over the closures and job losses led to a reprieve for several of the mines and an agreement to privatize any other mines slated for closure. The government also proposed a number of policies to subsidize domestic coal production and encourage the use of coal as an interim measure to improve competitiveness and stabilize the coal industry for privatization. The conversion from coal to natural gas occurred much more swiftly than the government had anticipated, and the Major government actually sought to slow the process and revive the coal industry, despite the slower reductions in CO_2 emissions that would result.

Renewable energy also held long-term potential for reducing GHG emissions. The Thatcher and Major governments devoted significant resources to promote renewable energy research. The 1989 Electricity Act created the "Non-Fossil Fuel Obligation" (NFFO) program, which required electricity companies to purchase minimum amounts of electricity from renewable sources. Recognizing that renewable energy sources would be unable to compete on price with fossil fuels, the government adopted a fossil fuel levy to subsidize the renewable energy industry through the NFFO program. The initial NFFO primarily required the purchase of nuclear power. Ninety-five percent of the fuel levies went to the nuclear industry.[49] Renewable energy and environmental interests heavily criticized the focus on nuclear power. To broaden support for the NFFO program, the DoE developed an additional NFFO in 1990 for other renewable energy sources. The second NFFO created contracts for seventy-five projects estimated to produce 250 MW of energy, primarily through wind, solar, waste gas, and tidal technologies. The third NFFO in 1991 created contracts for 122 projects with a total capacity of 572 MW. The government's goal in 1990 was to add 1,000 MW of renewable capacity by 2000. The goal was later increased to 1,500 MW of renewable energy.[50] The expansion of renewable energies created the potential for significant reductions in carbon emissions in the future.

The anticipated emission reductions from fuel switching renewed a cabinet row over the future of British climate policy. The government release revised figures in December 1991 that showed that emission rates would rise by 14 percent by 2005 as opposed to a 1989 prediction of a 20 percent increase. The downward revision was almost exclusively the result of plans by power companies to substitute natural gas for coal in energy production. The revised figures led to a public dispute between Energy Secretary John Wakeham and Environment Secretary Michael Heseltine. Heseltine recommended that the United Kingdom adopt the EC's stabilization target date of 2000. He argued that private and government studies had demonstrated that the United Kingdom could dramatically reduce its CO_2 emissions by adopting regulations to stimulate cost-effective energy efficiency investments. When combined with fuel switching, these measures should allow the United Kingdom to meet the 2000 target without harming Britain's economic position. Wakeham countered that the 2005 commitment remained "demanding and realistic" and should be kept.[51] The cabinet conflict represented a growing split between supporters of emission reductions and representatives of domestic economic concerns.

Energy Secretary Wakeham attempted to block new regulatory efforts by promoting a voluntary scheme to promote energy efficiency. Wakeham asserted that £10 billion per year could be saved if industry and the public adopted the best available energy technologies.[52] He put significant pressure on industry to sign a declaration voluntarily accepting new energy efficiency programs. Many of Britain's largest companies accepted the secretary's proposal and adopted policies to promote energy savings. The Wakeham/ Heseltine dispute erupted again in February 1992. Heseltine championed a

£120 million energy savings program to reduce power demand. He argued that the program was essential to stabilize CO_2 emissions at 1990 levels by 2005.[53] The government also faced a deadline of April 1992 to produce a CO_2 stabilization plan to meet its EC commitments. A failure to meet this deadline would reflect poorly on the Conservative government's environmental image and provide fodder for the Labour Party in the upcoming elections. Labour supported the year 2000 as the target for stabilizing emissions and argued that the government should initiate a national program to make this happen. Secretary Wakeham argued that the government could not support a program to reduce energy demand before the coal industry was privatized. He suggested that there would be no market for coal and thus no investors in the British coal industry if the government succeeded in the program that Secretary Heseltine was promoting. Secretary Wakeham proposed a more modest £20 million program to switch British homes to gas heat from more polluting fuels.[54]

The cabinet formally addressed its climate policy just prior to the INC meeting in New York and the EC deadline for submitting national plans to meet member state CO_2 reduction targets. The cabinet agreed that it would be willing to move up its target date if other countries (i.e., the United States) also accepted the same date, but otherwise it would maintain its existing target. The decision on Secretary Heseltine's energy savings plan was postponed and sent back to the Environment Ministry for further study. In the end, the cabinet was unable to produce a specific proposal for meeting its stabilization commitments and failed to submit a plan to the EC by the April deadline. Instead, the cabinet decided to leave the issue for the new government following the elections.[55]

The Conservative Party's victory in the election led to a shake-up of Prime Minister Major's cabinet. Michael Heseltine was moved from the Environment Ministry to the Ministry of Trade and Industry. The move was significant for climate policy because the Energy Ministry was to become a part of the Ministry of Trade and Industry under a restructuring of ministerial responsibilities. The disappearance of the Energy Ministry and the Heseltine appointment eliminated the Wakeham/Heseltine standoff, and it created the potential for a fundamental reevaluation of British climate policy in the future.

British Foreign Policy

The British position in the climate negotiations was the most complex of the developed countries. The Major government sought to promote an international agreement that was compatible with existing British policies and commitments. It wanted to maintain control of climate policy at an intergovernmental level and deny the expansion of European Community policy competence into taxation. To achieve these objectives it was imperative that the United States be a party to the climate treaty. Achieving these goals was complicated by a more activist EC policy, a consensus among its major European partners on the need for concrete international goals and time-tables, and a hardened American position against these very same targets and timetables. The result was a vast chasm between the American and European positions that British negotiators worked assiduously to bridge.

At INC I the United Kingdom (as co-coordinator of the IPCC's Legal Measures Group) presented a format for the climate convention. The proposal was based on the Vienna Convention and envisioned no concrete commitments. It anticipated a framework convention with protocols to be negotiated later. The convention would be acceptable to the United States and would provide limited justification for common action at the EC level. However, it was unacceptable to its European partners, who demanded the inclusion of concrete emission reduction targets and timetables either in the treaty or in a protocol to be adopted simultaneously. It was apparent from the initial negotiating session that finding a compromise acceptable to the United States and the European Community would be a daunting task.

In June 1991, Michael Heseltine traveled to the United States to present a compromise plan for establishing firm targets and timetables for cutting GHG emissions. The government proposed a "phased, comprehensive" pro-gram for reducing GHG emissions. Under the proposal, countries would be allowed to make "national commitments" to cut a range of GHGs, including methane and CFCs as the United States had proposed. Countries that went beyond commitments made under the Vienna Convention and its protocols would be allowed to take credit for these additional cuts and apply them toward the GHG target. In addition, the proposal would allow countries to include sinks in their calculations. The proposal went a long way toward meeting the American demands. However, the White House was unwilling to budge from its rejection of concrete limits on emissions—including limits that could be easily met under the British plan.

During the INC II negotiations in Geneva, the British negotiators attempted to appease the Americans by proposing, with Japanese, Norwe-gian, and Australian support, a system of "pledge and review." States would make individual commitments to cut GHG emissions, which would be bind-ing on the country. An independent body would evaluate the pledges to assure compliance. The convention itself would be a framework with no specific targets or timetables. The proposal was a further concession to the Americans, and it had the added advantage of allowing the United Kingdom to maintain its 2005 commitment date. Environmental NGOs derided the proposal as "hedge and retreat." The EC and its member states also rejected it, and the British government was forced to disavow it.

Conflicts within the Major cabinet over the British emission reduction target and energy efficiency proposals, as well as the distraction of the April 1992 elections, undermined the government's negotiating position. However, the postelection cabinet shakeup facilitated a shift in the British negotiating stance. Following an April 30 cabinet meeting, Prime Minister Major announced a shift in the British target date for stabilization of carbon emissions from 2005 to 2000, in line with the rest of the European Community. He reiterated that the target remained contingent upon other countries (i.e., the United States) accepting a similar target. New emissions data suggested that Britain would likely meet the 2000 target without significant additional policies.[56] British support for the 2000 target belied the simultaneous efforts of British diplomats to bridge the gap between the United States and the EC. In those discussions, the government made it clear that it was willing to accept an agreement without binding targets or timetables. During late April 1992, Environment Secretary Howard traveled to the United States and participated in negotiations with State Department officials that led to the language that INC Chairman Ripert eventually offered at the final INC meeting in New York. The British negotiated an agreement without targets or timetables—despite the recent acceptance of the 2000 target date (contingent upon American acceptance of a similar target). The Major government thus played a decisive role in negotiating the final content of the FCCC. Its efforts secured American acceptance of the convention, but in doing so, it abandoned the binding targets and timetables that it had been advocating and undermined the domestic commitment norm.

Conclusions from the British Case

British climate policy leading up to the conclusion of the FCCC is revealing. While the Major government continued to promote climate change as a significant threat, its domestic and foreign policies were not fully consistent with its rhetoric. The government was in the fortuitous position of being able to rely on fuel switching to produce the emission reductions required to meet its international commitments, but it was unwilling to undertake significant additional policies to reduce its GHG emissions. This is puzzling because government and private studies suggested that significant emission reductions were possible with minimal economic dislocation. The government appeared to be more concerned with protecting domestic economic interests, keeping the EC at bay, and assuring that the United States remained engaged in the climate negotiations. The international norm requiring an emission reduction commitment had influenced British foreign policy by pressing the government toward accepting the 2000 stabilization target. It had thus achieved a "Foreign Policy Impact," and the government was beginning to justify domestic policy changes based on the need to meet its commitment. However, the government continued to defer to the economic interests of those who would be adversely affected.

CONCLUSION

As the INC negotiations began, national leaders had already accepted that climate change was a significant problem that had to be addressed through a multilateral response. There was also broad acceptance of a set of norms to be included in the FCCC. For example, only developed states would be required to accept legally binding emission reduction commitments. The minimum first commitment should be to stabilize emissions at 1990 levels by 2000. Developed states would have a responsibility to transfer technologies and resources to developing states to facilitate emission reductions. The negotiation of the specific provisions to implement these norms would dictate the effects that the FCCC would have on both the future path of climate change and on domestic policy. Prior to 1991, international discussion of climate change could be conducted at a level of abstraction, but as negotiators began to create a legal framework, each state faced a set of tradeoffs among competing domestic interests. Each government had to establish the priority it placed on addressing climate change, determine the international commitments it was willing to support, and decide on the domestic policy changes that it was willing to undertake to achieve its international commitments.

There are some fascinating parallels across the three countries during this period. First, international competitiveness concerns and the potential domestic costs of adjustment to international commitments constrained foreign policy positions. None of the three states appeared willing to accept an international outcome that entailed significant changes to domestic policy or imposed substantial economic costs. Economic considerations clearly drove the foreign policy positions of all three states. Germany, the United States, and the United Kingdom were willing to go as far as existing domestic policies would permit. When there was a conflict between international and domestic policies, the adjustment was typically made at the international level. The internal dynamics of all three countries were very similar despite domestic institutional differences. The major decisions concerning both domestic and foreign climate policies were made at the cabinet level. In all three cases, the cabinets were divided between the environment ministries (often with support from the foreign ministries) and the economic and energy ministries. When policies with the potential for significant domestic economic and/or competitive costs were addressed, ministries with responsibility for energy and economic issues typically blocked these policies.

While all three states rejected policy changes that entailed significant competitive or redistributive consequences, rhetorical support for reducing GHG emissions and the willingness to undertake limited efforts to reduce emissions varied significantly. Differences in domestic institutional structures and approaches to environmental policy appear to explain this variation in the domestic political salience of international norms. The German electoral system and the prominence given to environmental issues by the Green Party led the Kohl government to place greater emphasis on climate policy. The German approach to environmental policy, in particular the precautionary principle, predisposed the government to address climate change. The manner in which the German political system aggregated scientific and economic information also facilitated a domestic consensus on the ability and desirability of reducing carbon emissions. Climate change achieved domestic political salience. The German government pursued policies aimed specifically at climate change. It marginally improved energy efficiency standards in the construction and electric appliance industries. It also promoted the development of renewable energy sources. These policies entailed limited costs to domestic economic actors, but for the most part, they would not have significant effects on the competitive positions of German manufacturers. The Kohl government refused to undertake the two policy options that would have had the greatest effect on carbon emissions. It rejected the unilateral imposition of a carbon tax, and it refused to reform the electricity generation and coal industries. Internationally, Germany pursued a more activist climate policy than either the United Kingdom or the United States. The German government was one of the foremost supporters of the emerging climate norms, and these norms were beginning to be translated into domestic policy changes, though economic concerns constrained their influence on policy.

While there was significant public support for addressing climate change, the Conservative Party in Britain did not face the same electoral pressures as the Kohl government due to the lack of a viable Green Party. British foreign policy was also influenced by the desire to maintain American participation in the negotiations. This goal was tied to broader economic and political objectives related to EC policy. The British hoped to restrict the expansion of EC competence over taxation policy, which limited the type of international and EC measures that would be acceptable. Domestic institutional structures were important for understanding British climate policy. The ability of the government to reform and privatize the electricity and coal sectors provided the carbon emission reductions to allow it to accept a stabilization target. The British reforms were not directed at climate change. Rather, the policies provided a fortuitous opportunity for the United Kingdom to dramatically reduce CO_2 emissions while achieving other policy goals. Regardless of the source of the emission reductions, the ability to meet the international target allowed the British government to pursue a more activist international climate policy. Under pressure, the Major government ultimately affirmed the norms requiring the developed states to act first and conditionally accepted a target of stabilizing emissions at 1990 levels by 2000, but these norms did not significantly affect domestic policy during this period.

A number of domestic institutional forces constrained American policy. The political power of the electricity generation industry, the manufacturing sector, the coal industry, and their relationships with key members of Congress and the Bush administration limited the range of politically viable domestic policies to achieve carbon reductions. The litigious nature of American environmental policy created an obstacle to accepting binding commitments, even when it looked like the United States could meet the proposed international target. The lack of an environmental party in American politics and the inability to establish a scientific and/or policy consensus on the need to address climate change also limited American policy. The American government refused to accept the major international climate norms in its foreign policy or its domestic policy. America's position as a dominant international power and domestic public apathy allowed the Bush administration to oppose the dominant norms and to attempt to reshape them to better reflect American preferences.

In the international negotiations, scientific advice and norm entrepreneurs played little role in determining the key provisions included in the FCCC or the policies pursued by the three countries. The IPCC along with the domestic scientific community in each of the states consistently warned of the dire consequences of a failure to aggressively reduce global GHG emissions. The 2000 stabilization target included in the FCCC had no scientific foundation. It was a political decision. Decisions on the policy mix to achieve carbon emission reductions also held only a tenuous relationship to economic research. Economic analyses (including government-sponsored analyses) suggested that all three countries could achieve large reductions in carbon emissions at little or no economic cost. None of the governments were willing to act on the economic and policy advice presented. Opposition from domestic groups to proposed policy changes and/or fear that the policies could have unintended effects on the competitiveness of industry obstructed attempts to pursue more aggressive emission reductions. The following chapters will look more closely at the effects of the nascent climate regime and its associated norms on the evolution of British, German, American, and European policy preferences and strategies.

CHAPTER FOUR

The Domestic Political Salience of International Norms?

(Rio to Berlin)

The climate negotiations from the 1992 Rio Earth Summit to the signing of the Kyoto Protocol in 1997 can be divided into two phases. The period from the signing of the FCCC in Rio through the negotiation of the 1995 Berlin Mandate was characterized by domestic debates over the feasibility of reducing GHG emission, which would determine the nature of the commitments in the Kyoto Protocol. Following an extended period of domestic political debate, the Berlin Conference of the Parties in 1995 established the negotiating mandate for the Kyoto Protocol. The second phase from Berlin to Kyoto shifted the focus from the domestic policy realm to the negotiation of new international commitments built on largely static domestic policy positions. This second phase will be addressed in chapter 5.

As of 1992, most industrial countries were unlikely to meet the FCCC's nonbinding goal of stabilizing GHG emissions at 1990 levels by 2000. The domestic difficulties led most industrial countries to reexamine their domestic and foreign policy positions. Existing FCCC commitments and growing scientific evidence supporting the warming of the Earth's atmosphere made it difficult to argue that GHG reductions were unnecessary or undesirable. Most governments faced a quandary. They were presented with growing scientific evidence that climate change was occurring and that GHG emission reductions were necessary, but they confronted significant domestic opposition to policies designed to reduce emissions.

Germany, the United Kingdom, and the United States conducted reviews of their national climate policies between 1992 and 1995. The 1992 presidential election appeared to portend a dramatic shift in American climate policy under the leadership of Bill Clinton and Al Gore. However, the new administration confronted significant obstacles to meeting the 2000 stabilization target and faced even more uncertainty for the period after

2000. Although the United Kingdom and Germany were both well positioned to meet the 2000 target, they too faced uncertainty for the period after 2000. Germany had already achieved the easiest CO_2 reductions available in the former East. Emissions in the former West were rising and would likely rise in the East as well unless new policies were enacted. In the United Kingdom, the potential for reducing CO_2 emissions through fuel switching was limited, and emissions from the transportation sector were rising rapidly. The British government would likely need to pursue additional domestic measures to significantly reduce emissions beyond 2000. The difficult policy trade-offs provide an opportunity to evaluate the political salience of international climate norms to the domestic policy debates.

This chapter is structured slightly differently than the last. During the INC process, international negotiations dominated climate policy with domestic policy playing a constraining role in the international discussions. During the period from Rio to Berlin, domestic politics predominated with international negotiations becoming central only toward the end of the period. This chapter thus deals with the formulation of domestic and foreign policies in the United States, the European Union, the United Kingdom, and Germany first and then analyzes the interplay of the various actors in the negotiations at the end of the chapter.

UNITED STATES

American domestic and foreign climate policy underwent intense scrutiny during the 1992 presidential campaign and during the first months of the Clinton presidency. This was a period of significant political debate over the costs and benefits of cutting GHG emissions. The Bush administration continued to argue that short-term domestic policies to address climate change would devastate the American economy. The Bush policy was essentially to reject additional domestic actions and rely on limited GHG emission reductions achieved through existing policies such as the Clean Air Act Amendments of 1990, the National Energy Policy Act, and the EPA's voluntary initiatives such as the Green Lights program. The Bush administration admitted that the United States was unable to return CO_2 emissions to 1990 levels by the year 2000, but it argued that it had made no binding commitment to achieve this goal.

The focus on the United States' inability to reduce GHG emissions was tied to the Bush campaign strategy. The administration sought to turn some of Senator Gore's policy positions on climate change against the Clinton/Gore campaign. In a vice presidential debate, Vice President Quayle attempted to define climate change as a choice between jobs and the environment and suggested that the Bush/Quayle campaign was squarely on the side of jobs. The Clinton/Gore campaign rejected the trade-off and argued that reducing emissions would improve the efficiency of the American economy while also safeguarding the environment.[1] The outcome of the race had very little to do with climate policy, but the election of President Bill Clinton and Vice President Al Gore created expectations among environmental groups and America's negotiating partners that the United States would assume a leadership position on climate change. The 1992 elections provided a window of opportunity for reform of American climate policy.

The Bush administration made one final attempt before leaving office to shape American climate policy. The administration published the American national action plan to address climate change, which was required under the FCCC. The White House released the report over the strong objections of the EPA, which argued that the plan was not publicly reviewed, hastily developed, and inadequate to meet the targets set forth in the FCCC.[2] The plan contained a catalog of existing policy measures that would influence GHG emissions. Environmentalists rejected the plan, and the Clinton administration pledged to revise it when it took office.

A number of early actions by the Clinton administration stoked the optimism that the United States would assume a leading role in the climate negotiations. During President Clinton's address to Congress in February 1993, he called for government-supported investment in energy efficiency, public transit, renewable energies, and most importantly a Btu tax on energy. Even though the modest tax would have only a marginal effect on emissions, it represented the first American attempt to address carbon emissions through taxation. The administration also announced that it would have a revised National Action Plan to present at the August 1993 INC 8 meeting in Geneva. The implication was that the United States would be prepared to commit to a concrete reduction target and undertake the domestic policies required to achieve that objective. This impression was strengthened by the appointment of Rafe Pomerantz of the World Resources Institute to head the American climate negotiating team.

In March 1993, the Clinton administration announced that it was undertaking a full review of American climate policy, but the enthusiasm for domestic and international climate policy had already begun to soften. Commenting on the climate policy review, American Permanent Representative to the United Nations, Madeline Albright, noted that "[w]e will reassess all options for reducing greenhouse gas emissions. Our goal is to determine *whether* we can at least stabilize our greenhouse gas emissions by the year 2000."[3] Ambassador Albright's comments reflected a growing conflict within the Clinton cabinet reminiscent of the debates in the Bush administration. Vice President Gore squared off against Treasury Secretary Bentsen and Energy Secretary O'Leary on the issue of accepting binding international emission reduction targets. Bentsen and O'Leary argued that there had been insufficient studies undertaken on what effect policies to reduce GHG emissions would have on the American economy.[4]

The differences between the Clinton and Bush climate policies began to blur following President Clinton's April 21, 1993 Earth Day speech where he addressed American climate policy. "I am instructing my administration to produce a cost-effective plan by August that can continue the trend of reduced emissions [of GHGs]. . . . Today, I reaffirm my personal, and announce our nation's commitment to reducing our emissions of greenhouse gases to their 1990 levels by the year 2000."[5] Although the president called for a return of GHG emissions to 1990 levels by 2000, he did not specify CO_2. He also did not specify that emissions would be stabilized at 1990 levels, which implied that emissions would increase again after 2000. The president's statements did not present any concrete differences from the Bush policy. President Bush's administration also noted that the United States would be likely to come close to returning total GHG emissions to 1990 levels by 2000—depending on which GHGs were counted. The primary difference was the rhetorical tone of President Clinton's remarks.

The similarity between the Bush and Clinton climate policies became more apparent when the EPA released its revised GHG emission inventory. The EPA continued the Bush administration's policy of counting reductions in CFCs required under the Montreal Protocol, but the EPA failed to count CFC substitutes, which are some of the most potent GHGs and whose emissions were increasing rapidly. The EPA also excluded methane from landfills, an important source of GHG emissions, and calculated net emissions, which included the effects of plant life in removing CO_2 from the air.[6] All of these actions were highly questionable under the reporting methodologies being developed under the FCCC. In essence, the Clinton administration adopted the Bush administration's strategy of creating the appearance of reductions in GHGs to facilitate its claim to the return of GHGs to 1990 levels. The question was whether the new administration would pursue new policies to achieve real reductions in the future.

American Energy Taxation

The 1992–1993 energy tax debate is an important episode for this study in two ways. First, it is a test of the strength of climate commitments as a catalyst for change in a vital area of domestic policy. Second, the debate occurred at approximately the same time as the fuel tax debate in the United Kingdom and the ongoing carbon/energy tax debate in the European Union. The parallel comparisons of these three cases of energy related tax reform offer some insight into the relationship between climate politics and taxation policy.

The issue of an energy tax emerged in the presidential campaign. The EPA had been studying the feasibility of a carbon tax to reduce CO_2 emissions. The National Commission on the Environment, a panel that included several Clinton advisors, called for the development of environmental taxes in its report. The commission asserted that a one dollar per gallon increase in the gasoline tax, the introduction of a carbon tax, and the elimination of federal subsidies for agriculture and natural resource extraction were all necessary for the United States to move toward a "sustainable growth" path.[7] President Clinton adopted the environmental taxation proposals as part of his campaign platform.

The proposed energy taxes emerged as part of the president-elect's policy agenda in January 1993. The Clinton administration's stated goal was to cut the budget deficit by $145 billion over its first term. To achieve this goal the administration would have to find significant sources of revenue and/or impose large budget cuts. The administration's options were further constrained by campaign pledges to cut taxes for the middle class. The proposal of a broad-based energy tax presented a number of opportunities. The administration could present the measure as an environmental policy. The tax would have the effect of raising energy prices and thus encouraging greater investments in energy efficiency and conservation measures, which should result in falling CO_2 emissions as well as other damaging emissions. In addition, it would produce significant new revenue for the government. As one Clinton administration official put it, "[t]he attraction on energy was that everyone thought you were doing good if you did it."[8]

The debate within the administration was over what type of energy tax to enact. Environmental groups along with Vice President Gore favored a carbon tax, but President Clinton and his advisors rejected that option on political grounds. A carbon tax would have hurt eastern coal producing states disproportionately, and these states were a crucial part of the president's election coalition. The debate came down to two proposals: a tax on the energy content of fuels measured in British thermal units (Btus) or a tax on the retail prices of fuels. The administration chose the Btu tax because the relationship between thermal content and fuel choice was such that the tax would be heaviest on imported oil while having a lesser impact on domestically produced natural gas and coal. It had the additional advantage of creating higher taxes on coal from Republican-dominated western states while imposing a relatively lower tax on eastern coal from Democratic states.[9]

Domestic opposition to energy taxes began to mobilize even before the administration made its taxation proposals. The US Chamber of Commerce, the American Petroleum Institute, the National Association of Manufacturers, as well as a large number of trade associations organized a grassroots and Washington lobbying strategy to block the proposed energy taxes.[10] The lobbying proved to be extremely successful. Republicans were already opposed to new energy taxes, and even prominent Democrats were uneasy with the proposal. Faced with aggressive lobbying from the business community, the Clinton administration began to take some of the "green" tint out of the tax package. The administration created exemptions for important energy interests including coal producers, oil refiners, the natural gas industry, ethanol producers, aluminum smelters, and chemical manufacturers, among others. Although the administration was able to move the revised tax through the House, a revolt by Senate Democrats doomed the proposal. In the end, the Senate forced the administration to accept a 4.3 cent per gallon increase in the gasoline tax. The tax would raise only $23 billion over five years compared to the $72 billion that the Btu tax would have raised.[11] The tax would also have a very limited effect on carbon emissions.

The tax debate is particularly interesting because it illustrates the difficulties of initiating new domestic policies to address climate change. President Clinton launched the tax initiative immediately after entering office during what should have been his "honeymoon." He also had a Democratically controlled House and Senate. This was the best opportunity to fundamentally alter the relationship between energy and environmental policy and achieve the president's broader deficit reduction goal. Initially, the need to reduce CO_2 emissions was used as a major justification for pursuing the Btu tax, but climate change fell to the wayside quickly as the distributive effects of the tax came to dominate the debate. In the end, the international norm requiring domestic reductions had no significant effect on the debate. However, the rejection of the tax left the Clinton administration with a gaping hole in its plans for cutting CO_2 emissions and sapped much of the administration's will to fight for policies to address climate change.

American Foreign Policy

In the face of the defeat of the Btu tax and substantial industrial lobbying, the Clinton administration scaled back its domestic policy proposals and assumed a position of rhetorical support for international action combined with limited commitment to domestic change. The failure to complete the revised climate action plan before the administration's self-imposed deadline of the August 1993 INC 8 meeting illustrated the waning support for reducing GHG emissions. When the plan was finally released in October 1993, President Clinton asserted that the revised action plan "re-establishes the United States as a world leader in protecting global climate. . . . I urge other industrialized countries to move rapidly to produce plans as detailed, as realistic, and as achievable as ours."[12] Although the rhetoric represented a significant shift from the Bush administration, the substance of the action plan was little changed. The focus was on *voluntary* measures directed at energy efficiency. There were to be no new taxes or regulatory measures to reduce GHG emissions. The federal government was to spend $1.9 billion on environmental technologies by 2000 with the private sector predicted to spend $61 billion. The private sector was predicted to receive a return of $207 billion between 2001 and 2010 on its investments through energy savings.[13] These investments were reminiscent of the "no regrets" policies advocated by the Bush administration. Even with the projected public and private spending, carbon emissions would continue to increase. The growth in CO_2 emissions was to be offset by reductions in other GHGs. The primary policy initiative was on the international side. President Clinton called for joint implementation to allow countries to reduce global emissions in the most cost-effective manner possible.

The revised American national action plan essentially set the American negotiating position for the ongoing INC process. The United States would be unwilling to agree to a legally binding target on CO_2 stabilization. It would seek to define GHGs in the broadest possible manner. There would be no attempts domestically to cut emissions through new regulations or taxes. Instead, voluntary measures and international investments would form the core of American climate policy. The Clinton administration's climate policy evolved into the Bush policy with more aggressive rhetorical support for the world's common interest in cutting GHG emissions. Ambassador Albright reflected this new viewpoint in comments to an INC meeting in New York. According to Albright, "[t]he new administration believes we must act with a sense of urgency to strengthen our common resolve for protecting the global climate. . . . The United States wants to help lead this effort."[14]

Although the Clinton administration articulated the view that climate change was a major threat to the United States and the world, it continued to block concrete targets or timetables in the INC process. The leadership the United States attempted to provide was in pushing developing countries to accept GHG reduction targets and concurrently to accept joint implementation as a means for the United States to meet its reduction targets by paying for emissions reductions elsewhere. In December 1993, the State Department issued ground rules for a joint implementation pilot program. The rules were to create the foundation for American companies to engage in JI immediately and potentially receive future credit for GHG reductions. The administration hoped to convince its partners to adopt its rules as the foundation for an international JI program.

As serious negotiations on the future of commitments under the FCCC began in August 1994, climate change had fallen off the domestic policy agenda. The administration focused on making international commitments consistent with American domestic policy requirements. This meant that there could be no legally binding targets or timetables, and the United States would demand provisions for joint implementation, emissions trading, and developing country participation before it would accept an international agreement. However, these positions ran counter to the two dominant international norms requiring developed states to act first and to pursue domestic emission reductions. It would be essential for the administration to reframe the international debate and alter the normative context for the negotiations if it was to succeed in achieving its objectives.

Conclusions from the American Case

This period of American climate policy provides a number of important insights into the domestic obstacles to the incorporation of international norms into domestic policy. First, the domestic institutional framework was a major constraint on the Clinton administration's climate strategy. The administration attempted to integrate climate policy with taxation to simultaneously reduce the deficit and cut CO_2 emissions, but the independence of Congress and the associated influence of economic interests over the policy process blocked the attempt. Subsequently, the administration made the calculation that domestic adjustment was too expensive politically and shifted its strategy to securing an international agreement consistent with the existing domestic policy situation.

Second, this period of American climate policy is particularly instructive, because it demonstrates the relative unimportance of the personal views of the members of the administration and the difficulties of altering the status quo in the American policy process. As a senator, Al Gore had been a leading advocate for an aggressive policy to address climate change. President Clinton had promised during the campaign to make climate change a top priority for his administration. American foreign environmental policy was coordinated in the State Department by former Senator Timothy Wirth, who was another advocate for action to address climate change. Finally, Rafe Pomerantz of the World Resources Institute initially led the American climate negotiating team. This group of policy makers had the potential to revolutionize American climate policy. The Democratic Party controlled the presidency and both houses of Congress, and yet American climate policy changed only marginally from the Bush policy. Climate change did not have sufficient political salience to alter the domestic policy equilibrium in the areas of energy policy, energy taxation, or transportation.

Third, expert policy advice continued to have a limited effect on American climate policy. Studies by the EPA and a number of NGOs demonstrated that energy and/or carbon taxes could reduce American CO_2

emissions with limited economic effects, and yet policy makers refused to act based on those studies. Economic and scientific evidence was used to bolster the existing positions of participants in the policy process, but it had little effect on policy outcomes. Finally, international pressure had only a marginal effect on American policy. The European Union and its member states all encouraged the United States to develop a program of energy taxation and to commit to internationally binding targets and timetables to reduce GHG emissions, but the pressure had no effect on American policy. The Clinton administration rhetorically affirmed the emergent international norm requiring GHG emission reductions, but it was unwilling or unable to accept the implications for domestic policy. The administration also sought to overturn the emerging norm that exempted developing states from GHG emission commitments. If the United States was to participate in the international climate regime, the normative framework would have to be shifted away from a primary focus on domestic emission reductions and toward a focus on economic efficiency and the participation of all states in the most cost effective strategies for reducing global emissions.

UNITED KINGDOM

Following the signing of the FCCC in Rio, the British government was in a position similar to that of the United States. In 1992, the Energy Ministry released a report noting that British carbon emissions in 2000 could range from 1990 levels up to an increase of 15 percent—assuming no additional government actions to reduce carbon emissions.[15] Four factors accounted for the broad range of possible emission levels. First, the British economic recession was constraining growth in emissions. The length and severity of the recession would have a significant impact on emission levels. Second, the structure of the British economy was changing. The energy sector was predicted to fall from 9 to 4 percent of GDP by 2020. In addition, energy intensive manufacturing was declining and being replaced by service industries. Third, changes in the fuel mix for electricity generation were producing fewer CO_2 emissions. Coal provided 68 percent of electricity in 1990. By 2020, energy experts predicted that it would provide only 27 percent. The contribution of natural gas to energy production was set to rise from 0 to 57 percent by 2020.[16] Finally, carbon emissions from the transportation sector were set to rise at an alarming rate unless the government took action in the near future.

The rapid shift from coal to natural gas was having a profound effect on British emissions. It was possible, under the most optimistic assumptions, that the government would not have to undertake any new domestic policies to meet its objectives. However, the Major government adopted a more proactive stance than the United States and assumed it would need to cut its emissions by ten million tons of CO_2 (mtc) by 2000 to return emissions to 1990 levels. The government prepared a broad ranging emission reduction plan to achieve its reduction target (proposed emission reductions included in parentheses): value-added tax on home fuel/electricity (1.5 mtc), value-added tax on transportation fuels (1.5 mtc), Energy Savings Trust investments (2.5 mtc), and building regulations and renewable energy promotion (1.0 mtc).[17] Each of these measures will be discussed below. However, it became apparent in the ensuing years that the changes occurring in the fuel mix for electricity production would obviate the need for significant additional measures to reduce GHG emissions. The rapidly declining CO_2 emissions would weaken the government's will to pursue additional politically costly measures to reduce GHG emissions.

British Value Added Taxes

In 1993, the Major government proposed an extension of the value-added tax to residential heating fuels. The VAT debate occurred concurrently with the Btu tax discussion in the United States. Similar to the Clinton administration, the Major government in 1993 faced a country in recession and a gaping hole in its budget. The government desperately needed a new source of revenue, but the Conservatives had campaigned on lowering taxes. The Major government believed that an extension of the value-added tax to residential heating fuels and an increase in automotive fuel taxes provided a viable solution to its dilemma. The taxes could be portrayed as "green" measures, rather than attempts to raise revenue. In addition, the tax had the advantage of preempting action at the EU level. The British government could point to its own domestic taxes as sufficient to meet its CO_2 reduction target and thus further undermine Commission arguments that states would not pursue energy taxes on their own.

Treasury Secretary Norman Lamont made the strategy behind the initiative quite clear in his presentation of the taxes. "Together with measures which have already been announced, these tax proposals should take Britain two-thirds of the way to meeting the Rio target. They will do so in a way that does the least possible damage to the competitiveness of British industry." Lamont also alluded to the latent rationale for pursuing the tax. "I remain unpersuaded of the need for a new European Union tax. Tax policy should continue to be decided here in this House—not in Brussels."[18] British industry was to be left untouched by the new taxes due to international competitiveness concerns, and the EU would be left with a major obstacle to an EU wide carbon/energy tax.

The government proposed to raise the VAT on heating fuels and domestic electricity over two years to 17.5 percent. The motor fuel duty was to increase by 3 percent per year for an indefinite period. Although the motor fuel tax was relatively uncontroversial, the domestic fuels duty created a storm of protest. The Labour Party attacked the Major government for balancing the budget on the backs of the poor. The Conservative government further provoked public opposition by initially failing to provide funding to cover the additional charges to pensioners and those on public assistance. The fact that the Major government was able to force through the tax, even over the opposition of many Conservative backbenchers, is a tribute to the power of the British parliamentary system to enact change when the ruling government deems it necessary.

A comparison between the Btu tax debacle in the United States and the domestic fuel tax in the United Kingdom illustrates a key distinction between the American and British political systems. In the British case, there was limited debate of the domestic fuel tax proposal. It was presented as part of the government's budget and came as a surprise to most political pundits. The short period between the proposal and the budget's passage limited the amount of time for opposition to organize against the tax. The party discipline of the British parliamentary system also provided the Major government with more leeway in pressing its agenda. In the American case, the Btu tax proposal was made in January and the gasoline tax compromise was not accepted until July. American interest groups had much more time to mobilize, and the nature of the American political system provided more access points to pursue their interests. Although the Democratic Party controlled the executive's office and both houses of Congress, the relative independence of congressional leaders and the lower level of party unity made it much more difficult for the Clinton administration to impose its agenda.

However, the following year's budget debate demonstrated equally the limitations of the government's ability to defy public opinion. In September 1993, the Conservative government faced a grassroots revolt over the VAT tax. In response, it offered additional aid to pensioners and those on public assistance to help cover the costs of the tax. Nevertheless, the Labour Party and eight Conservative backbenchers defeated the second stage of the domestic VAT. The action was a significant blow to the United Kingdom's CO_2 reduction plan, though it is unclear how much of an effect the increases would have had. Electricity prices had fallen considerably because of privatization of the electricity industry, and the motor fuel tax had not kept up with the rate of decline in fuel prices.

Carbon emissions and the British climate strategy were not significant issues in the VAT debate beyond the initial justifications by the Major government. This episode demonstrated the limited domestic political salience of GHG emission reduction commitments as a justification for broader domestic policies. Similar to the Clinton administration efforts on the Btu tax, the Major government was willing to use climate change as a justification for a politically difficult policy, but the public was unwilling to accept the justification.

Energy Savings Trust

The Energy Savings Trust (EST) was part of the Conservative's election manifesto and the centerpiece of the Major government's plan for cutting emissions prior to the VAT tax. The EST was officially launched in May 1992. It was to receive funding from British Gas and the regional electricity utilities, which would then pass the costs on to consumers as a surcharge in their utility bills. The funds were to be used to facilitate energy efficiency investments by consumers and to promote combined heat and power projects. The EST ran into difficulty from the very beginning. It had no chairman for the first five months of its existence as the government sought a high profile individual willing to take on the task. The EST made almost no investments in 1993 and disbursed less than £4 million in the first quarter of 1994.[19] Even with the slow start, the EST had the potential to achieve its target if it moved aggressively during the latter half of the 1990s. However, it ran into further trouble when OFGAS' director general refused to pass the costs of the EST on to consumers on the grounds that the program should be funded through the budget.[20] The program's funding was further imperiled when the director general of Offer, the electricity regulatory agency, refused to provide more than £25 million per year.

The funding dispute quickly emerged as a political issue. The Labour Party maintained that the increase in energy prices the EST would require was excessive on top of the proposed 17.5 percent increase in the VAT tax. Labour also argued that the EST was unfair because all consumers would pay into the fund, but only a small fraction would receive the benefits from the grants for energy efficiency measures.[21] The government had alternative means to fund the EST. It could have bypassed the regulators and directly applied a 2 to 4 percent levy on electricity and gas, but the growing political conflict over the VAT on heating fuels made a new tax politically unpalatable. It could also have funded it within the general budget, but this would have required finding additional revenue and/or budget cuts in other areas. Falling energy prices undermined the incentives for energy efficiency investments, and public support for government funded energy efficiency programs was also fading. The rapid conversion from coal to natural gas also meant that the British climate target could likely be met without the energy efficiency measures. The result was that the EST, once a centerpiece of the United Kingdom's climate strategy, was allowed to wither into a marginal program that provided limited funds for a small number of projects and promoted energy efficiency through publicly funded publicity campaigns.

The defeat of the VAT tax along with the failure of the Energy Savings Trust eliminated 40 percent of the projected cuts in CO_2 emissions included in the British climate strategy.

In addition to the EST savings, energy efficiency measures were supposed to provide 35 percent of the United Kingdom's total emissions reductions. The government did not specify how these reductions were to be achieved. The primary regulatory change was a bill requiring double-glazed windows and stricter regulation of the use of air conditioners. Rather than impose new regulations, the government launched a £6 million media campaign to raise public awareness of the need to conserve energy. The program, entitled "Wasting Energy Costs the Earth," targeted children and featured talking dinosaurs. Despite the ongoing attempts to raise public awareness, government studies revealed that public understanding of energy efficiency remained low. The government appeared unlikely to induce sufficient CO_2 emission reductions through energy conservation to meet its target. Even the government, which had pledged to cut its own energy use by 15 percent by 1997, found that its energy use had actually increased.[22]

Transportation

The one area where British emissions were set to rise significantly was in the transportation sector, which was conspicuously absent from the government's emission reduction plan. The Royal Commission on Environmental Pollution produced an alarming report on the future of British transportation. According to Commission Chairman, Professor John Lawton, "life, particularly in southern England, in thirty years will be . . . hell on earth. . . . Noise, smell, concrete, and impossible to go anywhere. Congestion means our cities will not work and our motorways will not work."[23] The Commission called for a number of measures to reduce road and air transport. British business leaders condemned the report on the grounds that its calls for increased taxes and restrictions on road building and road usage would raise production costs, lead to price increases for consumers, and reduce British competitiveness.

The primary government action to address transportation policy was the development of new "Planning Policy Guidelines" for local land use. The guidelines entailed recommendations for restrictions on parking spaces, limits on new out of town industrial parks, and limits on development on the edges of communities. According to Environment Minister Gummer, "The Government recognizes that forecast levels for traffic growth especially in urban areas cannot be met in full and that new road building or the upgrading of existing highways may be environmentally unacceptable."[24] Despite the recognition of the transport sector problems, the government continued with its program of road expansion. It was unwilling to take the politically unpopular actions necessary to address emissions from the transportation sector beyond imposing increases in gasoline taxes.

Conclusions from the British Case

Despite being more active than the United States in developing a domestic program to address GHG emissions, the United Kingdom ended up in a position very similar to that of the United States. The government successfully pursued an increase in the gasoline tax and half of its proposed VAT on household energy use, but Tory backbenchers blocked the larger VAT increases. On the other hand, the government was unable to overcome obstacles to effectively implement its Energy Savings Trust program, was unwilling to address industrial energy use through taxation due to competitiveness concerns, refused to tackle the transportation sector beyond raising the gasoline tax, and declined to impose significant new regulations to improve energy efficiency. The government essentially failed to implement the program that it had outlined to reduce GHG emissions. Rather than pursue additional regulatory or taxation measures, the Major government emphasized voluntary energy conservation measures and publicity campaigns.

Paralleling the American experience, the government charged its Foreign Ministry with the task of making international policy compatible with existing domestic policy. The Major government had to operate simultaneously within the EU and the INC. British negotiators fought to assure that international, particularly EU, climate policy was consistent with existing British policy. The Major government continued to block a European carbon/energy tax and opposed any sort of burden sharing that would require the United Kingdom to cut its emissions to compensate for higher emissions among the Eurpean Union's southern members. International forces had a limited effect on British climate policy. The EU carbon/energy tax debate created additional incentives for the Major government to expand its domestic VAT on fuels to preempt EU action, but the government was primarily motivated by the need to increase tax revenue.

The Major government assumed a much more proactive position on climate change than its American counterparts and supported the emerging international norms related to emission reduction commitments and the exemption of developing countries. It adopted a plan to reduce national emissions; however, it largely failed to implement the central components of the plan. In the end, the British domestic efforts were not that different from the American position. However, the Major government was able to rely on the rapid shift from coal to natural gas to obviate the need for immediate policy changes.

GERMANY

As the United States and the United Kingdom struggled with policies to achieve their emission reductions, Germany found itself in a similar position. Though returning CO_2 emissions to 1990 levels remained achievable, the more ambitious goal of cutting emissions by more than 25 percent by 2005 was slipping further from its grasp. Emissions were rising in the West and only the dramatic declines in the East created any prospect of meeting the 2005 target. For example, October 1992 projections by the Wuppertal Institute for Climate, Environment, and Energy Policies suggested that Germany as a whole was unlikely to cut its emissions by more than 10 percent under existing conditions.[25] Conflicts emerged in the Kohl cabinet over how to address CO_2 emissions. The Environment Ministry publicly reaffirmed Germany's reduction goal, while the Economics Ministry called the 25 to 30 percent target unachievable.[26]

Faced with the prospect of missing its CO_2 reduction target, the government responded by announcing a new interministerial study to determine the feasibility of additional policies to accelerate cuts in GHG emissions. The two prior reports, released in November 1990 and December 1991, cataloged long lists of policies directed at reducing carbon emissions. Of these proposals, only one, a requirement for electricity companies to purchase power from renewable energy sources, had been fully adopted by the end of 1992. The Kohl government either delayed or rejected proposals to encourage combined heat/power cogeneration plants, to increase building insulation standards, to establish minimum heating efficiency standards, to introduce a carbon and/or energy tax, and to convert vehicle taxes to taxes on vehicle emissions. The failure to enact these policies produced sharp criticism from the SPD, the Greens, and even Chancellor Kohl's own CDU/CSU party members. The government asserted that its interministerial report, due by the end of 1993, would contain sufficient measures to reduce all GHG emissions, including NO_x, CFCs, VOCs, and CO_2 by 50 percent by 2005. The government's ambitious CO_2 reduction target was beginning to soften as the government diluted the focus on carbon dioxide and included additional GHGs in the calculations. The tactic was very similar to that pursued by the American government; however, Germany's target remained much more ambitious than its American counterpart.

Between the signing of the FCCC in Rio and the first Conference of Parties (COP–1) in 1995, climate policy intersected with related domestic policy debates in four primary areas: energy efficiency, the carbon tax, nuclear power, and transportation policy. In each case, the government declined to impose new regulations or taxes and instead pursued voluntary agreements with the affected actors. The voluntary approach fit well with Germany's corporatist system, and it was possible that the strategy could provide the necessary emission reductions at a lower cost than government regulation. If the strategy succeeded, it would provide German corporations with a competitive advantage over foreign companies, which would be forced to reduce GHG emissions through government regulation or taxation. The German experiment thus provides an alternative approach to emission reductions.

German Carbon Tax Debate

The Kohl government continued to support the concept of a carbon tax, but it refused to introduce the tax unilaterally for fear of harming the competitiveness of German industry and due to strong opposition from industry. The SPD and Greens attempted to make the carbon tax a major election issue prior to the October 1994 federal elections, but it failed to resonate with the electorate. The Kohl government's opposition to imposing the carbon tax is interesting in light of research demonstrating that a properly implemented tax would have a positive effect on the economy and on carbon emissions. According to the German Institute for Economic Research (DIW), a continuous increase in the tax by 7 percent per year would produce a decline in carbon emissions and energy consumption of 20 percent by 2005. In addition, prices would remain stable, six hundred ten thousand new jobs would be created, and there would be no adverse redistribution of income so long as the new tax revenues were recycled back to tax payers to keep the tax revenue neutral.[27] Faced with extensive industrial lobbying, the Kohl government continued to reject the unilateral imposition of a carbon/energy tax. Following the October elections, the CDU/CSU and FDP declared in their coalition agreement that any unilaterally imposed carbon/energy tax would be unacceptable on competitiveness grounds, and they emphasized that, at a minimum, an EU-wide energy/carbon tax was essential.[28]

Voluntary agreements also became linked with the carbon tax issue. German industrial interest groups attempted to quash the carbon/energy tax debate indefinitely. The BDI, the association of energy intensive industries, announced that their members would collectively reduce their carbon emissions by 20 percent by 2015 if the government would suspend its regulatory and taxation proposals. In response, the government announced that it would delay a carbon/energy tax as well as the introduction of new energy efficiency regulations for at least two years pending progress toward Germany's carbon reduction objectives. The agreement further complicated efforts to develop a European energy tax and energy efficiency initiatives. The voluntary accord appeared to prevent the Kohl government from supporting EU initiatives that would supersede the domestic agreement. The government essentially forfeited regulatory control over its climate policy in return for the voluntary commitments by industry to produce the necessary emission reductions. The rapid emission reductions achieved in the former East reduced the pressure for the government to immediately adopt additional regulations to reduce GHG emissions. However, if industry failed to fulfill its commitments, the government would face significant difficulties in the future to achieve its more ambitious domestic target.

German Nuclear Energy

Nuclear power had long been a core component of Germany's energy strategy, but growing public discontent with nuclear energy and strident opposition by the Greens was undermining its long-term viability. In 1992, the political parties had initiated a review of the role of nuclear energy in the national energy strategy. The Greens entered the talks seeking commitments to phase out the nuclear industry. The parties were unable to achieve consensus, and the Greens eventually pulled out. The government attempted to revive the talks by utilizing climate change as a justification for maintaining the nuclear program, which touched off a raucous debate. The government argued that nuclear energy was critical to Germany's ability to meet its carbon reduction objectives. The SPD and Greens rejected the assertion and criticized the government's failure to adopt meaningful measures to cut Germany's emissions. The Kohl government accused the SPD of hypocrisy for supporting the expanded use of coal for energy production in the face of the threat of climate change.[29]

The political conflict surrounding nuclear energy continued throughout the climate negotiations. The government initiated new consensus talks in 1994 without achieving an agreement. The German electricity industry attempted to link the future of the nuclear industry to the government's CO_2 emission reduction target and the global response to climate change. The industry pledged to voluntarily reduce its emissions by 25 percent by the year 2015, but only on the condition that its nuclear plants would be allowed to function to the end of their designated life cycles. The nuclear debate remained deadlocked, and the status quo would prevail until the election of the new SPD/Greens government in 1998.

Conclusions from the German Case

Climate change was a much more prominent issue in German politics than it was in the United States or the United Kingdom during this period. The Green Party had been extremely active on climate issues, and the Kohl government had adopted climate change as one of its core "green" issues in the most recent elections. Of the three countries studied here, Germany should have been most politically predisposed to pursue policies to address climate change. Yet, the German case parallels the British and American climate policy debates. In all three countries, climate change was utilized to support domestically difficult policy proposals, and in all three cases, the governments failed to achieve the desired policy changes. The Kohl government continued to utilize climate change as a justification for nuclear energy, but public, SPD, and Green Party opposition constrained the ability of the government to promote nuclear power. The government exploited climate change to justify a carbon/energy tax and additional energy efficiency measures, but in both cases, it ultimately rejected the measures on competitiveness grounds. It also refused to address emissions from transportation.

The corporatist nature of interest representation in Germany provided an opportunity for addressing GHG emissions that was much more unlikely in the American context. Instead of pursuing regulation, the government worked with industry to develop voluntary agreements to reduce GHG emissions. Voluntary agreements had the potential to significantly cut emissions without creating the adverse competitive effects that regulations and taxes could create. If the voluntary accords were successful, they would provide German industry with a competitive advantage, because they would have reduced domestic emissions without creating regulatory burdens that other states would likely pursue to reduce GHG emissions.

Germany remained well placed to meet the FCCC's 2000-stabilization target, and it would achieve larger short-term emission reductions than any of its industrial partners. It did not face significant international pressure to change its policies and could continue to aggressively pursue binding international emission reduction targets. However, the German reductions were primarily derived from the restructuring of the former East German economy. Emissions in the East were already showing signs of increasing. Germany had an interest in assuring that over the long-term it would be able to meet future GHG reduction goals without significant domestic costs. Thus, during the latter part of this period of negotiations, Germany began to support American calls for including "flexibility mechanisms," such as joint implementation, in a protocol to the FCCC. This represented a shift away from the norm requiring emission reductions to be achieved domestically. Germany called for such mechanisms to be available for commitments after 2000, which fit with German emission reduction needs. The Kohl government maintained a strong rhetorical position on climate change, and it continued to support a meaningful international agreement to reduce GHG emissions. However, it largely deferred costly domestic actions to reduce emissions and placed its faith in voluntary accords and emission reductions in the East to meet its commitments.

THE EUROPEAN UNION

The European Union remained at the forefront of efforts to secure international commitments to reduce GHG emissions, and the Commission continued to use the climate negotiations to pressure member states to broaden its international and internal policy mandates. The European Union also increasingly became a battleground for the United Kingdom and Germany to pursue their interests. The United Kingdom sought to block EU climate proposals that contravened existing domestic policies, but it focused primarily on defeating the carbon tax initiative. The Kohl government was unwilling to pursue significant unilateral emission reduction measures, and it sought to promote common policies at the EU level to avoid adverse competitive effects. The European climate debates increasingly became a microcosm of the larger climate negotiations, and the member states repeatedly failed to achieve consensus on common measures to reduce GHG emissions. The Council, through budget cuts and the failure to adopt proposed measures, had emaciated the other climate-related programs (ALTENER, SAVE, THERMIE, and JOULE), which would not provide significant CO_2 emission reductions. The Commission faced a difficult situation in its climate policy. The combined carbon emissions of the member states were likely to lead the EU to miss the 2000 target. The Commission had to create a strategy that would achieve the required emission cuts in the face of a diversity of member state interests and a general reluctance to undertake major new environmental regulations during a period of economic downturn.

One of the most important issues that had to be resolved was whether each individual state would be required to meet the same emission reduction target or whether targets would be differentiated according to domestic circumstances. In addition, would the EU require all member states to accept the same common policies or would states pursue their own unique mixes of domestic policies? Discussion of European climate policy stagnated under the British presidency of the EU in the second half of 1992. In the first half of 1993, the Danish presidency and the Commission focused on establishing a standardized system of reporting member state emissions. The reporting program was intended to provide uniform data on member state emissions and create a foundation to develop emission reduction strategies.

The March 1993 Environment Council meeting agreed on a standard reporting methodology, but in the process, it opened up a dispute over the nature of the European Union's commitments under the FCCC. The Major government perceived the common reporting methodology to be the first step toward EU control of member state climate policies. The United Kingdom rejected EU control and refused to accept any sort of burden sharing between northern and southern member states to meet a common EU emissions reduction target. The British representatives negotiated an understanding that the Commission would not be able to impose changes to the national programs of a member state without the state's agreement. The British position led to a split with Germany, Belgium, Italy, Luxembourg, and the Netherlands who inserted a declaration in the meeting's minutes noting that they would block ratification of the FCCC if the EU was unable to develop a policy framework to achieve its emission cuts.[30] They argued that the EU's ratification would be meaningless unless the member states agreed to jointly develop a strategy to achieve the necessary emission reductions. The Council finally agreed that each state would be responsible for its own target, but progress would be monitored at the EU level. Presumably, if the member states failed to achieve sufficient reductions on their own, the EU would assume responsibility for coordinating national responses.

The agreement fit well with British interests, but it undermined the EU's claim to have a common climate policy. The burden sharing issue would become a major problem for the member states leading up to Kyoto. Following the agreement for individual states to pursue their own climate policies, EU attention shifted once again to the carbon/energy tax debate.

European Carbon/Energy Tax

Denmark revived the controversial carbon tax debate during its EU presidency. At the March 1993 Environment Council meeting, Denmark, Germany, Italy, Belgium, the Netherlands, and Luxembourg formally committed themselves to an EU energy tax, and eleven of the twelve member states expressed at least tentative support for the tax.[31] Tax supporters sought to build on the momentum created by President Clinton's recent Btu tax proposal. However, the United Kingdom continued to block the initiative. The British advocated a compromise that would allow any country able to meet its target without a tax (i.e., the United Kingdom) to opt out of the taxation requirement. Those member states unable to achieve their goal would be forced to accept the tax. The British position was unacceptable to the other member states. British Environment Minister Gummer emerged triumphantly from the Council meeting. He alleged that the meeting was an "ambush" designed to force the British to accept a carbon tax. Gummer claimed victory in blocking the tax proposal and noted that "[w]e believe our programs are already enough to meet our national commitments, and we see no reason for an EU-wide energy tax."[32]

The EU had the potential for eleven countries to move forward with a measure that would cut CO_2 emissions and take the EU a significant way toward its emission reduction objective. However, the member states apparently rejected the tax because it would give one country, the United Kingdom, an unfair competitive advantage. It is difficult to judge whether all eleven other states were truly willing to implement the tax if the British would not have blocked it. It is likely that several countries would have raised objections, but they were instead able to hide behind the United Kingdom's tenacious position. The June 1993 Finance Council rejection of the tax provides stronger evidence of the underlying opposition to the carbon tax. The failure of the American Btu tax created further uncertainty regarding the EU's proposal. French Energy Minister Gerard Longuet noted that the American failure to increase its taxes raised serious questions about the European effort, "we want to proceed at a rhythm no faster than our major competitors."[33]

Supporters of the tax brought the issue to a head in the fall of 1993. The EU had pledged to ratify the FCCC by the end of 1993. However, Germany and other tax supporters attempted to hold the ratification hostage in their efforts to create a common EU climate policy (including a carbon/energy tax). The failure to ratify the convention was becoming an embarrassment. At a December 1993 meeting of the Environment Council, fourteen hours of negotiations failed to resolve the issue, and the Netherlands, Denmark, and Germany continued to block ratification. An additional Council meeting was set for December 15 to find a compromise solution. At the meeting, the United Kingdom called the bluff of those member states blocking ratification and won. The EU ratified the convention without a common EU climate policy. Each member state would be responsible for its own emission reductions.

Without the carbon tax, the EU had limited options to meet its commitment. The SAVE program was supposed to provide one-third of the necessary CO_2 emission reductions, but the lack of funding and political support meant that it was unlikely to provide even a fraction of those reductions. The Environment Council made an additional attempt to produce a comprehensive, achievable program to meet the EU's climate commitments at the March 1994 Environment Council meeting. The Environment Council called on the Commission to prepare a 1990 baseline from which the EU could evaluate member state progress toward the 2000 commitment. In addition, the Commission was to estimate emission levels in 2000 based on existing member state policies. Should it appear that the member states would not jointly achieve their objectives with existing instruments, the Commission was instructed to offer proposals under the SAVE, ALTENER, THERMIE, and JOULE programs.[34] Finally, a high-level group was to be set up to once again study the carbon/energy tax. The Commission was to report its findings to the Council at a June 1994 Environment Council meeting.

The June meeting made no progress on the tax. The member states had divided into four camps on the issue with no clear compromise available. The United Kingdom rejected any tax. Another group of states was willing to consider a tax, but only if the United States and Japan implemented a similar tax. A third group sought a carbon tax but not an energy tax, and finally the fourth group was willing to accept a tax but only with burden sharing.[35] Questions surrounding the tax intensified as ECOFIN expressed great concern over the competitive effects of a carbon tax on European firms. The heads of state finally rejected the tax at the 1994 Essen Summit. Member states were left to pursue tax policies on their own, should they choose to do so. British Environment Minister Gummer pronounced himself "very pleased" at the outcome and noted that the energy tax was "dead in the water." [36] The failure to adopt a tax left the EU in a position where it would be unlikely to meet its emission reduction target, unless the United Kingdom and Germany significantly reduced their emissions beyond their national targets.

Conclusions from the European Case

The December 1994 Essen Summit of heads of state finalized the agreement on an EU climate action plan including measures under the SAVE, THERMIE, and ALTENER programs as well as additional efforts to achieve automobile fuel efficiency and to reduce other greenhouse gases. Though it was not officially acknowledged, the program, as formulated, was insufficient to achieve the necessary emission reductions. The heads of state implicitly accepted that the EU program was merely the summation of national programs. The failure to adopt common EU policies to address climate change undermined the Commission's negotiating position in the INC talks by opening it to charges of hypocrisy for its own failure to act.

The Commission and more progressive member states failed to overcome the opposition of member states disinclined to act on climate change. The United Kingdom was willing and able to protect its interests by vetoing the carbon/energy tax without significant political cost. The member states as a whole were loath to pursue common policies in other areas such as energy savings or fuel switching. Though the EU negotiated on behalf of the member states, there was little coordination of domestic policies. While the EU and its member states continued to affirm the norm requiring domestic emission reductions, the norm failed to achieve sufficient salience to alter EU policy.

The Commission attempted to use climate change to extend policy competence into energy taxation and broaden its power base in international affairs. Member states blocked its efforts and maintained control of national climate policies. Overall, the Commission forced member states to address climate policy more than many likely would have otherwise, but its effect on member state policies was limited. It could be argued that if the United Kingdom had been excluded from the EU decision making process, the EU would have been more likely to act. Although plausible, it is unlikely that the Commission would have achieved its objectives. France and Spain joined the United Kingdom at a number of points to block the carbon/energy tax, and Germany's voluntary agreements with domestic industry would seem to preclude German acceptance of a carbon/energy tax. In other climate-related areas such as the SAVE program, member states were also unable to find common ground even without the United Kingdom blocking agreement. The EU remained among the foremost supporters of international climate action, but the inability to achieve meaningful coordination of member state policies undermined its claim to leadership.

THE NEGOTIATIONS: RIO TO BERLIN

Traditionally, intergovernmental negotiating committees have been dissolved after the treaty is signed. The new treaty typically establishes subsidiary bodies, which become active after the initial conference of parties (COP). The climate negotiations represented the first time that the INC continued to meet after the treaty was signed. The signatories agreed that the climate negotiations could not wait for the new subsidiary bodies to be formed. The INC thus met six times between Rio and the March 1995 first Conference of the Parties (COP 1) in Berlin. The first three meetings were largely focused on institutional issues: the financial mechanism, interim arrangements, developing reporting methodologies, and organizational questions for COP 1. Most states remained preoccupied with domestic policy concerns. It was only in the weeks leading up to COP 1 that states began to focus on how the FCCC would evolve.

As COP 1 approached, Germany, the United Kingdom, the European Union, and the United States had demonstrated a general lack of political will to pursue significant domestic measures to reduce GHG emissions. The aversion to altering domestic policy meant that international policy had to be made compatible with existing domestic policies. For Germany and the United Kingdom this meant that the commitment to return carbon emissions to 1990 levels by the year 2000 was acceptable. Germany was potentially in the position to press for significant emission reductions beyond the year 2000, but the future path of British emissions was less clear. Fuel switching continued to provide CO_2 emission reductions, but it was unclear whether these reductions would persist. In addition, transportation sector emissions were rising rapidly, and the phasing out of some nuclear power plants could further increase emissions. The United States, on the other hand, had little chance of meeting the 2000 target and even worse prospects beyond 2000. Without changing domestic policy, it could not support action beyond 2000 in good faith. Even Germany was in somewhat of an awkward position, because it was open to charges of hypocrisy if it pressed too forcefully for emission reductions. The former West Germany's emissions were actually rising. Fortunately, the economic restructuring in the former East more than compensated for the increase in emissions from the West.

Only a handful of states were likely to meet the stabilization target by 2000, and even fewer had policies in place to reduce emissions beyond 2000. Few countries were eager to make additional commitments in the existing political and economic environment. The developed countries largely split into two groups. The European states supported a more aggressive approach to reducing GHG emissions; however, most of the member states hoped to rely on Germany and the United Kingdom to provide the bulk of emission reductions within the EU. The states that faced the greatest difficulty in reducing national emissions coalesced into a loose alliance known as the "JUSCANZ" group (Japan, United States, Canada, Australia, and New Zealand). Norway, Switzerland, and the former Communist states also co-operated with the group on various issues. For the developed countries, three primary issues dominated the INC negotiations between Rio and Berlin: the desirability of a new protocol and the nature of the commitments it would contain, the role of developing countries, and joint implementation.

It quickly became apparent that there was insufficient political will to finalize a protocol prior to COP 1. The debate shifted to what types of commitments should be included in a future protocol. The reluctance of most states to pursue significant CO_2 emission reductions led to a number of proposals to redefine how GHG emissions were calculated. Essentially, states sought to create an accounting framework that would allow them to claim GHG emission reductions while permitting CO_2 emissions to continue to increase. Four proposals had the greatest potential to achieve this goal. First, the political and economic potential for reducing methane, CFCs, HFCs, PFCs, NO_x, and VOCs was much greater than CO_2, because emissions of many of these gases were already being reduced for health and environmental reasons. Second, a focus on net emissions (emissions minus sinks), as opposed to total emissions, would provide relief to countries such as the United States and Canada that had significant forest and other biomass cover. Together, these two modifications would allow states to take credit for cuts in total GHG emissions and improved sinks, while still allowing CO_2 emissions to rise.

The third proposal was to include at least the largest developing countries in any future agreement to minimize adverse competitive effects and thus increase the potential to achieve simultaneous domestic policy changes across all parties. The final proposal was to permit the purchase of carbon emissions in other countries to cover excess domestic emissions through joint implementation and emissions trading. For most developed countries the marginal cost of emission reductions in developing countries or the former Communist states, was significantly lower than the cost of domestic action. It would thus make economic sense to fulfill domestic commitments through foreign investment. The inclusion of developing countries in the JI scheme would be particularly important to minimizing the costs of reducing GHG emissions. However, these initiatives would require a revision of the core climate policy norms. First, the primary supporters of an aggressive international climate policy had advocated a norm requiring states to reduce emissions domestically. The focus on economic efficiency posed a normative challenge. Should states be held responsible for reducing emissions domestically, or should global emissions be reduced in the most cost effective manner possible? The two are not necessarily compatible. Second, the developed states were historically responsible for the vast majority of emissions. Should they be obliged to reduce their emissions substantially before developing countries would be required to reduce their emissions? The sections below analyze the evolution of these normative debates in the negotiations leading up to the Berlin Mandate.

Adequacy of Commitments

According to Article 2 of the FCCC, the primary objective of the convention is to "achieve . . . stabilization of greenhouse gas concentrations in the atmosphere at a level that would prevent dangerous anthropogenic interference with the climate system."[37] Article 4.2d states that at the first Conference of the Parties (COP 1) the parties to the convention shall review the adequacy of commitments to determine whether they are sufficient to meet the objectives of the FCCC.[38] If they are found to be inadequate, then the COP has the obligation to amend the commitments. There was general agreement among industrial countries that existing commitments were inadequate. Even the United States accepted this view.

The rhetorical support for new commitments did not produce specific proposals for action. The deadline for proposals to amend the Convention or to create a protocol was September 28, 1994. In August, Germany tabled a "plan for a protocol." Under the proposed protocol, Annex I Parties would commit themselves to stabilizing carbon dioxide emissions by the year 2000 at 1990 levels (a legally binding version of the commitments contained in the FCCC). "Moreover it is necessary to undertake ambitious CO_2 reductions in the period after 2000. At COP 1, therefore, the Annex I Parties should commit themselves to reducing their CO_2 emissions by the year (x) individually or jointly by (y) percent."[39] In addition, Germany called for commitments governing other GHGs as well as agreement on common policies such as a carbon tax to be adopted by Annex I countries.

It is unclear how sincere the German proposal was. Not a single country voiced support for it. Even the Commission did not lend support. The German government felt some obligation to offer a proposal because it would be hosting COP 1. At INC 10, prior to the German proposal, there had been a consensus that no protocol would be adopted at COP 1. Instead, COP 1 would generate a negotiating mandate for a protocol to be completed for COP 3 in 1997. Support for immediate new commitments was nearly nonexistent among the developed countries.

Joint Implementation

The United States was one of the foremost supporters of the inclusion of joint implementation (JI) in a future protocol. The JI proposal fit well with the American emphasis on market mechanisms to achieve emission reductions. It also created the potential to avoid difficult domestic policies to reduce GHG emissions. Theoretically, JI should minimize the costs of reducing GHG emissions by equalizing the marginal costs of emission reductions across states. Actors would be able to invest in emission reduction projects in another country and receive credit for a portion of the emission reduction achieved.

Joint implementation was placed on the INC agenda at the seventh session. Initially, it was presented as applying only to projects conducted among Annex I countries. At the ninth session, the JUSCANZ group put forward proposals to incorporate developing countries in JI. The inclusion of developing countries would dramatically reduce the costs of cutting emissions. However, the Group of 77 rejected the proposal and appealed to the norm that developed countries were obligated to act first. Joint implementation should not be used to force reductions on developing countries, nor could financial flows under JI substitute for economic assistance and technology transfers. Industrial states also split over whether JI could be used to meet the 2000 target or not. The JUSCANZ group argued for the allocation of credits to meet the 2000 target. The EU rejected any credits prior to 2000, but supported the concept of JI.

During the intervening period between INC 8 and INC 9, the United States and other supporters of JI went on the diplomatic offensive to establish a viable program. A special discussion session was held in Bermuda in January 1994. The only participants were the INC bureau members, countries sympathetic to JI, and a few NGO representatives.[40] The participants discussed the secretariat's draft document on JI and made several significant changes. From the JUSCANZ perspective, the most important change was the deletion of language prohibiting JI with developing countries. The United Kingdom also joined the United States at INC 10 in holding out for the establishment of a JI pilot phase to begin immediately after COP 1. The JUSCANZ group introduced draft language at INC 11 that would allow a pilot phase for JI to begin following COP 1. The proposal called for JI to be voluntary, involving both Annex I (developed) and non-Annex I (developing) countries. The proposal also noted that JI should not modify existing commitments (Annex I or non-Annex I) and should provide financial transfers additional to existing official development assistance. According to the proposal, any JI project that addressed either sources or sinks of any GHG should be permitted. The only requirement for the JI project was that the reductions had to be measurable and verifiable. The United States made it clear that any strengthening of its commitments would be tied to acceptance of JI. The JI negotiations reached an impasse over the participation of developing countries and crediting of reductions prior to 2000.

The Berlin Mandate

As COP 1 approached, the INC meetings left several essential issues unresolved. There had been only superficial debate of the substance of future emission reduction commitments. Limited progress had been made on JI, and there had been only minimal progress on issues important to the G–77 such as technology transfer and the financial mechanism. It was clear that there would be no new commitments made at COP 1. The question was what would be achieved. The United States argued that the objective of COP 1 should be establishing a "new aim" to be negotiated by COP 3 in 1997. France, on behalf of the EU, called for a comprehensive protocol covering all GHGs and the coordination of policy measures wherever there were competitiveness concerns. Finally, China argued that additional commitments were a distraction until the existing commitments were met. The focus should be on enacting policies to meet current commitments.[41] Despite some opposition from China and a few developing countries, a consensus emerged that COP 1 should establish a negotiating mandate to develop a protocol to the FCCC. The so-called Berlin Mandate was intended to set the parameters for the negotiation of a future protocol containing additional commitments to be signed at COP 3 in 1997. The negotiations at COP 1 reflected attempts by countries to shape the negotiating mandate to make it consistent with their domestic interests. Considerable diplomatic effort went into developing as vague a mandate as possible. American negotiators argued that targets and timetables were premature and that the first step in developing new commitments had to be a thorough review of the environmental and economic trade-offs that various approaches to addressing climate change would entail. According to the leader of the American delegation, Rafe Pomerantz, "We haven't come here to support goals that we don't know we can meet. . . . We want to be realistic and we have to know what we are able to do in the future."[42] The American position seemed to require an extended period of analysis before the negotiation of a new protocol could begin.

The Major government stunned its partners when it called in early March 1995 for an agreement to cut emissions 5 to 10 percent below 1990 levels by 2010. The position gave Britain the moral high ground for the upcoming COP, but the position was rather cynical. The British government had recently determined that emissions levels were likely to fall even further and faster than predicted due to the switch from coal to gas.[43] The proposed emission cuts were thus easily achievable and would place the pressure on other states to block the proposal. The Kohl government faced a dilemma at the Berlin COP. The meeting was the first major UN conference to be held on German soil. The public and opposition parties were calling on the government to produce tangible results. Germany called on Annex I Parties to, at a minimum, pledge to stabilize their CO_2 emissions at 1990 levels by the year 2000.

The Berlin Mandate emerged from a contentious negotiating process. The first draft of the Mandate contained no finding of inadequacy of existing commitments and no specific commitment to negotiate GHG emission reductions. Instead, the parties were to undertake a period of analysis to decide how to reduce GHGs. There was no specific mention of a target; rather, the American terminology of an "aim" was included. There was no clear differentiation between developing country and developed country responsibilities. The proposed mandate represented a near complete capitulation to the American and the JUSCANZ position. The G–77 rejected the mandate and called for binding GHG reduction targets and time frames for Annex I countries and declared that there should be no additional commitment for developing countries.[44]

German Environment Minister Angela Merkel attempted to use JI as the means to reconcile the JUSCANZ and the G–77 positions.

[I]ndustrialized countries are attaching increasing importance to the question of cost efficiency. For the developing countries, it is crucial that joint implementation measures are linked to additional transfer of technology and knowledge. . . . Applied properly, joint implementation creates additional room for maneuver for the industrialized countries to adopt more stringent commitments and thus helps realize the Convention's objective.[45]

Ultimately, a compromise position on JI was agreed. The G–77 countries accepted the concept of JI, but they forced the JUSCANZ group to agree that JI would be tested in an open-ended pilot phase. No credits toward the 2000 goal would be allowed during the pilot phase. The agreement on JI led the United States to relax some of its opposition to the inclusion of targets and timetables in a negotiating mandate. However, the agreement effectively meant that the JI pilot phase could be held hostage by the developing countries. The United States had achieved some success in shifting the normative framework to emphasize economic efficiency as a central objective of climate policy.

The final version of the Berlin Mandate called for the parties to the FCCC "to elaborate policies and measures, as well as to set quantified limitation and reduction objectives within specified time frames, such as 2005, 2010, and 2020, for their anthropogenic emissions by sources and removals by sinks of greenhouse gases not controlled by the Montreal Protocol."[46] The mandate called for the creation of ad hoc groups to conduct the negotiation of quantified emission limitation and reduction objectives within specified time frames, but there was no reference point for emission levels such as 1990. The mandate also called for negotiations on all GHGs and not just CO_2. A protocol was to be prepared for signing at COP 3 in 1997.

The vague language in the mandate produced immediate conflict over its interpretation. According to Merkel, the mandate "means that after the year 2000 emissions will not rise but will be limited and reduced."[47] The American delegation rejected that position. According to U.S. Undersecretary of State Timothy Wirth, "[w]e agreed there are to be reductions, but the word 'target' does not appear and there is no specific timetable. . . . I don't think there's a baseline in this."[48] The American delegation succeeded in achieving an agreement sufficiently vague to assure that no immediate changes in domestic policy would be necessary, but it was also forced to accept a mandate that did not require developing country commitments and contained no assurances that JI crediting would be included in a final agreement. The EU and its member states achieved a mandate that could be interpreted as calling for specific reduction targets and thus be sold to the public as a victory over the United States. The disagreements over the interpretation of the Berlin Mandate set the stage for the contentious negotiations leading up to COP 3 in Kyoto.

CONCLUSIONS

Competitiveness concerns continued to play a major role in the climate policies of all three states. Each state rejected policies that would have forced costly adjustments on domestic industries. The German government maintained its opposition to the unilateral imposition of a carbon/energy tax.

The Major government enacted part of its proposed VAT on household energy consumption, but there was no attempt to impose the tax on corporate consumption. The United Kingdom also blocked EU attempts to implement a common energy taxation scheme, though it encouraged the other member states to pursue a tax without British participation. The other EU states rejected the option on competitiveness grounds. The Clinton administration appeared to be willing to impose a small tax on corporate energy use, but it would have been offset by breaks for energy intensive industries. None of the three enacted significant regulations to address energy efficiency, though all three encouraged voluntary measures.

This period also points to the tight constraints that domestic and international forces place on a government's ability to pursue policy changes. The Clinton administration entered office with the declared goal of bringing American climate commitments into line with international norms. It placed committed environmentalists into important positions over climate policy. Although American rhetoric changed dramatically, the underlying domestic and foreign policy positions remained basically consistent with those pursued by the Bush administration. The American political system heavily constrained the ability of the new Clinton administration to act—even though the Democratic Party controlled the executive and both houses of Congress. Partisan control did not appear to matter in the definition and pursuit of American climate policy. The importance of the transfer of power to the opposition will be further examined in the next chapter's analysis of the transition from Conservative to Labour governments in the United Kingdom.

The international negotiations were driven primarily by the policy proposals offered up by the most powerful states in the negotiations. The compromises contained in the Berlin Mandate were the result of hard negotiations among member states. There was no movement toward common policies to address climate change beyond the American push for flexibility mechanisms. The American initiative gained increasing support among industrial countries due to their inability to achieve sufficient domestic emission reductions. There was also little progress toward the incorporation of the international norms and principles contained in the FCCC into the policies of the United States, the United Kingdom, and Germany. The Berlin Mandate contained references to the FCCC's call for the development of climate policy on the basis of ". . . equity and in accordance with their common but differentiated responsibilities and respective capacities." The Mandate also noted that any new agreement will not "introduce any new commitments for Parties not included in Annex I," but the United States continued to fight for the inclusion of developing country commitments in any future agreement.[49] The Berlin Mandate also set up a conflict between national responsibility and economic efficiency. The unsettled normative debates would dominate the negotiations leading to the Kyoto Protocol.

CHAPTER FIVE

Domestic Conflict and International Normative Debates

(Berlin to Kyoto)

The period from the completion of the Berlin Mandate to the signing of the Kyoto Protocol involved intense international negotiations and domestic political conflict but limited domestic policy action. The dynamics of the negotiations were very similar to those leading up to the Berlin Mandate. Germany and the United Kingdom maintained their leadership positions internationally, but the United States and its JUSCANZ partners largely dictated the pace of the Kyoto negotiations. The United States took no significant domestic climate initiatives during this period, and American CO_2 emissions continued to rise at a rapid pace. The United States had no realistic chance to stabilize CO_2 emissions at 1990 levels. American policy focused almost entirely on shaping an international agreement compatible with domestic requirements. In practice, this meant recasting the normative debates by diluting the emphasis on national responsibility and domestic emission reduction commitments and developing "flexibility mechanisms" to allow the United States to avoid expensive domestic action by paying for cheaper reductions abroad.

Germany and the United Kingdom also pursued very limited domestic actions. The German government remained committed to its ambitious 25 percent CO_2 reduction goal, but it continued to rely on cuts achieved in the restructuring of the former East. The Kohl government advocated ambitious reductions in GHGs, even as it struggled with its domestic commitment. The British government also remained committed to its climate policies and pursued limited domestic actions to reduce its emissions. Climate change emerged as a politically salient issue in the May 1997 parliamentary elections. The Labour Party made climate change an important part of its election manifesto, but government policy failed to match the political rhetoric following Labour's victory. The British continued to rely primarily on the carbon reductions produced by the switch from coal to natural gas for electricity generation.

123

The European Union provided the primary impetus toward additional measures to reduce GHGs. In particular, the Commission aggressively promoted a carbon and/or energy tax to reduce carbon emissions over the concerted opposition of a number of member states. The Commission and the European Parliament played important roles in maintaining attention on climate issues and forcing member states to constantly respond to proposed climate measures. Without the EU's role in coordinating European climate policy, the Kyoto negotiations would have been much more difficult. Only Germany and the United Kingdom were likely to achieve the 2000 stabilization goal. Most of the other member states were supportive of international commitments; however, they expected Germany and the United Kingdom to provide the vast majority of the EU's emission reductions rather than pursue their own domestic reductions.

The economic conditions in the three countries differed slightly during this period. The British and American economies were on the upswing during the negotiations, while the German economy stagnated. German politics were preoccupied with unemployment, which constrained German climate policy. The Kohl government's domestic climate policy became much less ambitious as it began to characterize environmental policy as a drag on economic growth.

The period from Berlin to Kyoto was primarily devoted to finding an international solution consistent with the domestic policy requirements of the affected states. Much of the debate was couched in normative terms. Should states be held responsible for reducing domestic emissions, or should economic efficiency guide global emission reductions? Should developed states be held accountable for past emissions by forcing them to dramatically reduce their emissions, or should developing countries be expected to reduce their emissions, because they were becoming significant contributors to global GHG emissions? The first four sections of this chapter provide a brief overview of the evolution of German, British, European Union, and American climate policies. The remainder of the chapter links the domestic debates to the diplomatic strategies pursued by each of the governments in the Kyoto negotiations.

UNITED STATES

Congress set the tone for the post-Berlin Mandate climate debate. Following the conclusion of COP 1, Republican and Democratic congressmen alike assailed the administration for agreeing to a negotiating mandate that would require the United States to undertake expensive emission reductions while exempting developing countries that were "significant competitors." The Clinton administration defended the mandate and noted that it ensured that all parties would continue to be a part of the process. Developing countries would not be bound by the Berlin Mandate to take near-term action to reduce emissions, but they were not "off the hook." They would eventually be required to reduce their emissions. In addition, the mandate included an agreement to include joint implementation (JI) in a future protocol. The administration argued that JI would provide the United States with the flexibility to meet international targets without compromising economic competitiveness.[1]

American industrial interests aggressively sought to block GHG reduction commitments and domestic policy changes. In a letter to Secretary of State Warren Christopher, the Global Climate Coalition (GCC) argued that proposals for cuts in carbon emissions would result in "significant harm to the US economy and US competitiveness. . . . Of particular concern to the members of the Global Climate Coalition is the urgent need for a plan and timetable for a thorough analysis of the potential impacts on economic growth, trade competitiveness and jobs in the US and how they compare to the impact on nations in Asia and Europe that compete with the US."[2] The GCC's perspective resonated with congressional leaders. Industry leaders became very effective in framing the public debate and forcing the administration to respond to their claims.

The Clinton administration's climate policy reflected the intense opposition from large sectors of American industry, as well as the rather tepid support from most congressional Democrats and outright hostility from congressional Republicans. The administration pursued a two-pronged strategy of vocal support for international action while adopting a foreign policy strategy designed to delay progress in the climate negotiations and assure that future agreements would not require significant domestic action. The elections in November 1996 reinforced the administration's inclination to protect itself from charges of undermining America's international competitive position. The administration launched a public relations offensive to demonstrate American commitment to international environmental leadership. Secretary of State Christopher began a push in February 1996 to fully integrate environmental issues into American foreign policy. President Clinton also announced that environmental issues would top the agenda at the July 1996 Denver G–7 summit. The rhetorical support for environmental action was useful for the administration as it sought to bolster its green credentials for the upcoming elections. The combination of rhetorical support and international obstruction in the negotiations were viable as long as the negotiations continued in relative obscurity. By mid-1996 the administration faced rising international condemnation of its rejection of emission reduction commitments. In response to growing pressure, the Clinton administration finally affirmed the norm of accepting a legally binding GHG reduction target, but it was unwilling to articulate a position on what the target should be. The administration also refused to alter its demands for developing countries to assume international commitments and for the inclusion of flexibility mechanisms.

The administration's decision to support some form of legally binding targets resulted in a backlash from industrial interest groups and congressional Republicans as well as Democrats. Undersecretary of State Timothy Wirth challenged the criticisms. He accused industry leaders of creating "straw men" with their dire warnings of economic pain. "If you're opposed to doing anything under the climate treaty, you're going to fish for every argument you can. Just like auto companies saying airbags don't work and utilities saying there's no acid rain problem. They'll do everything they can to misinterpret what we've done."[3] However, the Clinton administration had to balance the defense of its policies with the need to maintain congressional support. Representative John Dingell, the ranking Democratic member of the Commerce Committee, voiced a common concern about the administration's climate policy. "If this is handled badly it could help promote the deindustrialization of the United States. I want to make sure that the interests of the United States are fully represented and I'm still not certain of that."[4] The administration attempted to build Democratic support in Congress, but it was becoming increasingly apparent that Congress would not support climate initiatives with the potential to inflict economic pain.

To counter the claims of industry, the administration attempted to reframe the debate by altering the economic analysis of climate policy. The administration put together an interagency analytical team chaired by the Commerce Department to guarantee that economic models used to evaluate the economic effects of emission reductions did not overstate the costs of controlling GHG emissions. The administration argued that conventional economic models typically underestimated industrial innovation and technological progress and overstated the negative effects on employment and income.[5] The administration was able to produce the results that it desired from its models, but the discrepancies between administration and private sector studies created public uncertainty and skepticism within Congress.

Climate change never became a major election issue in 1996. The Clinton administration successfully straddled the line between rhetorically supporting international climate policy and carefully avoiding policy proposals that would incite industrial interests to mobilize against it. Industrial interests criticized the administration's support of international action, but absent specific policy proposals, industrial groups did not have sufficient ammunition to sway public opinion on the costs of climate policy.

Following the election victory, the administration presented a more detailed plan for a climate agreement in December 1996. The plan introduced a number of provisions designed to delay action and provide "flexibility" to allow the United States to purchase emission reductions in other countries rather than pursue domestic action. In addition, the administration called for developing countries to accept emission reduction commitments. In essence, the United States was reopening the Berlin Mandate, which gave expression to the norm requiring developed countries to reduce their GHG emissions first. Article II.2.b of the Berlin Mandate specifically stated that the new protocol or amendment should "not introduce any new commitments for Parties not included in Annex I."[6] Vice President Gore echoed the Bush administration's call for developing country participation. Gore asserted that "[w]hile industrialized nations are responsible for [most] of the greenhouse gas emissions in the atmosphere today, we must keep in mind that the future emissions growth will come largely from the developing world . . . China, India, and the rest of the developing world must, too, have obligations."[7]

Vice President Gore also declared that climate policy could not be achieved at the expense of economic growth. Any climate agreement should "put us on a more sustainable energy path without sacrificing continued economic growth and development. . . . We must provide the maximum amount of flexibility to ensure that governments are given every opportunity to meet their commitments cost effectively and consistent with individual national circumstances."[8] The Clinton administration was attempting to recast the normative debate by reopening the question of developing country participation and promoting economic efficiency as a guiding principle of climate policy rather than national emission reduction commitments.

Building Domestic Support for GHG Reductions

In 1997, the administration attempted to reframe the domestic climate debate by focusing on the costs of not preventing climate change. Members of the administration argued that recent storms that had killed fifty people and caused more than $1 billion worth of property damage were warnings of worse events to come. "As we see increasingly severe storms, we begin to get a glimpse of what a post-climate-change world would look like."[9] The administration also initiated a campaign to demonstrate that the fears of climate policy critics were exaggerated. The Energy Department held a March 1997 press conference to announce the success of its voluntary "Climate Challenge Program." Members of the program had pledged to reduce their emissions of GHGs voluntarily. As of March 1997, the Energy Department had negotiated agreements with 117 corporations. Utility companies in the program pledged to cut their CO_2 emissions by 161 million metric tons per year by 2000.[10] The administration argued that the program demonstrated the potential for inexpensive reductions in emissions if climate policy was sufficiently flexible. Participants in the program pursued a broad range of policies including, energy efficiency, fuel switching, tree planting, and technological improvements.

As the Kyoto talks approached, the Clinton administration remained deeply divided over the acceptability of targets and timetables for GHG reductions. Congress and energy intensive industries were openly hostile to emission reduction commitments. The public was largely apathetic, and there was only limited political pressure to act coming from the insurance industry, the renewable energy industry, and environmental organizations. According to a September 1997 poll, nearly 75 percent of Americans believed climate change was occurring or would occur in the future. Sixty-six percent saw man-made climate change as a serious threat. An impressive 72 percent of respondents supported an international agreement to cut CO_2 emissions by 20 percent by 2005, but when specific policies to achieve these outcomes were included, support dropped off dramatically. A majority of respondents would not favor significantly higher utility bills or gasoline taxes to address climate change.[11]

The administration attempted to build popular support for action and to find an international equation that would minimize the domestic policy changes. It released studies indicating that the United States could stabilize GHG emissions in 2010 "or after" at a net cost or benefit to the American economy of 1 percent of the growth expected between 1997 and 2010.[12] The administration followed up its economic studies with a public relations program to educate American citizens about climate change. The president and vice president brought seven scientists to the White House to talk about climate change in July 1997. In remarks to the press, President Clinton said that

> We ask the American people to listen to the evidence, to measure it against their own experience, but not to discount the weight of scientific authority if their own experience does not yet confirm what the overwhelming percentage of scientists believe to be fact today. . . . We see the train coming. But most ordinary Americans in their day-to-day lives can't hear the whistle blowing.[13]

The president cautioned that failure to act could lead to widespread ecological disasters, including killer heat waves, severe floods and droughts, increases in infectious disease, and rising sea levels that could result in the loss of thousands of miles of coastline in Florida and Louisiana. The warnings were echoed in a letter signed by 2,600 scientists calling on the administration to take aggressive action to reduce GHG emissions.[14]

On the same day that President Clinton launched his climate publicity campaign, Ford Motor Company's chief, Alex Troutman, was in Washington, DC expressing the skepticism of American industry and announcing that the auto industry would begin its own public education campaign. Troutman said that the auto industry would present its own "equally eminent" experts to present "very forcibly our version of the science."[15] On the same day, the Senate passed a resolution containing minimum requirements for an acceptable international climate agreement:

> The United States should not be a signatory to any protocol . . . in Kyoto in December 1997, or thereafter, which would—(A) mandate new commitments to limit or reduce greenhouse gas emissions for the Annex I Parties, unless the protocol or other agreement also mandates new specific scheduled commitments to limit or reduce greenhouse gas emissions for Developing Country Parties within the same compliance period, or (B) would result in serious harm to the economy of the United States. . . .[16]

The resolution was bipartisan. Robert Byrd (D–WV), a cosponsor of the resolution and senior Democratic leader expressed the sense of the Senate, "I do not think the Senate should support a treaty that requires only . . . developed countries to endure the economic costs of reducing emissions, while developing countries are free to pollute the atmosphere, and, in so doing, siphon off American industries."[17] The administration did not oppose the resolution; in fact, Undersecretary of State Wirth suggested that the administration was "very strongly supportive of the Resolution. We believe it strengthens our hand [for the upcoming Kyoto negotiations]."[18]

President Clinton continued his education campaign throughout the summer. He met with Fortune 500 executives to address business' climate policy concerns. The president also sought to increase support for joint implementation and emissions trading as inexpensive mechanisms to achieve GHG reductions. To counter the administration's public relations campaign, trade groups representing automobile manufacturers, oil companies, and farmers launched a multimillion dollar print, radio, and television campaign that predicted dire economic consequences from current international proposals to curb GHG emissions. The ads asserted that energy prices would increase by more than 20 percent, which would have a devastating impact on America's standard of living. The campaign also assailed the lack of developing country participation. One ad showed a pair of scissors cutting countries out of a map, with the narrator asserting that "132 of 166 countries are exempt indefinitely. So while the United States is forced to make drastic cuts in energy use, countries like India, China, and Mexico are not."[19]

To counter the campaign, the Clinton administration recruited a cheap, and potentially effective, media force to disseminate its views. The administration invited leading weather forecasters from the nation's fifty largest television markets to the White House for a briefing on global warming by the president and vice president. As an incentive to attend, the administration allowed all of the forecasters to broadcast live from the White House. The administration and its industrial opponents were fighting to frame the domestic political debate and win the battle for public opinion, but the conflicting messages largely favored industry. In a further attempt to influence the economic debate, the Department of Energy released a study in September 1997 purporting to show that technology and energy efficiency could completely offset the costs of reducing greenhouse gas emissions.[20] The administration was at pains to note that it did not plan to propose this goal for the United States, but the study demonstrated that any cuts under 20 percent would be essentially cost free to the economy as a whole.

Even as the Department of Energy was suggesting that a 20 percent cut could be achieved at no cost, The National Center for Policy Analysis presented evidence to a Senate committee that "[c]hanges necessary for the United States to meet the proposed treaty commitments could reduce the nation's output of goods and services by $200 billion annually, do away with 600,000 jobs and increase the prices of almost all industrial and consumer products."[21] The vast discrepancies in predictions reflected the level of uncertainty surrounding the economic analysis of climate policy. A study by economist Robert Repetto examined 162 cost estimates from sixteen different economic models and found that 80 percent of the variation in cost projections could be explained by the differences in assumptions regarding economic uncertainties.[22] The vast range of economic predictions undermined attempts by the administration to build a domestic consensus on climate policy.

In the face of mounting industrial opposition, the persistent apathy of the American people, and escalating concern within the administration about the political consequences of climate policy, the Clinton administration began to hedge its support for binding commitments. Interior Secretary Bruce Babbitt told reporters that a "spirited debate [was] going on within the administration" on what the American position should be. Setting targets too low would yield a "whirlpool of disappointment" internationally, but if the target were too ambitious then the Senate would not ratify it.[23]

In October 1997, the administration began to publicly articulate its position. At the White House Conference on Climate Change, President Clinton announced that the United States would reject any short-term emissions cuts. "We can't do it all on the front end . . . because it either won't pass the Senate or it won't pass muster with the American people."[24] He also repeated his position that developing countries must participate. "The industrialized world alone cannot assume responsibility for reducing emissions. Otherwise, we will wind up with no reduction in emissions within a matter of a few decades. In Kyoto, therefore, we will ask for meaningful but equitable commitments from all nations [including developing nations]."[25]

The administration began to openly challenge the EU's emission reduction targets. In testimony before a Senate Foreign Relations subcommittee, Undersecretary Wirth attacked the EU plan as "fuzzy." "The EU has chosen what many analysts consider an unrealistic and unachievable target of a fifteen percent reduction by 2010 below 1990 levels. . . . Further complicating the negotiation, European member states have also insisted that they be allowed to 'bubble' their emissions. . . . Each individual country may not be required to meet that limit."[26] Wirth questioned the justice of allowing Spain to increase its emissions by 17 percent and Portugal by 40 percent while requiring the United States to reduce its emissions by 15 percent. However, even as the administration rejected the EU plan, it was unwilling to propose an alternative.

In part, the American reticence to put forward a proposal reflected its continuing efforts to test both domestic and international limits on an acceptable outcome. In a major coup for the administration, President Clinton secured the endorsement of President Carlos Menem of Argentina for a proposal to require developing countries to commit to reductions of GHG emissions. Menem announced during President Clinton's visit to Argentina that his government would support limitations on GHG emissions for developing countries so long as flexibility in how and when those targets would be met was maintained. Menem also expressed support for joint implementation. Argentina's support provided legitimacy to the American calls for developing country participation and created a crack in the formerly unified position of the G–77.

On October 22, 1997, President Clinton finally presented the American position for the Kyoto negotiations. The president announced that the United States would propose a stabilization of GHG emissions at 1990 levels between 2008 and 2012. This represented a retreat for the president. In 1993, he had called for GHG emission reductions by 2010. The president reiterated his claims that this goal could be achieved at no cost to the American economy. "If we do it right, protecting the climate will yield not costs, but profits, not burdens, but benefits, not sacrifice, but a higher standard of living."[27] The president announced a modest set of incentives to encourage cuts in GHG emissions, but the plan contained no new taxes or significant regulations. Firms would also be asked to voluntarily submit plans to cut GHG emissions. The plan would require developing country participation, though the president did not provide a precise definition of "participation." In addition, he called for emissions trading and joint implementation to provide flexibility in meeting the international targets. The political sparring began immediately after the president announced the American position. Republican Senator Frank Murkowski attacked the president's proposals as potentially devastating to the American economy. "To reach the President's targets, we will need a fifty dollar per ton carbon tax. American consumers and workers will pay dearly and, unless China, Mexico, and the other developing countries follow suit, global emissions will still increase."[28]

Even as the president announced the American position in the climate negotiations, the Department of Energy published a report predicting that American carbon emissions would be 17 percent above 1990 levels by the year 2000 and 34 percent above 1990 levels by 2010.[29] This represented a 5 percent increase over the prior year's forecast. The predictions cast doubt on the administration's policies for stabilizing emissions by 2010. The Department of Energy suggested that declining electricity prices due to deregulation, combined with rising energy consumption resulting from strong economic growth, would produce a rapid increase in carbon emissions over the coming decade.

Walking a Fine Line at Kyoto

On December 2, 1997, the administration announced that Vice President Gore would join the American negotiating team in Kyoto. To minimize his political exposure, he would only attend the talks for a single day, and he would not lead the American negotiating team. The vice president sounded a hard line on the American negotiating position prior to his departure. "I would like to make it clear that, as others have said, we are perfectly prepared to walk away from an agreement that we don't think will work."[30] Congress also sent more than a dozen members to the negotiations to make sure that the administration did not ignore congressional concerns.

The American position for Kyoto was in flux. The administration had been unable to generate support for policy reforms to reduce emissions. Congress continued to oppose American action on climate change—particularly if it was not accompanied by emission reductions in developing countries. There would be no new regulations or taxes domestically. The best that could be hoped for on the domestic policy side were voluntary initiatives by industry and tax incentives to promote reductions in GHGs. The international community would have to bear the weight of GHG reductions, or the United States would veto the agreement. Joint implementation and emissions trading would be essential to any agreement. In addition, developing countries would have to be brought on board before an agreement would be politically palatable for the Senate.

The United States was in the strongest position to shape the final agreement. It was the largest producer of GHGs, and according to its political leaders, it faced some of the highest economic and political costs of reducing GHG emissions. The Clinton administration could credibly threaten to veto an agreement if it did not meet its minimum requirements. The administration would be roundly condemned, but if it walked away, the agreement would be severely damaged. America's partners would be under considerable pressure to compromise to achieve an agreement and maintain momentum toward international action. The Clinton administration had to walk a fine line between committing to overly ambitious commitments that would be rejected domestically and mediocre commitments that would alienate its negotiating partners and undermine international progress. To succeed, the administration had to alter the normative debate to make all states (including developing countries) responsible for reducing GHG emissions, and it had to persuade its partners to focus on global emission reductions and cost effectiveness rather than national responsibility and domestic reduction commitments.

UNITED KINGDOM

For the British, the period from COP 1 to Kyoto involved a much more significant domestic component than American climate policy. Elections were due in May 1997, and the Labour Party made climate change a central component of its campaign. In July, Labour declared that, if elected, it would reduce British CO_2 emissions by 20 percent by 2010. The pledge was much more ambitious than the Conservative Party's goal. The EU also influenced the British climate debate. The Major government continued to oppose the EU's attempts to expand its policy competence through the proposed carbon/energy tax. The government hoped to maintain a strong position on climate change to avoid being labeled as a laggard and being pressed by the EU to adopt its climate program. Finally, the British government was in a position to accept international commitments and undertake limited domestic policy changes because the commitments did not represent a threat to British industry (with the notable exception of the coal industry). The British switch from coal to natural gas provided the vast majority of reductions in carbon emissions. Because costly new policies would not be necessary in the short term, there was limited domestic opposition to GHG emission reductions. British climate policy during this period focused on fuel taxes under the Conservatives and renewable energy and voluntary accords with industry under both parties.

British Voluntary Accords

Beyond the ongoing switch from coal to natural gas, the core element of British domestic climate policy was the negotiation of voluntary agreements with industry to cut GHG emissions. Industry supported the voluntary initiatives because the targets were not legally binding, and the agreements would presumably protect them against new regulations and taxes—unless the goals were not met. For the government, the voluntary agreements limited domestic opposition to climate policy from the groups with the most at stake economically, while simultaneously providing evidence that it was doing something to address GHG emissions. The voluntary agreements avoided the American situation where industry was constantly attacking government policy and undermining the government's position both domestically and internationally.

The push for voluntary agreements began in 1995 under the Major government. The Department of Energy (DoE) asserted that the objective of the voluntary agreements was to "devise an industry-led solution which is the most cost-effective way of meeting the government's environmental objectives and is less bureaucratic and more flexible than a solution centrally imposed by government."[31] In September 1996, the Conservative government initiated discussions on a voluntary agreement to improve energy efficiency with the chemical industry, which was responsible for a significant portion of total industrial energy consumption. The government was unable to finalize an agreement before the 1997 elections, but the new Labour government announced that it would continue the negotiations. The British Chemical Industries' Association (CIA) had proposed a 20 percent reduction in energy consumption per unit of production over the period 1990 to 2005. In return, the Association sought assurances that the government would not enact new energy taxes and would assist smaller chemical producers to meet the target. While the target appeared to be challenging, the commitment was somewhat misleading. Between 1990 and 1997, the CIA had already achieved reductions of 14 percent. The CIA was thus proposing an additional 6 percent improvement in eight years compared to a 14 percent improvement over seven years.[32]

In November 1997, the CIA and the government finalized an agreement to improve energy efficiency by 20 percent by 2005. The agreement would produce CO_2 emission reductions of between 550,000 and 900,000 metric tons per year.[33] This was the first voluntary accord to contain specific energy efficiency targets. The Labour government noted that it would monitor the industry's progress to assure success and would be willing to take other actions should the industry fail to meet its target. This was the first of a series of accords that the government would pursue.

British Energy Policy

The Major government had focused its climate related energy policy on two primary areas. It raised the VAT on fuel, principally as a source of revenue, but the action had the advantage of also cutting carbon emissions by reducing consumption. It also subsidized the development of renewable energy sources. The main mechanism for supporting renewable energy production was the Conservative Party's 1989 Non-Fossil Fuel Obligation program (NFFO). Under the program, electricity companies were responsible for purchasing electricity from renewable sources above market rates. A levy on consumer's electricity bills subsidized the difference between market rates and the NFFO rates. The Secretary of State established the obligations to be fulfilled, and potential electricity generators bid to be included in the program. Between 1990 and 1997, the Conservative government initiated four rounds of orders for renewable electricity generation capacity. The program achieved some success. Between the third and fourth rounds of NFFOs, the bid price for renewable energy generation fell by 20 percent.[34] The decline brought the price much closer to market rates. The NFFO projects included a wide variety of technologies, including: seventy landfill gas, sixteen waste incineration, sixty-five wind, thirty-one hydroelectric, six farm waste, and seven energy crop projects.[35] The Conservative Party's goal was for renewable energy to reduce carbon emissions by two million tons per year by the year 2000.

The Major government faced a very different political dynamic in energy policy than that confronted by the Clinton administration. In the United States, the energy industry posed a serious challenge to American climate commitments. In the United Kingdom on the other hand, British Petroleum (BP) broke ranks with the American energy industry. In October 1996, British Petroleum quit the Global Climate Coalition and announced that it would develop a strategy to measure and reduce its GHG emissions. The more cooperative stance of British Petroleum eliminated a significant obstacle to pursuing more ambitious climate targets. In contrast to the energy industry, the position of British business contained several anomalies. A November 1997 poll by the Confederation of British Industry (CBI) showed that 83 percent of the organization's members supported the EU's goal of a 15 percent reduction in CO_2 emissions between 1990 and 2010.[36] This acceptance of the need to act marginalized organized opposition to British climate policy.

Following the May 1997 elections, the new Labour government presented its strategy to reduce British CO_2 emissions by 20 percent by 2010. The strategy focused heavily on energy efficiency, combined heat and power (CHP), and renewable energy. The government set a target of creating an additional ten gigawatts of CHP capacity by 2010, which could provide six million tons of carbon (mtc) emission savings annually. The government also sought to build on the Conservative's renewable energy policy, by setting a target of renewable energy providing 10 percent of British electricity by 2010, which would provide a savings of 5.5 mtc per year. In 1997, renewables provided only 2 percent of electricity.[37] The primary mechanism for achieving the increase in renewable energy was to be additional NFFO rounds. The government launched the fifth NFFO round in November 1997. The largest contribution to emission reductions was supposed to be increased industrial, commercial, and public energy efficiency. The government relied heavily on voluntary commitments to achieve these reductions. Of the total reductions of thirty-three mtc that would be necessary to achieve the Labour government's goal, reductions of 22.6 mtc were to be achieved through energy efficiency improvements. The remainder was to be achieved through expansion of renewable energy sources and combined heat and power initiatives.[38] The strategy excluded transportation policy; yet, during the election campaign, Labour called for an integrated public transport system to cut CO_2 emissions as well as other pollutants. There was also no discussion of additional energy taxes or regulations. The strategy relied heavily on the decisions of private actors to cut their emissions, and it was not clear that the targets were achievable without significant government intervention. However, Labour was reluctant to pursue aggressive taxation and regulatory measures to produce GHG emission reductions. There was also less pressure on the Labour government to act because the United Kingdom would easily meet its existing international commitments, and the 20 percent target was a nonbinding domestic target.

An Envious British Position

The British government did not face the same constraints as the United States in its climate policy. Climate change had achieved a high level of domestic political salience, and there was a consensus across the political parties that GHG reductions were necessary. The United Kingdom was well placed to meet international commitments and thus could take a more aggressive position in the negotiations. The fact that additional domestic measures would not be necessary to meet international commitments minimized opposition to climate policy. Industries were willing to undertake voluntary emission reduction commitments, because they were secure in the knowledge that they would not face additional regulations or taxes. There was no incentive to undermine the domestic consensus to reduce emissions, and this allowed politicians in both parties to aggressively pursue an international leadership position.

GERMANY

The German government confronted a number of dilemmas as the Kyoto negotiations progressed. Climate change had achieved a high-level of domestic political salience, and the government was in a strong position to press for international GHG reduction commitments. Germany could easily meet any common reduction target acceptable to other industrial countries. The government capitalized on the circumstances to continue its international leadership position. Domestically, the Kohl government faced a very different situation. It had established a target of cutting CO_2 emissions by 25 percent by 2005. In 1995, Germany was half way toward its objective, but nearly all of the progress was due to reductions in the East. Western emissions were increasing, and eastern economic growth and rising automobile use were slowing the downward emissions trend. Achieving the 25 percent target would require additional domestic measures. The Kohl government claimed that Germany had already initiated more than one hundred measures to address GHG emissions.[39] The vast majority of these measures would have only minor effects on emissions, and it was becoming increasingly clear that they would be insufficient to meet Germany's target.

The Kohl government was constrained by a stagnating economy and unacceptably high unemployment. It faced growing opposition to its 7.5 percent "solidarity tax" that it had introduced to underwrite the costs of reunification. The budget deficit was increasing, which required spending cuts and increased tax revenues. Germany's economic problems dominated the domestic political agenda, and the debate intensified as the fall 1998 elections approached. Further complicating matters, the SPD controlled the Bundesrat, which allowed it to obstruct the CDU/CSU's policy initiatives. In the midst of these difficulties, the Kohl government was no longer prepared to view aggressive GHG emission reductions as compatible with German economic prosperity. The government maintained its strong international environmental rhetoric, but it began to backtrack on some of its environmental commitments.

The CDU/CSU's position on environmental policy reflected growing public apprehension about the economy and decreasing concern for environmental affairs. Opinion polls in 1996 revealed that Germans placed environmental matters well below economic problems on their list of priorities.[40] The Kohl government altered the terms of the German environmental debate by raising issues of balancing economic costs and environmental benefits. The government commissioned a study in 1995 to examine the economic costs of meeting the 25 percent emissions reduction target. The study by two German research institutes concluded that meeting the interim target of cutting CO_2 emissions by 17 percent by 2000 would cost one hundred twenty thousand jobs as a result of energy intensive industries scaling back their production and moving jobs overseas. In addition, one hundred fifty thousand jobs would be sacrificed to meet the 25 percent target by 2005. According to the report, German industry would need to spend an additional $489.1 billion to achieve the 25 percent reduction target by 2005.[41] German industries decried the absurdity of imposing the heavy costs of climate policy on them while foreign competitors faced no similar costs. German environmental organizations and opposition parties condemned the government's attempts to frame environmental policy as a choice between jobs and environmental quality and lambasted the government for abdicating its leadership role in environmental affairs and "Britainising" German environmental policy.[42]

This period of climate policy demonstrated the limits of German support for reductions in CO_2 emissions. Germany would continue to play a leadership role internationally. The Kohl government attempted to force other states to undertake major new commitments to cut CO_2 emissions even as it scaled back its domestic intiatives. The government also began to pave the way for meeting its future commitments by affirming the American emphasis on economic efficiency as a guiding principle of climate policy. Germany became a supporter of the American initiatives on JI and emissions trading, which would be essential to reduce the costs of meeting future international commitments. The following sections outline the most important domestic debates leading up to the Kyoto conference.

German Taxation

Given rising unemployment and the slowdown in the German economy, the major parties agreed that reducing relatively high taxes on employment was essential to tackle unemployment. The political divide that developed was over how to reduce the tax load without further expanding the budget deficit. The CDU/CSU's junior coalition partner, the Free Democratic Party (FDP), called for increases in energy taxes. The Economy Minister, Guenter Rexrodt (FDP), announced that he was developing a reform initiative that would raise taxes on energy and penalize CO_2 emissions. He argued that the initiative would help Germany meet its emission reduction target, and the revenue would allow the government to reduce taxes on employment.[43] The proposal ran into immediate opposition from the CDU/CSU and its industrial supporters. The party leadership was unwilling to risk raising taxes again in the face of determined public opposition to its solidarity tax increases to pay for reunification. In addition, the Kohl government had already acceded to voluntary agreements with industry groups to cut their emissions in return for the government's commitment not to pursue energy/carbon taxes.

Instead of raising energy taxes, the CDU/CSU proposed a reduction in taxes on business assets. The tax reductions would be paid for by reducing spending and closing tax loopholes. The initiative was a core part of the government's 1996 Tax Act, but the SPD controlled Bundesrat rejected the initiative. The SPD appropriated the energy tax proposal and used it to attack the government. At the SPD's November 1995 party congress, the party's leadership called for an "ecological tax reform." Using the same arguments that the FDP had used to support its initiative, the SPD argued that ecological tax reform was a silver bullet that would solve two major problems facing Germany. First, the tax would promote energy efficiency and CO_2 emission reductions by increasing the cost of energy. Second, the additional revenue would be used to reduce taxes on employment and thus raise employment levels.

The Greens adopted a very ambitious set of proposals at their party congress in March 1996. They proposed an "Alliance for Work and the Environment" to counter the Kohl government's "Alliance for Work." The Greens initiative proposed annual increases in taxes on energy and fossil fuels, which would raise $33 billion the first year and $165 billion after a decade. They also called for increasing gasoline prices to $12.60 per gallon in two years.[44] The size of the increases was politically impossible, but the proposals increased the pressure on the CDU/CSU, SPD, and FDP to articulate their own positions on energy taxation. The SPD pursued a more modest approach. It proposed much smaller increases in energy taxes that would rise gradually over time to avoid a severe shock to the economy.

The Kohl government opposed the taxes on competitiveness grounds and argued that they would lead to accelerated de-industrialization. In its place, the government called for an increase in the value-added tax to offset reductions in employment taxes. Tax reform created a window of opportunity to reduce CO_2 emissions, but the CDU/CSU refused to pursue energy taxation. However, the SPD and Greens were building the foundation for future energy tax reforms.

German Energy Policy

Two issues in particular dominated German energy policy during this period: coal and nuclear energy. A window of opportunity for linking climate policy to energy developed as a part of the worsening economic position and the debate over renewing German coal subsidies. In 1996, it cost $164 to produce a ton of German bituminous coal, but the world price was only $47 a ton.[45] Up until 1995, the subsidies for the coal industry were financed through the *Kohlepfennig* (coal levy). Following the abolition of the *Kohlepfennig*, the government paid the cost of the coal subsidy directly out of the budget. The government provided subsidies of more than ten billion deutsche marks (DM) to bridge the gap between domestic and international prices in 1996. That was more than DM100,000 for each of the country's ninety thousand miners.[46] The subsidies were a prime target for a government seeking to reduce the budget deficit and tax loads. A shift from coal to natural gas for electricity production would also provide emission reductions similar to those experienced by the United Kingdom.

The two primary bituminous coal producing states were Saarland and North Rhine-Westphalia, and coal mining continued to be an important source of employment and revenue for both. The SPD controlled both states and had long worked to protect the coal industry, but it faced a dilemma in the links between its coal and climate policies. The SPD attacked the government for not aggressively pursuing cuts in CO_2 emissions, and yet it could not support a reduced role for coal for political reasons. The coal miners' support for the SPD made the Kohl government's subsidy decision much easier. In March 1997, the government announced reductions in federal subsidies to western Germany's bituminous coal mining industry from DM ten billion to DM four billion by 2005. The cuts would reduce employment in the bituminous mines from eighty-five thousand to thirty thousand by 2005.[47] Following the announcement, fifteen thousand coal miners descended upon Bonn and held the government district hostage. The standoff eventually led to a compromise to reduce the subsidies but at a slower pace.

The decision to reduce the role of domestic hard coal in German energy supply would significantly reduce CO_2 emissions if natural gas were substituted for bituminous coal. However, German electricity producers faced different incentives than their British counterparts. German coal plants had already invested in expensive flue-gas desulfurization equipment and thus had little incentive to close the plants in favor of natural gas plants. Germany also maintained relatively high taxes on natural gas, which, when combined with an inefficient distribution network, kept natural gas prices relatively high. Germany maintained taxes of $20.3 per ton of oil equivalent of natural gas and no tax on the use of coal. The United Kingdom, on the other hand, had no tax on natural gas for industrial use.[48] The relatively high cost and the lack of incentives for building new natural gas plants deterred a wholesale switch to gas for electricity generation in Germany and led to the use of the more polluting domestic lignite coal and imported coal. The reduction in support for coal production produced a gradual decrease in CO_2 emissions as small amounts of nuclear, natural gas, fuel oil, and renewable energies replaced some coal for electricity generation.

Beyond the coal debates, nuclear energy remained an even more contentious political issue in Germany. Nuclear power provided 30 percent of German electricity, and the primary alternative to nuclear power was the expanded use of coal. The nuclear energy "consensus talks" resumed in March 1995. The Kohl government defended nuclear energy as indispensable to achieving Germany's international climate commitments. According to the government, nuclear power saved 150 million tons of CO_2 emissions per year.[49] A reduction in the role of nuclear power would require difficult and expensive CO_2 reduction measures to compensate for the additional emissions. The consensus talks coincided with the ninth anniversary of the 1986 Chernobyl disaster. Opponents of nuclear power were highly motivated and extremely vocal. For many Germans, nothing short of shutting down the nuclear industry was acceptable. The SPD and Greens rejected nuclear power as a strategy to reduce CO_2 emissions. They accorded priority to the elimination of nuclear energy over addressing climate change. During the April session of the consensus talks, the SPD presented a list of forty proposals covering energy conservation and renewable energy sources that they argued would provide the necessary emission reductions to meet the CO_2 target without relying on nuclear power over the long-term. The talks collapsed in June 1995 after the government refused to accept SPD demands for a moratorium on new nuclear power plants. The status quo in nuclear power would continue until the 1998 federal elections when the new SPD/Greens coalition would revisit the issue.

The last area of energy policy related to climate change was the promotion of renewable energy. The amount of renewable energy production continued its modest climb. The Electricity Feed Law required electricity producers to purchase electricity generated from renewable resources at a premium rate. The government did not pursue further promotion of renewable energy beyond small programs to provide funding for solar, hydroelectric, wind, photovoltaic, and biomass energy facilities. Total renewable energy production remained small at 1.7 percent of total energy supply in 1996.[50]

German Voluntary Measures

The Kohl government was reluctant to pursue aggressive regulatory or taxation measures to reduce GHG emissions. It abandoned the use of energy/carbon taxes and instead made a pact with the major industrial groups to voluntarily commit to emission reduction targets in exchange for a pledge that the government would not pursue additional energy taxes or regulations to reduce CO_2 emissions. These voluntary agreements were the foundation of the Kohl government's climate policy. Just prior to the adoption of the Berlin Mandate, thirteen industrial sectors, acting through the Federation of German Industries (BDI), committed to cut the group's total emissions by up to 20 percent by 2005 based on 1987 levels. The commitments varied by industry depending on the potential for emission reductions. These sectors accounted for nearly two-thirds of industrial energy consumption, so their commitments would have a significant effect on German emissions. In March 1996, industry groups committed themselves to a more specific target of reducing CO_2 emissions by 20 percent by 2005 based on a 1990 baseline.

This represented a strengthening of their commitment. Between 1990 and 1996, the sectors involved in the voluntary agreement achieved 77 percent of their reduction commitment. Most of the reductions were the result of economic restructuring in the eastern states and the slowdown in the German economy. For example, the chemical industry achieved its impressive reductions primarily by closing older factories—particularly in the eastern part of the country. The steel industry's reductions were largely the result of fewer orders caused by the economic slowdown.[51] Its emissions would rise as the economy picked up. The Kohl government extolled the efforts of these industries and argued that voluntary agreements would allow Germany to achieve its commitment without undermining German competitiveness.

The other major voluntary accord was between the government and the automobile industry. The industry committed to reduce fuel consumption of new cars by 25 percent between 1990 and 2005. The voluntary commitments allowed the government to claim significant progress in reducing emissions without harming the competitiveness of German industry or damaging the relationship between the CDU/CSU and its core supporters in the business community. For industry, the targets were not excessively difficult to meet, and they provided a means of avoiding higher energy taxes and more stringent regulations.

International Activism and Domestic Retreat in German Policy

The Kohl government faced a dilemma in its foreign climate policy. Germany had already cut its emission by 12 percent and thus could claim to be at the forefront of efforts to reduce CO_2 emissions. On the other hand, these reductions were almost entirely the result of the economic restructuring in the former East. The voluntary agreements with industry would not be sufficient to achieve the 25 percent reduction commitment. However, unilaterally enacting major new policies was unacceptable on competitiveness and political grounds.

Even as domestic emission reductions became increasingly difficult, Germany was at the forefront of efforts to secure substantial internationally binding emission reduction commitments. It proposed an international target of a 15 percent emission reduction by 2010. It pressed the EU and its member states to commit to stronger international action. The aggressive calls for international commitments to reduce GHG emissions paradoxically put Germany in a weak position in the negotiations. It had little leverage over opponents of its proposals. Germany attempted to seize the moral high ground and shame its negotiating partners into accepting substantial international commitments. Beyond the appeals to international norms, the most leverage that Germany could use to support its position in the negotiations was to threaten to veto an agreement if it believed it was too weak, which would be an extremely blunt instrument in the negotiations and would play into the hands of opponents of the protocol.

EUROPEAN UNION

At the European Union level, climate change continued to be a divisive issue. There was broad support among the member states for an aggressive international negotiating position, but when discussions turned to EU policies, the consensus broke down. Following the adoption of the Berlin Mandate, the first task facing the EU was agreeing upon a common European emission reduction commitment. The Commission had proposed an target of cutting GHG emissions by 10 percent between 2000 and 2010. The United Kingdom proposed a 5 to 10 percent cut by 2010, and other European countries suggested a variety of other targets. At the December 1995 Environment Council meeting, the member states accepted that every state could not adopt the same target. Variations in levels of development and other domestic circumstances made such an approach impossible. The EU would thus have to adopt a "burden sharing" agreement.

Though there was general acceptance of the principle of burden sharing, there was little consensus on what it would mean. The southern member states pressed for an explicit statement that the richer states would shoulder the bulk of the commitment, but the northern states rejected this idea. The EU held monthly ad hoc meetings on climate policy, but endless debates on burden sharing stalled the process. Germany, Denmark, and the Netherlands stressed that their individual reduction commitments would only apply to the EU's 2000 stabilization goal. These countries maintained that they would only commit to a burden sharing agreement beyond 2000 if the other states agreed to at least stabilize their emissions.[52] The burden sharing issue became more problematic when the Commission reported in the spring of 1996 that EU emissions were likely to be above 1990 levels by 2000.[53] Only Austrian, German, and British CO_2 emissions had declined. The rest of the member states were unlikely to meet the 2000 stabilization target.

When the Netherlands assumed the presidency of the EU in January 1997, one of the government's top priorities was securing an agreement on a reduction target and burden sharing. At the end of January, the Dutch presidency proposed a set of GHG emissions reduction targets as well as a model for distributing the reductions across the member states. The proposed burden sharing model, called the "Triple Approach," divided each member state's emissions into three groups: transport and housing, energy production, and heavy industry. The model then allocated emission reduction targets across the member states based on national circumstances. The

Dutch proposed an EU goal of cutting a basket of six GHGs by 10 percent by 2005 and 15 percent by 2010. Within the broader commitment, the Dutch proposed to cut CO_2 emissions by 8 percent by 2005 and 13 percent by 2010.[54] The Commission and the Dutch presidency hoped that an agreement could be achieved that would clear the way for formal approval of an EU negotiating position prior to the March AGBM meeting. Several states felt the EU target was too ambitious, and a majority of states rejected the individual targets. The member states rejected the plan at the February meeting.

In response, the Dutch called a special Council meeting just prior to the March AGBM session to negotiate an EU reduction target minus the burden sharing agreement. To the surprise of many observers and member state delegations, the Council agreed on a 15 percent GHG emission reduction target by 2010. The agreement contained a number of compromises that weakened the original Dutch proposal. It reduced the number of GHGs from six to three (CO_2, methane, and NO_x). The Council dropped the 2005 target as well as the specific target for CO_2. While the Council was willing to accept an aggregate 15 percent commitment for GHG emission reductions, member states were only willing to commit to individual reductions worth two-thirds of the 15 percent target. The commitments ranged from a reduction of 30 percent for Luxembourg and 25 percent for Germany, Denmark, and Austria to increases of 17 percent for Spain and 40 percent for Portugal.[55] The sincerity of the Council agreement is questionable. The 15 percent target was unrealistic. The United States and Japan were unwilling to accept such a target. The environment ministers also made it clear that the EU reductions were contingent upon similar action by the other industrial states. The EU position was a negotiating ploy to put pressure on the United States and Japan in the upcoming AGBM meeting. The member states did not have to seriously consider narrowing the 5 percent gap between member state commitments and the aggregate EU commitment. It was unlikely that the EU would even need to meet the 10 percent reduction commitment that the member states were offering.

The Commission anticipated that the new burden sharing accord would create momentum toward new EU policies to reduce GHG emissions. The agreement contained an outline of common and coordinated policies to reduce GHG emissions. The list of potential policies included renewable energy initiatives, combined heat and power, fuel switching, improved energy efficiency standards, reductions in transportation emissions, and taxation mechanisms. In October 1997 the Commission submitted a revised climate strategy communiqué to the Council. According to the Commission, a 15 percent emission reduction by 2010 "can be achieved without disruption of the economy, at low or zero costs. . . . [This] should help to convince other industrialized countries . . . that their economic development will not be impaired by such a reduction target."[56] The Commission also continued to claim that the EU was on track to meet its reduction targets. The claims contradicted emission predictions by the European Environment Agency (5 percent above 1990 levels by 2000) and the Commission's energy directorate, (2 percent above 1990 levels).[57] One European Environment Agency official expressed surprise at the Commission's predictions, calling them "wishful thinking."[58] The Commission plan would reduce CO_2 emissions by 800 million metric tons by improving automobile efficiency standards, developing renewable energy sources, promoting rail as an alternative to road and air travel, and improving energy efficiency. In addition the Commission continued to argue that a carbon/energy tax would be essential for the EU to meet its longer term emission reduction goals. The onus was now on the member states to either accept the Commission's plan or provide an alternative.

European Energy Policy

EU energy policy, as it related to climate change, involved three primary issues: energy efficiency standards, renewable energy promotion, and voluntary efficiency agreements with industry. The most important of these areas was the potential for energy efficiency savings. The EU's SAVE program was the principal vehicle for addressing energy efficiency, but the program had been chronically underfunded and lacked significant political support within the Council. In 1996, the SAVE program was to be renewed with a new five year mandate, but the Council slashed the SAVE II program budget from $192 million to $58 million over five years.[59] With the support of the Commission, the European Parliament fought the cuts; however, the Council unanimously rejected the Parliament's attempts to restore funding. Once again, the member states slashed a central part of the EU's climate policy.

The SAVE program could claim some limited success. The creation of new refrigerator standards were SAVE's most important contribution. Refrigerators accounted for 7 percent of the total electricity consumption in the EU and 20 percent of total household electricity consumption.[60] The directive thus had the potential to have a significant effect on EU emissions over time. The Commission had proposed a draft directive on refrigerator efficiency in December 1994, which would have required a two-step improvement in energy efficiency. The first stage mandated a 10 percent improvement in minimum efficiency standards by 1998, which was to be followed by a 20 to 30 percent improvement by 2001. Criticism from refrigerator manufacturers and opposition from EU Industry Commissioner Martin Bangemann forced the Commission to weaken the proposal and to postpone the second stage requirements for at least four years.[61] The European Parliament put significant pressure on the Commission to strengthen the directive.

It proposed a number of amendments to toughen the standards, bring forward the implementation dates, and add a third stage of emission reductions. The Council rejected the Parliament's amendments. The final directive, approved in August 1996, required a 15 percent improvement in energy efficiency standards within three years. This represented a slight increase from the initial proposal, but the Council dropped the second stage reductions in favor of a review of standards to be conducted four years after the directive came into force.

Environmental groups and members of the European Parliament roundly condemned the failure to take more aggressive action. Danish MEP Niels Snidal expressed the frustration with the slow progress of EU energy efficiency policy. "In 1998, the United States will have a third phase of energy requirements for these appliances which is far more ambitious, and that's in the liberal U.S.A. so we are lagging far behind."[62] The refrigerator efficiency standards debate again demonstrated the questionable level of commitment behind the EU's climate policy.

The May 1997 Energy Council conclusions offer further evidence of the limited political salience of the EU's climate commitments. The Commission recommended that the fifteen member states adopt a series of common and coordinated policies to achieve the EU's GHG emission reduction target. The list of measures included the promotion of renewable energies and cogeneration, improved energy efficiency standards for electrical products, energy efficiency agreements with industry, and reductions in fossil fuel subsidies. The Council conclusions did not call for these policies to be enacted but merely noted that they should be studied further.[63] While the Commission and the European Parliament continued to support common policies and measures to reduce GHG emissions in theory, the member states repeatedly blocked Commission proposals and stymied efforts for a common European climate policy.

European Energy Taxation

The most promising and most controversial EU policy for addressing CO_2 emissions continued to be a carbon/energy tax. The Finance Council and the heads of state rejected the tax proposal in December 1994. However, the Commission, along with a number of member states that either had recently imposed such a tax or desired to do so, continued to press for some form of common energy taxation. The tax proposals faced stiff opposition from European companies and a number of member states, particularly the United Kingdom. In May 1995, the Commission launched a new strategy for achieving a common energy tax. The Commission proposed a taxation directive that would create a harmonized framework for energy taxes by the year

2000. The proposal would provide guidance to member states on how to apply an energy/carbon tax, and the taxes would eventually be harmonized in 2000. The expectation was that the proposal would be less threatening and provide sufficient time for the approach to be accepted by all member states.

The proposal failed miserably. In October 1995, the Finance Council rejected the plan. The United Kingdom again led a group of member states in defeating the proposal. The British spokesman emphatically rejected any plan to apply a common EU energy tax.

> We feel that the current proposal as presented by the Spanish presidency was prejudicial as it would commit us to a harmonized tax in the future. . . . We will in no shape or form agree to a mandatory CO_2 tax. We feel that we have already taken painful measures such as our value-added tax on domestic fuel. By our calculation, we will meet our requirements under the climate change convention. We feel we have documented that in detailed reports—and these reports are far more detailed than those of the member states that are pushing for the carbon tax. . . . We are not opposed in any way if other countries want to implement a carbon tax. . . . The goal is to meet the climate change requirements, and whatever measures individual countries need to take is their option.[64]

The Council sent the measure back to the Commission for further study. Germany, supported by states with some form of energy/carbon tax (Finland, the Netherlands, Denmark, and Sweden), continued to lobby vigorously for a common tax structure.

The Commission again sought approval for a harmonized energy taxation directive in February 1997. The revised plan would create minimum levels of taxation on electricity, natural gas, coal, and other nonrenewable energy sources. The Commission attempted to recast the tax plan to address competitiveness concerns by focusing on the positive effects of the tax on employment, economic growth, and reductions in CO_2 emissions. The Internal Market Commissioner Mario Monti reflected the new "spin" on the proposal. "The proposal will not increase taxes in member states. . . . It is designed to help improve the environment and reduce unemployment."[65] The Commissioner noted that member states would be encouraged to use the additional tax receipts to reduce taxation on employment to improve the EU's competitive position. The proposal also allowed exemptions for companies with high energy requirements.

In practice, the tax would have had little short-term impact because most member states already had taxes higher than the minimum's proposed. However, once established, it would be easier to raise the tax rates over time to reduce European energy use. The UK rejected the proposal. According to Finance Minister Kenneth Clarke, "We would not hesitate to use our veto if these proposals stay in their present form. I think it is important to make this clear straight away, before we even start detailed discussions in the Council of Finance Ministers."[66] The proposal also faced stiff opposition from southern member states on competitiveness grounds and from the French who were pushing a carbon-based tax to take advantage of the role of nuclear energy in the French economy.

The Commission claimed that an energy tax would create a "triple dividend." It would create jobs, boost economic growth, and cut CO_2 emissions. The Commission produced three studies that estimated that the tax would produce economic gains worth .02 percent to .2 percent of GDP, the creation of between 155,000 and 457,000 jobs, and CO_2 emission reductions of .5 percent to 1.6 percent.[67] The Council continued to refuse to adopt the proposal, and the EU entered the Kyoto talks without its primary policy to address GHG emissions and significant questions regarding its ability to meet its proposed emission reduction commitments.

Eastern Expansion

The EU's best chance for technically meeting its targets would not require any additional regulation or taxation. Just as Germany had been able to make steep cuts in its aggregate CO_2 emissions by restructuring the former East Germany's electricity industry and industrial base, the EU had the option of expansion to the east. These countries could provide the cost-free reductions that the EU would likely need to technically meet its 15 percent reduction commitment. A spokesman for Environment Commissioner Bjerregaard rejected the view that the EU would utilize expansion to meet its international commitments. "The Commission, I am sure, would consider it a form of cheating, and therefore [Commissioner Bjerregaard] would do what she could to prevent it."[68] On the other hand, the Commission President's spokesman, Nikolaus van der Pas, did not rule out such a scenario. When questioned about the effects of eastward expansion on the EU's climate policy, van der Pas asserted that "[t]he Eastern and Central European countries will ultimately become EU members, and they will be treated no different from any other members. . . . They have to abide by the Community Acquis. There will be no exceptions. There will be no second-class members. Whatever the commitment of the EU is, it will apply to the new members."[69]

The candidate countries did nothing to dispel the view that they could provide CO_2 emission reductions for the European Union. In September 1997, environment ministers from the applicant countries met with the European Commission in Brussels to discuss climate policy. A majority of the ten countries adopted the EU's 15 percent reduction target by the year 2010. During the meeting, the applicants pressed for a joint implementation scheme between the EU and the applicants to facilitate the investments needed to achieve the 15 percent target. The joint implementation initiative received significant support from the Commission. Environment Commissioner Bjerregaard noted that,

> Due to economic restructuring, a number of no- and low-cost emissions [reduction schemes] are available in your countries. However, due to a lack of capital for the necessary investments, it might be difficult to implement these measures. Joint implementation, in my opinion could be an instrument which would attract the necessary financial flow to tap these options and to ensure high overall emission reductions at lower costs.[70]

Joint implementation and eastward expansion could potentially obviate the need for additional emission reductions within the existing member states. However, such an approach ran counter to the positions that the EU had taken on the use of flexibility mechanisms and on the norm requiring domestic emission reductions.

European Self-delusion

The European Commission refused to acknowledge the fact that it would not achieve its target of stabilizing emissions at 1990 levels by 2000. It failed to enact common policies to reduce GHG emissions (with the exception of the long-delayed refrigerator directive) and faced constant obstruction of its policy proposals by a number of member states. Yet, despite the internal struggles, the EU maintained a forceful position in the climate negotiations. Individually, only two of the member states (Germany and the United Kingdom) were likely to meet the target of stabilizing GHG emissions at 1990 levels by the year 2000. As individual states, only a minority of governments would have been willing to propose aggressive international GHG reduction targets, but jointly the member states provided a counterweight to the United States and its JUSCANZ group. Without the EU, it is doubtful that the Kyoto targets would have been as substantial as they were. The EU established a strong position of moral authority in the negotiations, even though there was little substance to its internal policy. Beyond the appeals to international norms, it had little leverage over its opponents beyond the ability to veto an agreement, but such a strategy was of limited use.

NEGOTIATING THE KYOTO PROTOCOL

The forces shaping the Kyoto Protocol negotiations were basically unchanged from the pre-Berlin Mandate period. The major states had not fundamentally altered their positions. However, in 1995 the IPCC released its second assessment report, which strengthened the view that human induced climate change was occurring. Opponents of international action faced greater difficulty in arguing that the science did not justify international action. The question was what sort of action was politically feasible. Four primary issues dominated the negotiations among developed states between the Berlin Conference of the Parties in 1995 (COP 1) and the December 1997 third Conference of the Parties (COP 3) in Kyoto. The first issue was the nature of GHG reduction commitments. What gases would be included in the calculations (CO_2, NO_X, methane, etc.)? Germany argued for a specific CO_2 reduction target with individual targets to be agreed for other GHGs. The United Kingdom and United States argued for a "basket" approach. Including a larger number of GHGs in a common target would provide flexibility to reduce emissions other than just CO_2. The Europeans continued to support the norm requiring a flat percentage reduction commitment using 1990 as a base year. A number of countries, which included at various points the United States, France, Japan, Australia, Norway, and Switzerland, argued that the targets should vary by state based on a set of criteria such as emission growth trends, per capita emissions, or carbon intensity of the domestic economy. What target dates would be used (i.e., 2005, 2010, 2015)? Germany and the EU wanted near-term targets to force immediate action, while the United States argued that short-term targets were unachievable.

A second set of issues related to the inclusion of binding policies and measures in the protocol. Germany and the European Union pressed for the negotiation of a set of common policies that all Annex I parties would be required to adopt. Because many of these policies would affect competitiveness, Germany argued that it was necessary for all industrial states to adopt the measures concurrently to minimize the competitive effects. The United States argued that common policy requirements could not account for the unique circumstances of each individual country and were therefore unacceptable.

Third, the United States and its allied argued that flexibility mechanisms would be essential for achieving cost-effective emission reductions. These countries proposed provisions for joint implementation, emissions trading, and emission budgets that would permit borrowing against future emission reduction commitments. The flexibility mechanisms were controversial, both between developed and developing countries and among developed countries. Would developing countries be able/willing to participate? The cheapest emission reductions could be achieved in the developing world, but many developing countries worried that the developed world would fail to undertake domestic actions and would instead rely on developing country emission reductions. Could flexibility measures be used to meet early reduction targets? Germany and the EU eventually accepted the principle of flexibility mechanisms, but they argued that the mechanisms should only be used to meet longer term targets after states had already taken domestic actions to reduce emissions.

The last issue was whether developing countries would be required to accept obligations to reduce emissions under the new protocol. The Berlin Mandate had ostensibly settled this issue, but the United States attempted to reopen it. The Clinton administration argued that developing countries had to participate in the protocol because their emissions were rising rapidly and the failure to include them would give them an unfair advantage. Developing countries were adamant that they would not accept binding emission commitments, though some states offered to voluntarily participate in the flexibility mechanisms.

The resolution of these issues was intimately linked to the domestic climate policies of each state. The developed countries split into two primary groupings on most issues. Germany and the EU formed the core of the first group that argued consistently for more aggressive reduction targets and common policies and measures to achieve those targets. The members of the JUSCANZ group would have difficulty achieving meaningful GHG emission reduction targets, and they attempted to minimize specific international commitments and maximize the use of flexibility mechanisms. Each side attempted to frame the international debate and the emerging norms to fit their domestic needs.

The Clinton administration was well aware of the narrow range of agreements capable of being ratified domestically. It was unable to pursue major new policy initiatives to reduce GHG emissions and was unlikely to do so in the near future. The American public was apathetic about climate change. American business interests were lobbying vigorously against an agreement, and Congress expressed outright hostility toward strengthening American commitments. Congressional Democrats and Republicans alike were skeptical of international commitments that did not include major developing countries such as China, South Korea, and India. The Clinton administration attempted to pursue a two-pronged strategy. Domestically, it sought to raise public awareness and concern about climate change to build support for emission reductions. In the negotiations, the administration sought to delay and obfuscate to buy time.

Germany and the United Kingdom were in much better positions to pursue meaningful international commitments. Germany could meet any target that would be acceptable to its negotiating partners, so it took a very aggressive negotiating stance and pressed for binding emission reduction targets for all Annex I countries. However, Germany was unlikely to meet its domestic 25 percent reduction commitment unless the government pursued additional domestic measures, which it was loathe to do unilaterally. The Kohl government was thus one of the foremost supporters of binding policy commitments in the future protocol. It believed that if all countries were required to enact a set of common policies, Germany could do so most efficiently. The promotion of common policies and measures had the added advantage of placing the onus on other countries to respond to the proposals. If the United States and its partners blocked the proposals, the government could point to the obstructionist tactics of the Americans and argue that it could not proceed unilaterally because of the effects on the German economy. The Kohl government was also open to proposals for flexibility mechanisms because it realized that future emission reductions would be much more difficult to achieve. It argued that these mechanisms should be developed for the post 2010 period, after Annex I countries had taken domestic actions to reduce their emissions. This position fit well with Germany's long-term interests. It would force other states to take costly short-term actions from which Germany would be exempt, while providing a longer term solution for reducing German emissions, but it also undermined the domestic emission reduction commitment norm.

The British government faced a similar set of incentives. It supported binding international GHG reduction commitments, although its proposed commitments were less ambitious and included all GHG emissions. It was also sensitive to the interests of the United States and continued to play a role as a mediator between the United States and its European partners. The Major government supported the concept of common policies and measures, as long as they were consistent with the Conservative government's policy agenda. For example, the government was unwilling to accept a carbon/energy tax, but it was willing to discuss policies for renewable energy, energy deregulation, and energy efficiency.

Both Germany and the United Kingdom had to operate internationally at two levels: the EU and the FCCC negotiations. Both countries pressed the EU to adopt an aggressive emission reduction commitment, but they were also reluctant to allow the other member states to "free-ride" on their emission reductions. The EU was unable to agree on a common position on emission reduction targets until 1997, which limited its ability to shape the negotiations. Germany and the Commission were also major proponents of developing a binding set of common policies and measures for the protocol, but yet again, the member states were unable to formulate a common position. The lack of a common EU position allowed the JUSCANZ group to seize the initiative, and it left the EU states on the defensive throughout the latter half of the negotiations.

The negotiations developed in three phases. After the Berlin Mandate was agreed, the United States attempted to delay concrete negotiations as it pressed for "analysis and assessment" of the economic effects of addressing climate change. Under significant international pressure, the Americans relented, and the first phase of negotiations leading up to COP 2 focused on narrowing a broad range of proposals into a manageable negotiating text. More serious negotiations began after the American elections in 1996. The United States put forth its proposal, and the outlines of a final agreement began to take shape. The final phase involved the mad rush to hammer out an agreement in Kyoto. Almost all of the crucial issues were left to the very last minute, and it required a marathon negotiating session to produce the Kyoto Protocol.

The Second Conference of the Parties

Substantive negotiations began in earnest at the third session of the AGBM in March 1996, and they gained momentum through the second Conference of the Parties in July. The heart of the negotiations centered on two issues: common policies and measures (P&Ms) and the nature of emission reduction targets. Most developed countries accepted that a number of policies could not be enacted unilaterally because of their effects on competitiveness and international trade. Germany and the EU thus argued that the new protocol should contain a set of common policies that all states would be required to enact. Germany presented its proposal on policies and measures (P&Ms) at AGBM 2. The United States and a number of other developed countries were skeptical of the P&Ms initiative.

At the July 1996 second Conference of the Parties (COP 2), the EU made a more detailed presentation of its P&Ms proposal. It called for the negotiation of three annexes to the protocol. The first would contain a small number of policies that all Annex I countries would be required to implement. The second would contain policies that would be most effective if widely implemented, and the third would include policies that states would be encouraged to pursue. The criteria for establishing the mandatory common policies would be large GHG reduction potential, competitiveness concerns that would prevent unilateral implementation, and long-term effectiveness. The United States rejected the EU's approach and continued to argue that a single set of policies could not possibly meet the needs of all affected states. The American delegation argued that an approach containing strong monitoring and reporting requirements would be much more cost-effective and successful in reducing emissions. During COP 2, the American delegation flatly rejected the inclusion of binding policies and measures in a final agreement. Germany and the EU continued to press for binding commitments, but the American position made their inclusion in the final agreement unlikely. The rejection represented a weakening of the norm requiring domestic responsibility and common emission reductions.

The most important issue was how to define emission reduction targets and schedules, which was where the clash of preferences and the unique circumstances of the primary actors were most apparent. Unsurprisingly,

Germany and the United Kingdom both offered specific emission reduction targets in the negotiations. Substantial German and British emission reductions also created the foundation for the EU as a whole to pursue a significant international target by offsetting smaller reductions or increases by other member states. The issue of burden sharing within the EU was a complex and difficult problem, but its eventual resolution allowed the EU to claim significant aggregate emission reductions. At AGBM 1, the British delegation proposed a target of 5 to 10 percent GHG reductions based on a 1990 baseline. The United Kingdom was already on track to meet this target. At AGBM 3, Germany proposed targets of a 10 percent CO_2 reduction by 2005 and 15 to 20 percent by 2010. A common flat percentage reduction target was appealing to the United Kingdom, Germany, and the EU, because it was straightforward and easy to explain to the public, and it did not require any complex agreements on criteria for determining emission levels on a case by case basis. It also fit well with the dominant norm requiring domestic emission reduction commitments, which most developing states, environmental NGOs, and the European public perceived as the only legitimate foundation on which to build the new protocol. The Europeans argued that the commitment would apply to the EU as a whole, which would permit differentiation within the EU, but other states would be required to achieve a common target. The JUSCANZ members rejected the flat rate targets and consistently argued that the EU approach was unjust and created a double standard. They argued for differentiation based on a number of potential criteria including: per capita emissions, carbon intensity of the economy, equitable costs of reductions across countries, and emission trend lines.

A second major issue was whether to agree to an aggregate reduction in a "basket" of gases or to reduce GHGs on a gas by gas basis. The United Kingdom argued that a basket approach would maximize flexibility by allowing reductions in whatever gases were most cost effective for the individual country. Other countries were skeptical of the approach because of the complexities of comparing the warming potentials of various GHGs. The United States supported the approach because reductions in GHGs, other than CO_2, were occurring as a result of policies enacted for other purposes, such as regulations under the CAAA of 1990. These reductions could offset increases in CO_2 emissions.

Finally, there was significant debate regarding whether to utilize net or gross GHG emissions. The United States argued that changes in domestic land use, which resulted in removals of CO_2 from the atmosphere, should be deducted from gross emissions. Calculations of net emissions would thus promote more sustainable land use and provide broader environmental benefits beyond the removal of CO_2. Environmental groups, developing countries, and some developed countries criticized the proposal as a loophole to allow states to emit larger amounts of CO_2.

Parties to the FCCC proposed a variety of reduction targets and timetables, but as the negotiations progressed, the debate centered on three issues: time frames for reductions, whether differentiation would be permitted, and the indicators to be used for differentiation. Most parties argued for some form of differentiation in emission targets that would take account of specific domestic circumstances. The issue of binding emission reduction commitments came to a head at the July 1996 COP 2. Countries were reluctant to offer specific commitments until the nature of the targets was clearer and other questions concerning differentiation were sorted out. Germany, the United Kingdom, and the small island states had offered the only concrete proposals. Even the EU had been unable to agree on a common target prior to COP 2. Delegates continued to debate the desirability of binding emission reduction commitments. France and Japan argued for differentiation based on per capita emissions or CO_2 emissions per unit of GDP. Other countries supported equalizing marginal emission abatement costs of parties.

The United States broke the commitments deadlock during one of the final COP 2 sessions. U.S. Undersecretary of State, Timothy Wirth, announced that the United States would support a "realistic, verifiable, and binding medium-term emissions target," but he then proceeded to assert that the targets being discussed were "neither realistic nor achievable."[71] The last minute nature of the concession minimized the amount of time devoted to exploring what the new commitment would actually mean to the negotiations. The timing of the announcement and the lack of details could be perceived to be a cynical attempt to bolster the administration's green credentials going into the fall elections. Wirth offered no comment on what a "realistic and achievable" target might be. Instead, he deferred the question until after the elections. Wirth also identified two primary conditions that the United States would place on the final agreement. First, there should be no binding policies and measures. Second, the administration demanded the inclusion of "maximum flexibility" in meeting the target, including joint implementation and emissions trading.[72]

Qualified American support for a binding commitment created an opening for a compromise. The final conference declaration called for the negotiation of "quantified legally-binding objectives for emission limitations and significant overall reductions within specified time frames, such as 2005, 2010, 2020, with respect to their anthropogenic emissions by sources and removals by sinks of greenhouse gases not controlled by the Montreal Protocol."[73] The declaration continued to include sinks in the calculation of emissions, and it contained no baseline for measuring emission reductions after the United States insisted on deleting references to 1990. There was also no specific call for binding policies and measures.

Targets and Loopholes

Discussion of emission reduction targets and flexibility mechanisms dominated the period from COP 2 through the final December 1997 negotiations in Kyoto. After accepting, in principle, binding emission targets at COP 2 and winning the 1996 election, the Clinton administration provided greater detail on its negotiating position. The administration sought to defer commitments as long as possible and to create loopholes to avoid near-term emission reductions. At the December 1996 fifth meeting of the AGBM, the United States presented a position paper outlining its views on binding targets and timetables. First, the administration rejected any reduction targets prior to 2010. The American paper then went on to propose "emission budgets," which would allow states to "borrow" emissions from subsequent periods. Under the proposal, parties to the protocol would not have to reduce emissions for nearly twenty-five years, and even then, they could "borrow" emissions from a future period to avoid reducing emissions. The American paper also called for credits to be provided for joint implementation projects and for enhancing sinks.[74] The proposal was clearly unacceptable to most of the other delegations, but it served as an extreme starting point from which to compromise.

Related to the emission reduction commitments was a second set of issues linked to incorporating flexibility mechanisms into the final agreement. The United States was instrumental in shaping the agreement on the pilot phase for activities implemented jointly (AIJ) at the first Conference of the Parties. The American delegation, with support from its JUSCANZ partners, continued to press for early agreement on converting the pilot phase into an official component of the future protocol. A number of states developed domestic joint implementation programs to explore their effectiveness and test procedures. By the July 1996 COP 2 meeting, six countries (Australia, Canada, Germany, the Netherlands, Norway, and the United States) had developed JI programs involving thirty-two projects in a wide range of sectors including energy efficiency, renewable energy, fuel switching, forestry, and fugitive gas capture program. Nearly all of the developed countries began to support the creation of a JI program, but there continued to be disagreements over crucial details, including reporting requirements, whether developing countries could participate, how reduction credits would be distributed, and when such a program could begin.

The United States expanded the conditions for accepting a binding GHG emission reduction target beyond the inclusion of JI. At COP 2, it also demanded the development of an emission trading program. Emission trading had been a point of discussion in the past, but the United States was the first country to officially call for the incorporation of such a program into the FCCC. The program raised a number of technical issues that would be difficult to resolve and resulted in opposition from both developed and developing countries who perceived the program as an American attempt to buy its way out of reducing domestic emissions. The JUSCANZ group supported the proposal, but the EU and many of its member states wanted to delay any trading until after Annex I countries had undertaken domestic efforts to reduce emissions. The Clinton administration gradually built support for the program, but it remained controversial, because it required a shift from the dominant norm of national responsibility and domestic reductions toward a nascent norm focusing on efficiency and cost-effectiveness of global reductions.

If the administration expected the Senate to ratify a future protocol, it would also be essential to incorporate developing country commitments in some meaningful way. At the December 1996 fifth meeting of the AGBM, the American delegation made a proposal for developing country commitments. The AGBM chairman immediately rejected further debate on the topic and noted that the AGBM mandate did not include a review of developing country commitments.[75] The American delegation continued to raise the issue and proposed the attachment of an "Annex B" that would allow developing countries to voluntarily accept emission reduction commitments. Developing countries rejected the proposal as an attempt to smuggle developing country commitments into the protocol.

The negotiations remained at an impasse over the question of targets and timelines. The United States, Japan, and the European Union had not proposed specific reductions by the beginning of 1997. The EU member states finally achieved consensus on a target in March 1997. The EU proposed a target of reducing a basket of three GHGs (CO_2, methane, and NO_x) by 15 percent by 2010 based on a 1990 baseline. The EU proposal allowed differentiation within the EU while other states would have to meet common targets. The American delegation ridiculed the EU for allowing differences of up to 70 percent among member states' targets. The American delegation proposed that the commitments of each member state be included in the negotiating text. The listing of individual member state targets would provide a range of options in the negotiating text extending from a 30 percent reduction (Luxembourg) to a 40 percent increase (Portugal). The United States hoped that such a list could build the foundation for flexibility in setting targets for other states. The EU responded that individual commitments were not part of the proposal and would not be included.[76] The EU challenged the critics to place their own proposals on the table to facilitate more meaningful discussion.

The United States held the key to the final agreement. Four primary issues remained to be resolved. First, would the Americans accept the EU's proposals for binding policies and measures? Second, would the EU and developing countries accept the American JI, emissions trading, and emissions banking/borrowing initiatives? Third, would developing countries accept some form of future commitment to reduce emissions? Finally, what was the American bottom line target for reducing emissions and would a compromise be possible with the EU countries? The Clinton administration sought to delay its proposal in an attempt to build domestic support and to test the political waters for an agreement acceptable to both domestic and international constituencies.

The AGBM process reached a deadlock as the Clinton administration continued to delay the release of its negotiating position. EU member states and developing countries declined to compromise on the flexibility mechanisms until the United States made a specific emission reduction proposal. The EU accepted that emission trading was a possibility, if the emission reduction targets pledged by the United States and other Annex I countries were adequate. However, the Clinton administration argued that it could not announce a target until there was some agreement on flexibility mechanisms.[77]

The JUSCANZ group worked throughout September and October to coordinate its position for the final session of the AGBM prior to Kyoto. The group agreed at a ministerial meeting in early October that the EU position on emission reductions was too ambitious and unacceptable. It also agreed that developing countries had to assume some obligations in the new agreement. After the meeting, Japan announced its position that developed countries should reduce their GHG emissions by a maximum of 5 percent some time between 2008 and 2012 based on a 1990 baseline. The level of reduction would be determined by taking into account emissions per unit of GDP and population growth rates. According to Japanese calculations, the United States, Japan, and Australia would have to reduce emissions respectively by 2.6 percent, 2.5 percent, and 1.8 percent.[78] The Japanese plan also included the American proposals for emission banking and borrowing, as well as provisions for joint implementation and emissions trading. The EU and environmentalists attacked the plan for failing to take emission reductions seriously, while the Clinton administration praised the proposal as thoughtful and realistic. The United States followed the Japanese proposal with its own two weeks later. President Clinton announced on October 22, 1997 that the United States was willing to commit to returning GHG emissions to 1990 levels between 2008 and 2012, reducing net emissions of GHGs below 1990 levels between 2013 and 2018, and discussing emission reductions after 2018. American support for binding targets was qualified by the demands for meaningful participation by developing countries and the inclusion of emissions trading and joint implementation.

The degree of coordination between Japan and the United States prior to the announcement of both plans suggests that they hoped to use the Japanese proposal as a compromise between the American and EU target proposals. Environmental groups and the European Commission lambasted the American proposal. European Commission spokesman, Peter Jorgensen noted that the United States had agreed in the FCCC to stabilize its emissions at 1990 levels by 2000. "Now it is saying it will stabilize by 2012.... That is not acceptable. In fact it is totally inadequate and downright irresponsible."[79] Other European states were less critical. British Environment Minister, John Prescott commended President Clinton for putting forward a specific proposal. "Given the opposition that he has faced from some quarters within his own country on climate change, I know that this has not been easy for him. Obviously, we would like more, but this is a useful first step towards Kyoto."[80] Germany also welcomed the proposal, while acknowledging that it hoped the United States would strengthen it.

As the Kyoto negotiations began, the United States and the European Union refused to budge from their positions. It was only in the final two days that both sides initiated compromises. The United States committed to a much larger emission reduction target than it had originally offered. The American delegation agreed to a 7 percent emission reduction commitment to be achieved between 2008 and 2012, and the EU member states agreed to reduce their emissions by 8 percent jointly. This represented a major concession on the part of the United States, but in return, it received even greater concessions from its negotiating partners. First, the basket of GHGs was expanded from the EU's proposed three gases (CO_2, methane, and NO_x) to include three others favored by the United States (HFCs, PFCs, and sulfur hexafluoride).[81] The inclusion of all six substances provided additional flexibility in reducing emissions. Second, the targets were defined as net emission reductions as opposed to gross reductions. The expansion of CO_2 sinks could thus offset emission increases. According to the 1997 American submission to the FCCC, the inclusion of sinks reduced American emissions by 8.2 percent (428 million metric tons) in 1995.[82] This represented substantial savings that could be applied toward the 7 percent commitment. The United States also received a number of compromises in terms of the flexibility mechanisms. In the face of strong opposition from developing countries, the United States was forced to abandon its attempts to include developing countries in its proposed joint implementation and emissions trading programs. Instead, Article 6 of the Kyoto Protocol provided for joint implementation among Annex I countries, though the rules and procedures for implementing the program were deferred to future negotiations. During the final debate China, India, and Indonesia also blocked American proposals for emissions trading. In a last minute compromise, the delegates accepted Article 17, which acknowledged the principle of emissions trading but deferred decisions on its operation to future negotiations.

The G–77 and China also blocked American proposals to include an article on voluntary commitments from developing countries, but the American delegation successfully bypassed China and split the G–77 to achieve a significant victory. While the G–77 tried to block the American initiatives on emissions trading and developing country commitments, the United States adopted a proposal by Brazil to create a "Clean Development Mechanism" (CDM). Brazil had originally proposed that states that did not meet their commitments under the new protocol would be forced to pay penalties to a fund to finance emission reduction projects in developing countries. The American delegation secured support from a number of other developing countries to turn the mechanism into a hybrid joint implementation and emissions trading mechanism. Under the new proposal, developed countries would undertake investments in developing countries that would result in certified emission reduction credits. A portion of these credits would then be transferred back to the developed country to fulfill part of its commitment. Developing countries would not have to assume binding commitments, but they could voluntarily participate in the program. As in the cases of joint implementation among Annex I countries and emissions trading, the rules governing the functioning of the CDM were left to future negotiations. Through the CDM, the United States was able to achieve most of the advantages it had sought through emissions trading and JI and was able to convince a number of developing countries to participate in the CDM.

The Kyoto Protocol established a set of binding emission reductions that fell well short of what scientists claimed were necessary, and they were less than half of what the EU and developing countries had proposed. Though the Kyoto commitments were not as demanding as many had hoped, they would be legally binding if the protocol came into force, and Kyoto created a framework for strengthening future emission reduction commitments. The problem was that the agreement was unlikely to be ratified by the developed states until the questions surrounding JI, emissions trading, the CDM, and sink credits were resolved. From a legal perspective, the Kyoto Protocol was a work in progress, but perhaps more importantly the agreement altered the normative framework for the ongoing negotiations. Economic efficiency became a guiding principle, which facilitated agreement on the flexibility mechanisms and undermined the norm requiring developed states to focus on reducing domestic GHG emissions. The norm requiring quantitative domestic emission reduction commitments remained, but the inclusion of credits for sinks and the introduction of flexibility mechanisms undermined the spirit of the norm. The conclusion of the Kyoto Protocol had the potential to increase the domestic political salience of climate change, but the introduction of the flexibility mechanisms also reduced the pressure to achieve domestic emission reductions. The Kyoto Protocol was a work in progress. The negotiations to define the rules that would govern it would be essential for determining whether it would have a significant effect on the future path of climate change. These negotiations would also establish the normative framework that would underlie its implementation. Would the primary focus be on national responsibility and domestic emission reductions, or would economic efficiency and cost-effectiveness guide its implementation? The resolution of this normative debate would be crucial in determining the rules that would govern Kyoto. These normative battles will be evaluated in chapter six.

CHAPTER SIX

Rhetoric and Reality:
The United States vs. the World?

(Kyoto to Marrakech)

The signing of the Kyoto Protocol was a high point of international action to address climate change. In the weeks after the Kyoto conference, nearly all of the major industrial states retreated from the commitments contained in the Protocol. None of them directly challenged the headline emission reduction commitments. However, the United States and its allies made it clear that they would demand very liberal rules for sink credits and the maximum use of flexibility mechanisms to minimize the need for domestic emission reductions. While the EU opposed the American tactics, most member states were also in retreat from their earlier commitments. The pre-Kyoto EU burden sharing agreement committed member states to achieve aggregate emission reductions of 10 percent (across three GHGs). The Kyoto Protocol reduced the EU's commitment to an 8 percent emission reduction (across six GHGs). The easing of the EU commitment produced a scramble among member states to secure reductions in their commitments. Even Germany secured a decrease in its EU emission reduction commitment from 25 percent to 21 percent. The parties to the Kyoto Protocol appeared to be having second thoughts about their commitments and the domestic emission reductions they could require.

The post-Kyoto negotiations can be divided into two periods. The period from Kyoto to the 2000 COP 6 meeting at The Hague produced intense negotiations over sinks and flexibility mechanisms that pitted the European Union against the United States and its allies. It was apparent that the United States was unlikely to achieve significant emission reductions and would need to rely on sinks and flexibility mechanisms to meet its commitment. Germany and the EU argued that the United States was creating loopholes to avoid domestic action and continued to appeal to a norm requiring domestic emission reductions before countries resorted to the flexibility mechanisms. International climate norms achieved greater levels of domestic political salience in Germany and the United Kingdom after Kyoto. Both countries used their Kyoto commitments to justify controversial domestic policy changes. In particular, both countries launched new energy taxes to fund reductions in taxes on labor. However, Germany continued to rely primarily on emission reductions from restructuring in the East, and the United Kingdom continued to depend on emission reductions from fuel switching to meet its target.

While the negotiations leading up to The Hague were contentious, the participants believed that an agreement was achievable and that the Kyoto Protocol could be ratified and enter into force in the near future. However, the remarkable failure of The Hague negotiations and the election of George W. Bush in 2000 launched a new phase in the negotiations. The period from The Hague failure to the Marrakech negotiations in the fall of 2001 produced a new dynamic. The Bush administration rejected the Kyoto Protocol as unfair and potentially devastating to the American economy. The American rejection forced the other states to decide whether to scrap the Protocol and pursue new negotiations or proceed without the United States in the hope that it would eventually return to the Protocol. Germany and the EU led the effort to complete the Protocol. The Protocol required ratification by fifty-five countries representing 55 percent of developed country CO_2 emissions. For Kyoto to enter into force without the United States, it would be necessary for the EU plus Russia and Japan to ratify the agreement.[1] After The Hague, the negotiations focused on EU efforts to offer sufficient incentives to Russia and Japan to ratify the Protocol. Domestic policy became a less important issue. The focus was on achieving a ratifiable agreement. The headline commitments would remain the same, but behind the scenes the states would eviscerate the agreement with various loopholes that minimized domestic emission reductions and undermined the norms that underpinned the Protocol.

UNITED STATES

The conclusion of the Kyoto negotiations changed little in the American climate policy debate. The Protocol contained no new commitments for developing countries, which remained a fundamental requirement for Senate ratification. Public apathy, industrial hostility, and congressional opposition combined to undermine meaningful attempts to reduce domestic emissions. Unless there was a dramatic shift in the domestic political situation, the United States would have to rely extensively on the flexibility mechanisms and liberal accounting standards for sinks to meet its Kyoto commitment. The post-Kyoto negotiations were thus critical to American participation in the Protocol. The administration had to find a means of inducing developing country participation. It had to negotiate a set of international rules governing joint implementation, emissions trading, and the Clean Development Mechanism that would allow the United States to achieve the vast majority of emissions reductions through the actions of other states. Additionally, the administration needed to negotiate an agreement to count emission offsets achieved through the use of carbon sinks. This would prove to be an exceedingly difficult agenda. America's negotiating partners in Europe and among the developing countries were adamantly opposed to allowing the United States to purchase its emission reductions without undertaking significant domestic action. It was thus vital that the administration demonstrate a commitment to reducing domestic GHG emissions. In the meantime, President Clinton notified the Senate that he would not submit the treaty for ratification until he secured developing country participation and finalized the rules for the flexibility mechanisms.

The only other major change in the forces shaping American climate policy was an ongoing reevaluation of the opposition to reducing GHG emissions among major American corporations. Corporate leaders increasingly worried that opposition to reductions in GHG emissions was hurting their public images. In addition, several companies came to the conclusion that there were potential profits available through the creation of a domestic market in GHG emission credits. The formerly monolithic front put forward by major businesses began to crack following the negotiation of the Kyoto Protocol, which created opportunities for the administration to exploit in revising America's climate policy.

The Clinton administration would once again be walking a fine line. It had to negotiate international rules to allow the United States to achieve its commitments, while also inducing significant domestic action to reassure its international partners that it was serious about the problem of climate change. However, following the contested election of 2000 and the selection of George W. Bush as president, the dynamics of both domestic and international climate policy fundamentally changed. The first section of the chapter evaluates the Clinton administration's response to Kyoto. The Bush transition is intimately intertwined with the post-Hague negotiations and will be addressed in the final section of the chapter.

Congress vs. the President

Congress squared off against the president immediately after the conclusion of the Kyoto negotiations. The confrontation revolved around two primary issues. First, many in Congress accused the administration of attempting to implement the Kyoto Protocol without seeking Senate ratification. The second area of confrontation involved the climate initiatives that the president outlined just prior to the Kyoto negotiations, which included energy efficiency tax credits and research funding, electricity industry deregulation, and voluntary agreements with industry to measure and reduce GHG emissions. The administration wanted to avoid an immediate rejection by the Senate so it withheld submitting the Protocol for ratification until a mechanism for developing country participation could be established and the rules for the flexibility mechanisms were finalized. It also sought to reemphasize the minimal costs of achieving the Kyoto target. The administration hoped that the political environment would shift to permit a more activist approach to reducing emissions in the future.

The Clinton administration's approach to climate policy was most comprehensively expressed in the March 1998 congressional testimony of Janet Yellen, the chair of the President's Council of Economic Advisors. Yellen testified that the costs of achieving the commitments contained in the Kyoto Protocol would be moderate. She emphasized that the administration had successfully negotiated an agreement that would allow the United States to address the problem in a manner consistent with continued economic growth. She focused on five issues that were critical to achieving the America's Kyoto commitments: international emissions trading, meaningful developing country participation, inclusion of "sinks" in the calculation of net emissions, the expansion of the number of regulated GHGs from the original three to six, and domestic initiatives proposed by President Clinton. Four of the five issues related to international matters that would not actually reduce American emissions but would rather provide the United States with credits for reductions achieved in other countries or for changes in American land use. Yellen asserted that if the administration achieved satisfactory outcomes in all five areas, the Kyoto commitment could be met at a cost of $7 to 12 billion per year between 2008 and 2012 or one-tenth of 1 percent of American GDP per year. Household energy prices would likely increase by 3 to 5 percent; fuel oil prices by 5 to 9 percent; gasoline prices by 3 to 4 percent; and electricity prices by 3 to 4 percent.[2] The costs of meeting the Kyoto targets would be barely perceptible.

The administration's cost estimates proved to be a political lightning rod. Several congressional committees requested the supporting materials for the cost estimates. The Clinton administration initially refused. The White House argued that the materials reflected deliberations internal to the Executive Office and could affect the ongoing international negotiations. In May, House Republicans informed the White House that they would seek a subpoena for the documents unless they were turned over. The primary issue in dispute was the question of how much of the United States' Kyoto commitment would be met by purchasing credits for reductions achieved by other countries. Yellen had repeatedly evaded questions regarding the size of the purchases.

Finally, on July 31, 1998 the administration released the supporting materials for its cost estimates. It became immediately apparent why it had hoped to avoid releasing the documents. The administration assumed that 75 percent of the American reductions would be achieved through emissions trading with other countries. It also assumed that the requisite credits would cost between $14 and $23 per ton of carbon equivalent.[3] The study reinforced the absolute necessity for the United States to achieve meaningful international emissions trading if it was to fulfill its Kyoto commitments. Environmental as well as business groups roundly criticized the study's assumptions, and congressional Republicans decried the vast transfer of wealth that was implied by the purchase of credits. Rather than building support for action, the administration's cost estimates further alienated an already skeptical Congress.

In the midst of the debate over the costs of achieving the Kyoto targets, President Clinton released his fiscal year 1999 budget proposal. Facing a skeptical Congress that would be hostile to major new climate initiatives, the administration chose to expand on the existing energy related climate research programs and to create a new set of tax credits to promote energy efficiency and renewable energies. The administration bundled the proposals into what it promoted as a five year, 6.3 billion dollar "Climate Change Technology Initiative" (CCTI). The package was based on the climate initiatives that the president had outlined in October 1997, but the package was $1.3 billion larger than the original $5 billion proposal. The core of the package was a set of tax credits totaling $3.6 billion over five years to encourage the purchase of highly efficient vehicles, energy efficient homes, and rooftop solar equipment. In addition, the administration proposed $2.7 billion to be used for research into improving energy efficiency in the building, transportation, and industrial sectors.[4] The administration attempted to demonstrate to its international partners and domestic environmental groups that it was acting to reduce American emissions. It also sought to defuse the hostility that was building against climate policy in Congress. The proposed measures were popular with several industry groups and with many environmental organizations.

The proposed CCTI measures were meager, representing one-tenth of 1 percent of the federal budget in FY1999, and they were unlikely to bring the United States much closer to achieving its Kyoto commitments. A General Accounting Office report on the proposals was highly critical. The report noted that the CCTI failed to provide a cost-benefit analysis, omitted any plan for coordinating the various initiatives across the fourteen agencies involved in the climate program, and failed to demonstrate the extent to which the proposals would assist the United States in meeting its Kyoto commitments.[5] The CCTI proposal allowed the administration to argue that it was doing something to reduce American GHG emissions while also avoiding a major battle with Congress over climate policy.

Congressional members from both parties found the research spending and tax credits to be enticing, because they had broad support from industry. Therefore, even in the face of extensive opposition to the administration's climate position, the Republican controlled Senate and House approved over $1 billion for the president's CCTI program. The spending total was slightly less than the president had requested, but it still represented a 25 percent increase over the 1998 funding levels.[6] However, Congress rejected the president's energy efficiency tax credit plans.

The administration substantially increased its climate change funding requests in its fiscal year 2000 and 2001 budget requests. The president proposed increasing the CCTI spending by more than one-third to nearly $1.4 billion in 2000 and reintroduced his proposals for tax credits worth $3.6 billion over five years.[7] However, the Republican controlled Congress again rejected the tax incentives and provided only a minor increase in CCTI spending. The FY2001 budget debate produced a similar outcome. The budgetary component of the president's climate plan was not going to provide significant emission reductions in the near-term.

While Democratic and Republican members of both chambers expressed concerns about the Kyoto Protocol, a small number of Republican members aggressively challenged the Clinton administration and fought to stop it from pursuing any policies to reduce American emissions or to undertake preparations for future reductions, which included educational efforts. These Republicans pursued their efforts under the banner of "No Implementation without Ratification." The first major conflict erupted in March 1998. An EPA proposal to regulate CO_2 emissions from power plants under the Clean Air Act was leaked to the press. The document linked the initiative to the Kyoto Protocol. The EPA asserted that it already possessed the regulatory authority under the Clean Air Act to regulate CO_2 emissions, but the document noted that additional authorization from Congress would facilitate the regulatory process.[8] The EPA document produced a firestorm in Congress.

In response to perceived implementation attempts by the Clinton administration, Republican Senator John Ashcroft and Republican Representative Joseph Knollenberg introduced bills that would make it illegal for federal agencies to regulate CO_2 emissions without the express authority of Congress. While neither bill received a hearing, they were the precursors to a series of environmental riders that were attached to spending bills for fiscal years 1999 and 2000. Knollenberg successfully attached language to the EPA's funding bill that barred the use of any EPA funds "to develop, propose, or issue rules, regulations, decrees, or orders for the purpose of implementation, or in contemplation of implementation of the Kyoto Protocol."[9] The amendment would also bar the administration from "conducting educational outreach or informational seminars on policies underlying the Kyoto Protocol."[10]

The administration decried the rider. Vice President Gore asserted that "[t]hat bunch over there in the Congress that's playing politics with this needs to go outside and feel the temperature. . . . They would not only keep us from acting against global warming; they would even keep us from informing the public about the dangers that are faced by our country. They don't even want us to talk about it."[11] A modified version of the rider was passed as a part of the final budget. The rider stated: "That none of the funds appropriated by this Act shall be used to propose or issue rules, regulations, decrees, or orders for the purpose of implementation, or in preparation for implementation, of the Kyoto Protocol which was adopted on December 11, 1997, in Kyoto, Japan. . . . "[12] Republicans continued this strategy in the 2000 budget and successfully attached similar riders to six appropriations bills. Congressional opponents of the Kyoto Protocol continued to level charges and hold hearings on alleged implementation throughout the period leading up to the Hague negotiations. The stalemate that developed between Congress and the president dramatically illustrated the potential for small numbers of committed legislators to thwart the will of the executive.

The final piece of the administration's climate change initiative involved the deregulation of the electricity industry, which had been discussed for several years. The administration saw deregulation as an opportunity to realize efficiency improvements and cost reductions in electricity markets while also achieving a number of environmental objectives. However, the effort bogged down in cabinet level disputes involving the regulation of CO_2 emissions. The Energy Department argued that competition would force energy companies to become more efficient and would produce reductions in emissions of CO_2 and smog producing pollutants. The EPA countered that without environmental mandates deregulation would force power companies to switch to cheaper and dirtier coal, which would produce more emissions.[13] As a natural gas industry analyst noted at the time, "[y]ou could save $20 billion [in electricity rates] if you use excess coal capacity, but that would give the EPA a heart-attack. . . . If you have a renewables [fuels] mandate and try to reduce carbon gases, then the saving is all over. They definitely do not want to come up with a bill that's going to cost you more."[14] The electricity deregulation debate languished in Congress during 1998. It briefly reemerged in 1999 with a new administration initiative, but there was little public demand for electricity deregulation, and the administration's commitment appeared lacking. The deregulation debate thus continued to languish in Congress with little prospect of near-term action. It became apparent that the administration's climate programs would not produce meaningful emission reductions.

Shifting Forces in the American Private Sector

The most interesting transformation in the American climate policy debate was the reevaluation by several major American corporations of the potential for voluntary GHG emission reductions and eventual emission trading.

During the Kyoto negotiations, American corporations presented a relatively unified position against American GHG emission reduction commitments. The front began to fragment in 1998. A number of corporations concluded that opposition to GHG emission reductions was hurting their public images. Furthermore, there appeared to be significant benefits for undertaking near-term action to address their GHG emissions. Voluntary actions could potentially forestall regulation and create profits from the sale of GHG emission reduction credits in a future carbon trading system.

Several events in the spring of 1998 were indicative of the shifting incentives that corporations faced on climate policy. In May 1998 the Pew Charitable Trust created the Pew Center on Global Climate Change, which sought to entice corporations to voluntarily reduce GHG emissions. The center's primary objectives were to conduct research into cost-effective emission reduction measures for industry and to promote voluntary emission reductions. A number of companies from industries that had traditionally opposed emission reduction initiatives affiliated themselves with the new center, including: oil companies Sunoco, British Petroleum, and Enron; power generators American Electric Power and US Generating Company; aerospace firms Boeing and Lockheed Martin; appliance makers Maytag and Whirlpool; auto maker Toyota; and the chemical company 3M. The companies did not commit resources to the new center, but they all agreed to cooperate with it to advance its agenda.[15]

A sharp divide was developing within these industries. At the same time that these firms were signing up to support the new Pew Center, the Business Roundtable and a number of associated industry groups announced a new lobbying campaign. A draft plan discussed by the groups called for giving climate change dissenters "the logistical and moral support they have been lacking." Specifically, the groups planned to spend $5 million over two years to "maximize the impact of scientific views consistent with ours on Congress, the media, and other key audiences."[16] Many of the companies that signed on with the new Pew Center were also members of the industry groups that were developing the anticlimate policy media campaign.

Beginning in 1992, the Clinton administration had developed a series of voluntary programs to promote GHG emission reductions. The 1992 Energy Policy Act established a voluntary GHG reporting program within the Department of Energy to record baseline emissions for individual firms and subsequent changes in emissions. In 1992, the EPA had launched the Energy Star program to work with industry to promote energy efficient products. The Climate Challenge Program was launched in 1994 to promote nonbinding commitments between the Department of Energy and power utilities to reduce GHG emissions. These programs did not involve legally binding commitments. They were designed to assist companies in analyzing their GHG emissions, to encourage cost-effective emission reductions and the development of more energy efficient products, and to offer public recognition of efforts to reduce emissions. Participation in the programs became much more enticing as momentum built to provide credits to companies that reduced their GHGs. These credits could eventually be worth a significant amount of money if the United States ever capped GHG emissions and created a market to trade them.

Industry groups and environmental organizations began to work closely with members of Congress to develop a crediting program for emission reductions. In October 1998, a bipartisan group of senators introduced a bill to provide credits to companies for GHG emission reductions. The existing voluntary reporting program at the Department of Energy would document emission reductions and assign the associated credits. Corporations would be entitled to sell the credits in a future emissions market. The National Association of Manufacturers as well as a number of power companies supported the bill. The White House released a set of guiding principles on crediting in December 1998. Such a program would be complicated to develop and administer, but it had the potential to form the foundation for more aggressive domestic emission reductions. DuPont calculated that it had reduced its GHG emissions by ninety million tons of CO_2 equivalent between 1991 and 1998.[17] Assuming that it received full credit for the reported reductions and that the reductions could be sold at the modest prices predicted by the White House, the credits could be worth at least $2 billion.[18]

As the debate over GHG crediting developed, the initial support from environmental and industry groups began to fray as the focus shifted to the rules of how such a system would work. In 1997, the 156 companies participating in the voluntary GHG reporting program claimed 137 million tons of carbon equivalent reductions.[19] Under the Senate bill, all of them would be eligible for credits for their reductions. However, the Energy Department did not audit these claims beyond checking arithmetic and the consistency of the data. A study by the GAO claimed that the emission reduction totals were almost certainly substantially exaggerated.[20] Several hearings were held on the crediting proposal, but the political tide began to turn against crediting. Skeptics charged that the early crediting strategy was part of an administration strategy to create a constituency for ratifying the Kyoto Protocol. The emission reduction credits would only have value if emissions were regulated and a market established. The crediting program was thus creating incentives for industry to support GHG regulations. Environmental groups were also critical of the crediting mechanism. They argued that it would reward companies for pursuing investments that they would have undertaken regardless of the new program and penalize companies that took those measures prior to the introduction of the program. The debate over early crediting stalled in both the House and the Senate. By late 1999 it was apparent that action on the initiative would have to wait until after the presidential elections in 2000.

The prospect of emission reduction crediting as well as positive public exposure for American companies led to a number of voluntary accords between the Clinton administration and industry. In November 1998, the electric power and magnesium casting industries agreed to undertake voluntary reductions in their emissions of sulfur hexaflouride (SF6), a powerful GHG included in the Kyoto Protocol. By April 1999, forty-eight electric utilities had signed memoranda of understanding with the EPA under the program. In May 2000, leading home appliance manufacturers, including Whirlpool, Maytag, and General Electric, concluded an agreement with the Department of Energy under the Energy Star program that would improve the energy efficiency of washing machines by 50 percent by 2007. The EPA predicted that the agreement would produce energy savings of five quadrillion Btu or the equivalent of eliminating the GHG emissions of three million cars every year.[21]

A number of companies were also experimenting with emissions trading to demonstrate its viability. In 1999 American and Canadian companies in cooperation with several northeastern states and environmental organizations developed the "Greenhouse Gas Trading Demonstration Project" that claimed to have prevented two million tons of GHG emissions.[22] In October 2000, Dupont, British Petroleum, Shell, Suncor Energy, Ontario Power Generation, Alcan (a Canadian aluminum company), and Pechiney (a French aluminum company) joined with the Environmental Defense Fund to create the "Partnership for Climate Action." Under the program, the companies jointly committed to reduce their GHG emissions by 15 percent by 2010. The joint goal would be met through direct reductions by participating companies as well as emission trading among the companies. If the joint target was met, the companies would cut their annual GHG emissions by ninety million tons a year.[23]

The automotive industry was also promoting voluntary efforts to reduce GHG emissions through the Clinton administration's "Partnership for a New Generation of Vehicles." The research program, funded jointly by the automakers and the federal government, was intended to develop technologies that would produce cars with a fuel efficiency rating of eighty miles per gallon by 2004. In January 2000, the big three American automakers introduced prototype automobiles that would be capable of achieving the eighty miles per gallon efficiency rating. Ford Motor followed up the auto show with an announcement that all of its future light trucks would meet American auto efficiency standards. GM and Ford also announced that they would significantly increase the fuel efficiency of their SUVs. While supportive of the introduction of more fuel-efficient automobiles, the automakers were also adamant that federal regulations should not mandate higher fuel efficiency. The automakers successfully lobbied congressional members to include riders in every transportation appropriations bill between FY1996 and FY2000 that prevented the administration from raising vehicle fuel efficiency standards. Environmental groups had appealed repeatedly to President Clinton to veto the measures, but they were rebuffed each time.

The shifts in the perception of corporate interests reflected the increased domestic political salience of climate change and an evolving perception of the costs and benefits of reducing GHG emissions. The changes created the potential for the Clinton administration to pursue a more aggressive climate policy. However, it was unclear whether public opinion and the views of congressional opponents had shifted sufficiently to create the foundation for action.

The 2000 American Elections

The 2000 elections would be critical to American climate policy. Climate change was an issue that clearly divided the Republican and Democratic presidential candidates. The Republican platform rejected the Kyoto Protocol and suggested that the United States would pursue a radically different climate policy under a Bush administration. The platform stated:

> Complex and contentious issues like global warming call for a far more realistic approach than that of the Kyoto Conference. Its deliberations were not based on the best science; its proposed agreements would be ineffective and unfair inasmuch as they do not apply to the developing world; and the current administration is still trying to implement it, without authority of law. More research is needed to understand both the cause and the impact of global warming. That is why the Kyoto treaty was repudiated in a lopsided, bipartisan Senate vote. A Republican president will work with businesses and with other nations to reduce harmful emissions through new technologies without compromising America's sovereignty or competitiveness—and without forcing Americans to walk to work.[24]

The Democratic Platform, on the other hand, was rhetorically more supportive of action but just as vague in policy terms:

> And we must dramatically reduce climate-disrupting and health-threatening pollution in this country, while making sure that all nations of the world participate in this effort. . . . Eight of the ten hottest years ever recorded have occurred during the past ten years. Scientists predict a daunting range of likely effects from global warming. Much of Florida and Louisiana

submerged underwater. More record floods, droughts, heat waves, and wildfires. Diseases and pests spreading to new areas. Crop failures and famines. Melting glaciers, stronger storms, and rising seas. These are not Biblical plagues. They are the predicted result of human actions. They can be prevented only with a new set of human actions—big choices and new thinking.[25]

While there were clear differences between the presidential candidates on climate change, there were very few specific policies that either candidate was willing to discuss. In the end, the issue was of minor importance to the outcome of the election, but the election would have a profound impact on American climate policy. The Hague negotiations were conducted in the midst of the contested Bush-Gore election. The Clinton administration was responsible for the American negotiating position; however, the election uncertainty loomed over the negotiations. The full consequences of the election of George W. Bush on American climate policy and the international negotiations did not emerge until after the failure of the negotiations in The Hague, which will be discussed in the final section of the chapter.

The American Negotiating Position

The Clinton administration was in a difficult position. The administration had decided to accept the Kyoto Protocol rather than allow the negotiations to fail. However, the prospect of Congress enacting major initiatives to reduce American GHG emissions was remote, and there did not appear to be sufficient public interest to alter congressional political calculations. The Clinton administration concluded that it would have to rely principally on the flexibility mechanisms contained in the Protocol to meet its Kyoto commitment. The primary international issues for the United States were the participation of developing countries, the development of rules to govern the use of the flexibility mechanisms (emissions trading, the clean development mechanism, and joint implementation), and the creation of accounting regulations for the use of carbon sinks to offset emissions of CO_2.

Developing country participation in the Protocol was a critical issue for the administration. The Senate was on record demanding developing country participation. The issue had achieved significant political salience with the American public, and critics frequently used it to condemn the treaty as patently unfair and damaging to American competitiveness. The administration's strategy was negotiate GHG emission agreements with major developing states, (i.e., China, India, South Korea, and Brazil). However, in the final hours of the Kyoto negotiations, developing states had successfully deleted the provisions that would have allowed developing countries to voluntarily assume emission reduction commitments. The existing Protocol did not appear to provide a mechanism to include developing countries, and there was no agreement on the rules for amending the Protocol. Even if rules for amendment could be negotiated, the Protocol would likely have to come into force before it could be amended, which was doubtful unless the United States ratified it. The legal obstacles to achieving developing country participation were daunting. The administration's strategy appeared to be designed to induce sufficient voluntary commitments, as opposed to legally binding commitments, on the part of developing countries in the hope of satisfying congressional demands.

Between the end of the Kyoto negotiations and the 2000 negotiations in The Hague, the administration pursued an aggressive bilateral strategy to induce developing country participation. In addition, it worked to build support among developed states to add further pressure for developing country participation. Secretary of State Albright raised the issue in visits to Korea and China, as well as pursuing the initiative at meetings of the G–8, ASEAN, and the UN General Assembly. The United States also tried to incorporate developing country participation into the agenda for the ongoing climate negotiations, but the G–77 consistently rebuffed the American efforts and reaffirmed the norm that developed states had to act first.

The American policy achieved a number of successes in fragmenting the monolithic developing country opposition. In April 1998, President Clinton and Chilean President Eduardo Frei issued a joint statement asserting that "developing countries should participate meaningfully in efforts to address climate change, for example, by taking on emissions targets whenever possible."[26] In June, Canada, Mexico, and the United States agreed to cooperate to develop emission offset projects in Mexico that could be utilized to meet American and Canadian Kyoto targets. During a June 1998 trip to China, President Clinton raised the issue of GHG emission reductions with Chinese President Jiang Zemin and Prime Minister Zhu Rongji.[27] President Clinton did not achieve agreement on emission reduction measures, but he did receive a commitment to begin a senior-level dialogue on climate change. In October 1999, the United States signed an agreement with India to expand collaboration on cleaner energy resources. For the first time, India also committed itself to implementing the Clean Development Mechanism.[28] The Clinton administration had created an opening to pursue developing country participation in the Kyoto Protocol. It remained unlikely that the major developing countries would accept binding commitments, but they acknowledged that they would need to cooperate to reduce global emissions. The administration was positioning itself to claim that it had achieved meaningful developing country participation.

Emissions trading was also critical for the United States, but the European Union remained the primary obstacle to an agreement. The EU repeatedly appealed to a norm that required states to pursue domestic emission reductions as the primary policy response to climate change. The United States accused the EU of applying a double standard. The Kyoto agreement treated the EU as a single unit. Under the EU's internal burden sharing agreement, there was broad variation in the emission reductions required of each individual member. The Clinton administration argued that the European "bubble" represented a form of emissions trading. In response, the United States, along with Japan, Russia, Canada, Australia, New Zealand, and the Ukraine, joined together to form the "Umbrella Group." This group sought to devise common rules for emissions trading and to coordinate negotiating positions on other important issues.

The EU-Umbrella Group split over emissions trading widened at the June 1998 Bonn negotiations. The EU demanded a cap on the portion of a country's target that could be met through emissions trading. The American delegation argued that a cap would undermine the efficient functioning of international markets. The issue would bedevil the emission trading negotiations leading up to The Hague conference. In the face of EU intransigence over emissions trading, the United States proposed that the Umbrella Group should form a "bubble" as an alternative to the EU's bubble. The proposal would essentially allow all of the countries to meet their targets by using excess Russian credits. The proposal was meant to put pressure on the Europeans to relent in their opposition to trading. Stuart Eizenstat laid out the administration's rationale for the proposal.

> If [the EU states] are developing their own internal mechanism, those of us outside the bubble ought to be able to trade emission rights and participate in joint implementation projects among ourselves or Clean Development Mechanisms with developing countries without restrictions. . . . If the EU insists—and we hope they won't—on quantitative caps or ceilings on the amount of trading that can be done through any of these flexible mechanisms . . . [we reserve] the option of trading among [the umbrella group].[29]

The United States asserted that it could proceed with emissions trading without the EU's approval.

As the 2000 Hague negotiations approached, the administration had made some progress in convincing developing countries to cooperate in establishing rules to govern the Clean Development Mechanism. It had also consolidated the Umbrella Group's support of the flexibility mechanisms and had begun to exploit cracks emerging among the EU member states. However, the administration was a long way from achieving a final agreement on the Kyoto flexibility mechanisms. It also further complicated the negotiations when it submitted a proposal that would provide substantial credits for the enhancement and protection of carbon sinks. The administration insisted that carbon sinks would be an important part of its strategy to meet its Kyoto commitment. The EU rejected the American position on sinks, which paved the way for a showdown at The Hague.

Domestically, the administration also faced a difficult situation. Congress rejected the president's tax credit initiatives to promote emission reductions, made significant cuts in proposed spending for the CCTI, and failed to enact electricity deregulation. There was little evidence that the United States was making significant attempts to reduce its emissions, and the administration faced mounting criticism from the EU, G–77 countries, and NGOs over the lack of domestic action. The White House attempted to counter the international criticism by issuing a series of executive orders that did not require congressional approval. American negotiators touted these measures as part of a substantial domestic effort to reduce emissions. American negotiators pointed to an executive order that required the federal government to cut its GHG emissions by 30 percent below 1990 levels by 2010. A second order sought to build a foundation for biomass energy production. A third was intended to improve fuel efficiency in the government's fleet of cars.[30] In a final attempt to demonstrate American domestic action, the president called for new federal regulations to limit power plant emissions of CO_2. Specifically, the president proposed adopting a "cap and trade" approach. The government would cap national emissions of CO_2 and allocate emission credits by industry. Companies could then buy and sell the credits to meet their individual needs. The initiative may have been a useful ploy for American negotiators, but Congress was unlikely to approve it in the near future. The negotiations were further complicated by the electoral crisis in the United States and the uncertainty about the future of American climate policy. The Clinton administration faced an extremely daunting task if it hoped to achieve a ratifiable agreement at The Hague.

UNITED KINGDOM

The new Labour government had been elected on a platform that included a commitment to cut British CO_2 emissions by 20 percent by 2010. Prior to 1997, the switch from coal to natural gas for electricity production had produced the vast majority of British CO_2 emission reductions. There were limits to further fuel switching, and rapidly increasing transportation emissions threatened to undermine the progress that had been made. Achieving the 20 percent reduction target would require significant additional policy changes. Initially, the Blair government wavered in its support for the 20 percent target. It refused to make the target a legally binding part of the EU burden sharing agreement. An October 1998 draft climate change consultation paper asserted that the government's aim was to "start a national debate on how we can move beyond our legally binding target [the EU burden sharing target] towards a 20 percent reduction." The paper also emphasized that while compliance with the Kyoto Protocol "cannot be jeopardized, we will not introduce measures that would damage competitiveness, nor will we take any action that would bring unacceptable social costs."[31] The rhetoric fell considerably short of accepting the 20 percent target as binding.

The early months of the new Blair government were a blur of policy reviews, which had the potential to produce significant policy changes in areas relevant to climate change, including green taxation, transportation, renewable energy, combined heat and power generation, electricity markets, as well as an aggregate review of measures necessary to meet the United Kingdom's GHG emission reduction target. Reconciling the competing interests across the various policy areas with the government's climate policy proved to be an extremely difficult proposition. The Labour government did not produce its strategy to achieve these reductions until November 2000. The strategy emerged following a long and difficult consultation phase that continued after most of the policy reviews related to GHG emissions had already been completed. The government predicted that emissions would fall by approximately 8 percent by 2010 without further policy changes. The government thus needed to achieve an additional 12 percent cut in emissions. The Labour government's climate strategy focused on four policy initiatives: the climate levy and associated voluntary agreements, the fuel duty escalator, renewable energy promotion, and transportation policy.[32] Each of these policies will be discussed below.

British Energy Policy

The new Blair government faced a number of difficult decisions that required trade-offs among its energy and climate policy goals: preserve the domestic coal industry, reform electricity markets, promote renewable energy, and reduce CO_2 emissions. The first crisis was in the coal industry. At the end of 1997, up to eight coal mines were expected to close and several thousand coal miners were to lose their jobs. Coal miners had been a traditional constituency for the Labour Party, and the government was loath to allow the mining industry to deteriorate further. In response to the threatened closures, the government initiated a moratorium on the building of gas-fired power stations and negotiated a deal with power generators to purchase enough domestic coal to support the industry until at least the summer of 1998. During that period, the government intended to finish an energy policy review. The moratorium created difficulties for the government's CO_2 reduction commitment. The shift from coal to natural gas was responsible for the vast majority of the reductions in CO_2 emissions prior to 1997. The moratorium would weaken this trend, and it would substantially increase the emission reductions that would have to be achieved through other policies.

The government released its energy review in June 1998. It announced that it would allow some existing proposals for gas-fired plants to go forward, but it intended to continue, what was in effect, a moratorium on the building of gas-fired power plants. Natural gas provided 30 percent of the United Kingdom's electricity in 1998, and anticipated gas-fired power plants could have increased total capacity by 78 percent.[33] The government argued that the role of gas had to be restricted on the grounds of security and diversity of energy supply. It was important to both conserve the United Kingdom's gas reserves and also maintain a viable domestic coal industry. Independent analysts predicted that the restrictions on gas would produce an additional ten million tons of CO_2 emissions in 2010 relative to a scenario of unfettered expansion of gas-fired generation.[34] This represented nearly a quarter of the emission reductions that the government needed to meet its 20 percent target. In addition, all but three of the United Kingdom's nuclear power stations would be closed by 2015, which would create a shortfall in energy production as well as significantly higher carbon emissions as fossil fuels replaced nuclear power.

In addition, the prospects for achieving the government's goal of renewable energy providing 10 percent of electricity were growing dimmer as well. In September 1998, the government awarded its fifth round of NFFO orders. It was the largest and also provided the most inexpensive electricity prices to date. The bids fell by 22 percent from the NFFO–4 order. While the government continued to trumpet the successes of the program, problems were emerging. Only 26 percent of the 2,094 MW of energy capacity awarded under the first four NFFO auctions was generating electricity in 1998.[35] The government acknowledged that many bidders had submitted speculative bids that were unlikely to lead to new investments under existing conditions. The United Kingdom had the greatest potential of any EU member state to expand its renewable energy production, particularly through offshore wind generation. However, it possessed only 130 megawatts of installed capacity in 1998. Between 1996 and 1998, Germany had installed six times the wind power capacity as the United Kingdom.[36] The German government had devoted significantly more resources to promoting renewable energy than the British. The Blair government was reluctant to create costly new programs to subsidize the development of wind energy through the national budget. Instead, it relied on indirect spending measures such as the NFFO program and the promotion of the voluntary "green electricity tariffs." Under the "green tariff" program, customers could choose to pay more for their electricity and in return power companies would produce or purchase an equivalent amount of electricity generated by renewable sources. However, market research suggested that only 2 percent of customers were willing to pay a premium for "green" electricity.[37]

Boosting renewable energy demanded additional government support that created trade-offs among the goals of fiscal discipline, support for the coal industry, and the promotion of renewable energy. The government released its paper on the promotion of renewable energy in April 1999 after twenty months of delay and internal debate. The final document contained no new policy decisions and merely reaffirmed the government's support for renewable energy and launched a new consultation on a future policy. It contained a commitment to review the planning system to ease the approval process for new wind generation projects, but beyond that there was only minimal policy relevance.[38]

British climate policy would be further undermined by the proposed electricity market reforms. In August 1999, the Department of Trade and Industry (DTI) released an outline of its proposals for reforming the electricity market. The initial proposal would have the effect of creating additional competition in the market and would likely produce significant reductions in electricity prices. Unfortunately, the proposal also had the effect of discriminating against renewable energy production as well as combined heat and power, and the fall in electricity prices would undermine the government's energy efficiency goals. The net effect would likely be to substantially increase GHG emissions. In October, the government acknowledged that its plan "will reduce the market value of renewables generation and the incentives to invest in new CHP, with a resulting detrimental environmental impact." However, the DTI went on to argue that these effects "must be considered in the context of [the reform's] expected benefits for industry, consumers and the economy as a whole."[39] The DTI pledged to find a means to continue to support CHP and renewable energy production, but it refused to alter the plan.

In February 2000, the government introduced a support mechanism for renewable energy to be included in the new utility regulations. The government intended to replace the NFFO program with a requirement for electricity suppliers to acquire a percentage of their power from renewable sources. The commitment could be met by contracting directly with renewable energy producers or by purchasing "green certificates" for renewable energy produced by other companies. In theory, the program would allow the government to slowly raise the renewables requirement over time to achieve the 10 percent target by 2010. However, concerns that the program could dramatically increase energy prices, led the government to cap the potential price that suppliers would have to pay. If the price rose above the cap, the supplier could merely pay the cap price and purchase additional fossil fuel electricity. The long-term problem was that new renewable technologies, such as offshore wind and solar power, would cost significantly more than the cap price. These technologies were unlikely to be exploited. Instead, land-fill gas recovery, sewage gas, and onshore wind power were likely to be the primary sources of renewable energy, but the total capacity of these technologies was limited. Though hydroelectric and waste to energy capacity was not included in the renewables obligation, the government did intend to count their contributions toward the 10 percent target.[40] The government was unlikely to meet the 10 percent target without enhancing support for renewables.

British Green Taxation

Environmental taxation proved to be the primary element of the government's climate strategy. In July 1997 the new Blair Government set forth a "Statement of Intent on Environmental Taxation" in which it committed itself to shifting the burden of taxation from "goods" to "bads" (i.e., from employment, savings, and investment to pollution). Between 1997 and 2000 the Blair Government introduced a series of "green taxes." The most important of the taxes for climate policy were the increases in the gasoline tax escalator and the taxation of industrial and commercial energy use.

The Major government had introduced the gasoline tax escalator in 1993, which increased gasoline taxes by 3 (and later 5) percent above inflation. In 1997 the Blair government announced an increase in the gasoline tax escalator to 6 percent above inflation. In March 1998, Finance Minister, Gordon Brown announced that gasoline prices would immediately be increased by 9.2 percent and diesel taxes by 11.7 percent. He also announced a set of tax initiatives to reduce CO_2 emissions from cars owned by corporations. The government trumpeted the initiatives as critical components of its climate strategy.

The United Kingdom had the highest gasoline taxes in Europe, and the escalator continued to widen the gap with the rest of the continent, which created a number of political difficulties when world oil prices began to rise dramatically in 1999 and 2000. In July 1999, the government faced large demonstrations and demands for the elimination of the escalator and a reduction in the tax. Treasury department officials defended the tax and noted that it was essential to reduce CO_2 emissions in the transportation sector.[41] In the face of public demonstrations and political pressure from the Conservative Party, the Major government eventually dropped the escalator from its 2000 budget. The escalator had been predicted to reduce carbon emissions by between two and five million tons of carbon by 2010. The government admitted that the loss of the escalator would modify the potential reduction to between one and 3.3 mtc.[42]

In addition to the increase in gasoline taxes included in the 1998 budget proposal, Gordon Brown announced the creation of a panel to analyze the potential for a tax on industrial and commercial energy use to stimulate CO_2 emission reductions. The government chose Colin Marshall, president and chairman of British Airways, to head the task force. Marshall, a longtime supporter of environmental action, would play an important role in building momentum for the new tax. He restricted the task force's membership to civil servants and excluded representation from environmental and industrial groups. The task force concluded in its November 1998 report that existing measures were insufficient to achieve the government's GHG emission reduction target and that economic instruments would be necessary. The report highlighted the need to introduce a tax on industrial and commercial energy consumption and raised the possibility of an emission trading scheme.[43]

Business interests, led by the Confederation of British Industry (CBI), condemned the plan. The CBI argued that the taxes would have to be exceptionally high to change behavior, which would harm industrial competitiveness. The business community maintained that negotiated agreements, emissions trading, and energy efficiency incentives offered a more efficient and certain way to achieve the emission reductions. The most determined opposition to the tax emerged from energy intensive industries, which alleged that the tax would be devastating to their competitive positions and demanded that they be exempted from it.

Despite the determined opposition from industry, the Blair Government announced in March 1999 that it would introduce a tax on commercial and industrial energy use in 2001. The tax would raise nearly £1.75 billion (approximately $2.8 billion) and would cover natural gas, coal, and electricity consumption by business, agriculture, and the public sector. The tax excluded fuels used for electricity generation. Most of the revenue would be recycled back to businesses through a reduction in employers' national insurance contributions. A small portion of the revenue was reserved for the creation of a new "carbon trust" to promote the introduction of energy efficient technologies. The government acknowledged the potential competitive effects of the levy on energy intensive industries, and it offered to reduce the tax rates for industries that accepted agreements to reduce their GHG emissions.

The tax proposal set off a prolonged period of fractious negotiations between the government and industry over which sectors would be allowed tax reductions as well as how large the reductions would be. Initially, the government offered to reduce the tax rate by 50 percent for energy intensive industries if they accepted significant GHG emission reduction commitments. The government sought to negotiate the agreements with nine trade associations, representing energy intensive industries. The CBI rejected the offer and asserted that even the reduced rate would have a substantial effect on competitiveness. The negotiations began in April 1999 and did not conclude until mid-2001. The government sought to force each industry to adopt all "cost-effective energy efficiency investments" to qualify for a 50 percent cut in the energy tax. The government also held out the possibility of additional reductions in the tax if the industries adopted all "technically possible measures."[44] The CBI demanded that energy intensive industries receive a 70 to 80 percent reduction. The steel and aluminum industries demanded full exemption on the grounds that even an 80 percent tax reduction would leave them unable to compete internationally. The CBI claimed that the tax would lead to the emigration of jobs and investments to countries with lower taxes and ultimately would hollow out the United Kingdom's manufacturing base.[45]

If the government was primarily interested in reducing CO_2 emissions, a tax on the carbon content of fuels would have been much more effective. By 1999 Norway, Sweden, Finland, Denmark, Austria, the Netherlands, Germany, and Italy had introduced or were considering, a tax on the carbon content of fuels. Energy and carbon taxes both raise the costs of energy and promote energy conservation, but a carbon tax also creates a bias in favor of natural gas, nuclear, and renewable energy sources that produce less CO_2. The Blair government did not give serious consideration to this option, because it would have favored natural gas and nuclear energy over coal, which was politically unacceptable.

Between 1999 and 2001, industrial interests gradually chipped away at the government's tax plans. In July 1999, the government announced that the aluminum smelting and the chlor-alkali industries would be exempted from the tax. The government also announced that industries accepting GHG reduction plans negotiated with the government would be allowed to use international flexibility mechanisms to meet their obligations, which created the potential for greatly reducing the costs of achieving emission reductions. The government's new emphasis on flexibility mechanisms created incentives to finalize rules on the use of the mechanisms in the international negotiations, undermined the norm requiring domestic emission reductions, and legitimized the American focus on economic efficiency.

In October 1999, the government announced that a domestic trading program would also be developed to provide additional flexibility for industries to meet their obligations. This was followed in November by a retreat by the government in the prebudget report. The proposed levy rate was cut by nearly 30 percent. Energy intensive sectors would receive an 80 percent reduction in energy taxes after concluding energy efficiency agreements with the government. Renewable energy and combined heat and power sources were excluded from the energy tax. As a result of the changes, the predicted revenue from the tax was revised downward from £1.75 to one billion per year, which also cut the national insurance contribution reduction by 40 percent.[46] Amazingly, the prebudget report asserted that the modified tax and the energy efficiency taxes would together reduce CO_2 emissions by four mtc, a higher total than predicted in the original proposal. According to the Department of the Environment, Transport and the Regions, the tax itself would reduce emissions by one mtc; the exemption for renewable energy and CHP would reduce emissions by one mtc; and the negotiated agreements would provide at least an additional two mtc of reductions.[47]

The sectors initially eligible to negotiate agreements with the government concluded memoranda of understanding in December 1999 covering the size of the emission reduction commitments, but disputes remained over how the commitments would be enforced and how penalties would be imposed for failure to achieve the targets. In addition, it was unclear whether the EU would invalidate the agreements on the grounds of unfair state aid to industry. The green taxation retreat reflected the political effects that the taxes were having. As a treasury official put it, "[t]he papers have been full of the threat to industrial competitiveness and there has been virtually nothing about the environment. What we needed was fewer stories about threatened steel plants and more about threatened seal pups."[48]

The negotiations with the affected sectors continued with growing acrimony into 2001. Over time, the list of sectors eligible for the rebates expanded, and the government successfully completed negotiations with most of the forty eligible sectors by mid-February 2001. Each of the agreements contained intermediate targets that had to be met for the sectors to continue to receive their 80 percent tax rebate. The various agreements could be met either through internal reductions in energy use or through the purchase of carbon credits in an emissions trading system that the government was developing.

The retreat on energy taxation and the gasoline tax escalator created new holes in the United Kingdom's climate strategy that were threatening the 20 percent reduction target.

The British Negotiating Position

The Blair government placed the United Kingdom in a leadership position within the climate negotiations. The commitment to reduce British emissions by 20 percent was among the most ambitious of the developed states. However, the government also faced a number of dilemmas. It had accepted a 10 percent emission reduction target within the EU's burden sharing agreement. Labour had asserted during the election that it would contribute substantially more toward the EU target. However, after the Kyoto agreement the government argued that if it included its 20 percent commitment in the EU bubble, there would be much less pressure on the other member states to undertake emission reductions. The British found themselves in a difficult position. They held the EU's rotating presidency during the first half of 1998, and one of the primary issues that had to be addressed was a revision of the burden sharing agreement in light of the Kyoto Protocol commitments. The burden sharing debate is discussed in detail later. The primary problem for the British government was that it needed to secure an agreement in the face of attempts by most member states to reduce their individual commitments. These states argued that the United Kingdom should contribute more to offset the reductions in their commitments. Finessing this issue would be a difficult foreign policy challenge.

The United Kingdom also continued to play an important role as a bridge between the United States and the European Union. British diplomats aggressively promoted a compromise between the EU and the United States at The Hague and in the ensuing negotiations. The Blair government shared the American desire to conclude negotiations on the flexibility mechanisms. It also understood the political constraints that the Clinton administration faced. The government sought to soften European opposition to the American positions on sinks and the flexibility mechanisms. In the end the government failed to elicit EU support for a compromise position in The Hague that it had negotiated with the Americans. The failure of the compromise produced a nasty split between the British negotiators and their European counterparts.

GERMANY

The September 1998 German elections held the potential for profound changes in energy, taxation, and climate policy. Climate policy was not a divisive issue. All of the major parties remained committed to Germany's domestic emission reduction target and its international leadership position. However, divisions among the parties on the issues of energy taxation and the future of nuclear energy would significantly impact Germany's GHG emissions.

In March 1998, the Greens set forth their platform for the upcoming campaign. Three proposals that would affect climate policy included tripling gasoline prices through tax increases over a ten year period, closing all nuclear power plants within five years, and establishing a one hundred kilometer per hour speed limit. With the exception of the phaseout of nuclear power, these positions conflicted with Schroeder's positioning of the SPD for the election. The public reacted with abhorrence to the proposed restrictions on motoring and the increase in energy prices. The CDU denounced the Greens as irresponsible and launched a scare campaign to "educate" voters about the potential effects of a SPD/Green coalition government.[49] The SPD leadership quickly condemned the proposals, and Schroeder went so far as to declare the Greens "unfit to govern" after their rejection of NATO expansion. "The radical-pacifist wing can expect to play no role in a government of mine. . . . Nonsense will not become government policy."[50] The German electorate recoiled at the possibility of a coalition government including the Greens, which damaged the prospects of the SPD gaining power. The Greens repudiated their proposal to triple gasoline taxes and shifted their emphasis to raising energy taxes to fund a reduction in taxes on labor. The Green Party leadership perceived that it had an opportunity to govern in coalition and reframed its policies to accommodate the SPD's positions.

The SPD secured 298 seats in parliament (45 percent of the total) and the Greens forty-seven seats (7 percent), which allowed the two parties to form a coalition government. The Greens made two core policy demands in the coalition agreement negotiations: the rapid closure of all nuclear power plants and the introduction of energy taxes to fund a reduction in taxes on labor. The ensuing policy debates dominated the early months of the new government.

German Energy Taxes

The coalition negotiations launched a debate over "ecological tax reform." The primary goal of the taxes was to provide sufficient additional revenue to offset reductions in the taxes on labor through reduced social security contributions. For the Greens, the introduction of the taxes was also a first step toward altering German energy consumption through a series of tax increases over time. The Greens and SPD agreed upon a three-step increase in taxes on gasoline, heating oil, electricity, and natural gas. The total increase in revenue would allow the government to reduce nonwage labor taxes.[51] The coalition argued that the reductions would promote new jobs to reduce Germany's high unemployment rate.

The secondary concern for environmental goals in the tax reform was apparent in the decision to exempt coal (the dirtiest of the fossil fuels) from the tax but to tax natural gas (the cleanest). The proposal also covered all electricity, including electricity generated from renewable sources. If the government was mainly interested in environmental goals, particularly CO_2 emission reductions, a carbon tax would have been a more appropriate mechanism, but such an approach was unacceptable to the SPD's supporters in the coal industry. Both parties emphasized the importance of eco-taxes to improve the environment, but the relatively small increases were unlikely to stimulate significant reductions in CO_2 emissions. The tax increases were clearly designed to increase revenue in a manner that was acceptable to the electorate.

Despite the coalition agreement, disputes between the Greens and the SPD quickly emerged over the tax. German industrial groups lobbied aggressively against the taxes and argued that they would undermine the competitiveness of German industry. The new economic minister, Werner Müller, acknowledged the business community's concerns and demanded tax exemptions for German manufacturers. New Green Party Environment Minister Jürgen Trittin rejected exemptions from the tax and argued that such concessions would undermine the centerpiece of the new coalition's initiatives.[52] The conflicts delayed the implementation of the tax from its original target of January 1, 1999 to April 1.

Trittin and Finance Minister, Oskar Lafontaine, eventually negotiated a compromise, which would exempt energy intensive industries from the tax and reduce the rate for manufacturers to 20 to 25 percent of the basic rate. The government's proposal received broad criticism from business and environmental interests alike. Critics asserted that the small tax increases would have minimal effects on employment, and the exemptions for business would undermine CO_2 emission reductions. Schroeder attempted to deflect some of the criticism by promoting the energy tax at the EU level to minimize the domestic competitive effects of the tax. The German government placed environmental taxes near the top of its agenda for its EU presidency in the first half of 1999, but British opposition blocked progress at the EU level.

Ecological tax reform continued to be a contentious issue in German politics. The second stage of the tax increases in 2000 became bound up in debates over whether some of the revenue could be used to offset the growing budget deficit. This debate reinforced arguments by business interests that the "ecological taxes" had nothing to do with environmental improvement but were instead merely cynical mechanisms to increase revenue. Further complicating the taxation debate, the European Commission in March 1989 forced the government to abandon the tax exemptions for energy intensive industries. The Commission ruled that the exemptions amounted to illegal government subsidies and forced the Schroeder government to revise the tax. Under the final agreement all manufacturers would only pay 20 percent of the basic rate. However, in an attempt to continue to aid energy intensive industries, all companies that paid more in energy taxes than they received in labor tax reductions would be entitled to receive an 80 percent rebate of the difference. The new system was deemed acceptable by the EU.

The "eco-taxation" debate further demonstrated the secondary importance of climate change to national policy making. While the new SPD/Green government aggressively marketed the new taxes as environmentally friendly and necessary for Germany to meet its national climate commitments, the design and implementation of the taxes exposed the political imperatives that drove the policy process. The norm requiring domestic emission reductions remained at the sixth level of norm salience, "domestic policy impact." The government continued to justify policy changes with references to the international norm, but the interests of adversely affected groups continued to trump the norm in policy debates. The taxes would have only a marginal impact on German CO_2 emissions.

The End of German Nuclear Energy?

The elimination of nuclear energy was one of the founding goals of the German Green Party, and the new coalition government offered the Greens their best opportunity to realize its goal. When the Greens entered into coalition negotiations with the SPD, they sought a precise framework and timetable to close all nuclear power plants. They preferred that the government immediately introduce legislation to achieve this objective. The SPD, however, desired a negotiated solution with the energy industry. A negotiated solution was important to preserve Germany's consensual policy process and to avoid lawsuits and demands for compensation that would likely follow unilateral action by the government. The coalition agreement presented a compromise. The government would immediately introduce legislation to strengthen the security and safety of nuclear plants, and simultaneously, the government would pursue "consensus talks" with the energy industry during 1999 to establish a framework and timetable for closing the nuclear plants.

The nuclear issue came to a head in July 1999, the Economics Ministry and energy executives reached a tentative agreement that would allow nuclear power plants to operate for a total of thirty-five years, which would have meant that the last reactor would not close until 2024. The Green Party rejected the agreement and threatened to withdraw from the coalition, though the party later played down the possibility.[53] The SPD responded that unless the Greens scaled back their demands, the coalition would likely dissolve. The coalition clash led the Green Party to reevaluate its priorities. Faced with the possibility of losing power, the Greens began to compromise on the nuclear issue. The negotiations continued to flounder until June 2000. In the end, the SPD and Greens accepted nearly all of the industry's demands in return for a commitment to phaseout nuclear energy. The final agreement assigned each nuclear plant a total electricity output quota based on the plant running at 90 percent capacity for thirty-two years. The quota was transferable across plants, which would allow energy companies to close less efficient and more costly plants and transfer their quotas to extend the lives of newer plants. In addition, most plants operated at an average capacity of 85 percent, which would extend plant life by another three years. It was possible that a few nuclear plants could continue to operate far beyond the headline thirty-two year maximum included in the agreement.[54] New safety and security requirements were scaled back, and the industry would not face new punitive taxes. Hard-line Greens urged a rejection of the proposal in the upcoming Green Party conference. However, the pragmatic Green leadership prevailed in the party vote and accepted the agreement.

This episode demonstrated the severe constraints under which governments operate when they attempt to radically alter domestic policy. It also illustrates the secondary status of climate policy. GHG emissions played a minor role in the debate. Nuclear supporters appealed to the need to reduce CO_2 emissions to justify the continued use of the energy source, but the argument was not sufficient to alter the policy outcome.

German Energy Policy

The decision to phaseout nuclear power created a number of difficulties for German climate policy. How would the lost electricity production capacity be replaced? This was not an immediate issue because the final nuclear agreement postponed the closing of much of the nuclear capacity, but it would be essential to eventually provide a nonfossil fuel alternative energy source to meet the CO_2 reduction target. The government asserted that Germany could replace the lost capacity through a combination of renewable energy and more efficient use of energy through improved product efficiency and enhanced building standards. Most experts rejected this approach as unrealistic. The government established a goal to raise renewable energy sources to 10 percent of total production by 2010. The promotion of renewable energy and combined heat and power capacity became a significant goal of the SPD/Green government.

In 1991, the Kohl government had established a renewable energy program that created generous minimum prices above market rates that utilities were required to pay for electricity produced from renewable sources. The program achieved some success, and Germany emerged as a world leader in wind generation. The program, however, engendered strong opposition from German utilities that had to pay the higher prices. The utilities launched a number of legal challenges to undermine the system. In addition, following a EU Competition Directorate review, the Commission sent Germany a letter warning it that its program was not consistent with the liberalization of the EU's energy market. The Commission was at the same time developing a directive to harmonize national renewable support schemes across the EU, which could potentially force Germany to alter its program. The growing opposition to the system created significant uncertainty among renewable energy producers and posed a challenge to the government's attempts to expand renewable energy production.

The new Schroeder government sought to shape the EU directive to accommodate its domestic support system. The government made the achievement of a common position on the directive one of the primary objectives for its EU presidency. However, the diversity of the various national support schemes and the differences between the German government and the Commission on the types of support systems that would be tolerated led to an impasse. The Commission's draft directive would have set a requirement that each state achieve a minimum of 5 percent of its national electricity consumption from renewable sources by 2005. States already near the 5 percent threshold would have to achieve a minimum of a 3 percent increase in the share of renewables. One of the core principles that the Commission set forth in its program was that the system had to ensure competition among producers to progressively force down the price of renewable electricity. The United Kingdom's NFFO program met this requirement, but Germany's system of generous fixed rates for renewable electricity would not. Responding to the hostile reaction by its domestic wind energy industry, the Schroeder government blocked the directive and sought additional changes that would protect the German system.

Faced with Commission challenges to its renewable support scheme, the Schroeder government undertook a revision of its renewable energy law during 2000. Under the new scheme, the government kept the fixed price for electricity produced by renewable sources and expanded the scope of renewable sources covered by the program. The primary change was that the prices were no longer linked to the average price of energy, but rather would decline gradually over a twenty year period, which the government argued would make the support consistent with EU regulations. The government's stated goal was to double the share of renewable energy by 2010, and it placed an emphasis on the development of solar technologies. The new support program raised the guaranteed price for solar electricity from eight cents per kilowatt hour under the old law to nearly fifty cents under the new law.[55] The government also launched a program to install solar roofs on one hundred thousand roofs.

Beyond renewable energy support, the government also faced significant challenges from the CHP sector. European energy liberalization led to falling electricity prices, which made German CHP producers uncompetitive. By March 2000, 15 percent of German CHP capacity had been completely or partially shut down, and a significant portion of the remaining capacity was in danger of being shut down.[56] The government responded by establishing above market rates for electricity produced from CHP. In addition, it set forth a proposal later in 2000 to set a minimum amount of electricity that utilities had to purchase from CHP producers. The proposal was met with significant opposition from the energy industry. Economics Minister

Werner Müller, to the great consternation of Jürgen Trittin and Green Party members, supported the industry in its opposition.[57] In the place of CHP quotas, the energy industry proposed to undertake voluntary cuts in GHG emissions. The Green Party and environmental organizations condemned the proposal as vague and unenforceable.

The final agreement was concluded in June 2001. German energy producers agreed to cut approximately twenty to twenty-three million tons of CO_2 emissions by 2010 through increased investment in CHP and fuel cell technologies. Taken together with prior commitments to reduce CO_2 emissions by twenty-five million tons, energy producers had jointly committed themselves to approximately forty-five million tons of voluntary emission reductions.[58] The voluntary commitments successfully avoided the imposition of national regulations.

The 2000 German National Climate Strategy

As the controversies over the nuclear phaseout, energy taxes, and renewable energy support began to subside, the Schroeder government undertook a review of its strategy to meet its emission reduction commitments. The government admitted that CO_2 emissions were not falling rapidly enough to meet the 25 percent reduction target in 2005 and additional policy changes were urgently required. The Environment Ministry leaked its draft strategy to the press in April 2000. The draft contained nearly three dozen measures designed to improve energy efficiency, lower transportation emissions, and reduce industrial and energy transformation emissions. In total, the draft asserted that the identified measures could produce the one hundred million ton reduction in CO_2 emissions by 2005 necessary to meet Germany's domestic commitment. The draft contained a number of controversial elements, including the establishment of a national speed limit and an increase in levies on air travel.[59] The leak was an attempt to shape the national debate before the draft was reviewed by the government as a whole. Speaking to reporters, Environment Minister Trittin noted that not every proposed measure would necessarily be included in the final strategy, but he asserted that for every one dropped or modified additional measures would have to be found to compensate. Trittin announced that an interministerial panel would review the draft and finalize a strategy by June.[60] The CDU and CSU blasted the plan. They rejected the extremely unpopular 130 kilometer per hour speed limit and the levy on air travel. They argued that even if the government implemented all of the proposed measures, it would still fail to fulfill the national CO_2 commitment. Most of the reductions would be offset by increased emissions as nuclear power plants were closed and replaced by fossil fuels. Even within the Schroeder government, the proposal resulted in significant conflict.

The renewed focus on climate policy fit well with a growing interest in the issue among the German public. A June 2000 public opinion poll revealed that 98 percent of respondents perceived climate change to be an important problem. In addition, 58 percent said the government needed to do more to address the problem.[61] The Greens highlighted the public support to pressure the SPD to accept the climate strategy. After extensive internal debate, the cabinet approved a climate strategy that contained a set of measures to cut German CO_2 emissions by fifty to seventy million tons by 2005. This was less than the one hundred million tons contained in the earlier draft and reflected a reduction in the number of measures and estimates of achievable emission reductions contained in the strategy.

The strategy combined a number of initiatives under a single program to theoretically provide the emission reductions necessary to meet the 25 percent target. One of the new initiatives was an "Energy Saving Ordinance" designed to improve energy efficiency standards in new construction and to promote renovations in older structures. The government introduced the initiative in December 2000. The strategy also included a number of traffic related measures, including additional funding for rail infrastructure, the promotion of fuel efficient cars, and public education campaigns. The strategy did not include a call for a national speed limit.[62]

The strategy also included commitments from nineteen German industrial groups to increase their contribution to GHG emission reductions. In 1996 these groups had committed themselves to reducing their emissions by 20 percent by 2005. By 1999 they had already achieved aggregate CO_2 emission reductions of 23 percent. The groups committed themselves to cut their CO_2 emissions by 28 percent by 2005 and all GHG emissions by 35 percent by 2012. In return, the government committed itself to ". . . not take any initiative to achieve the climate protection targets through command and control measures. . . . The Federal Government will endeavour to ensure that German Business will not suffer any competitive disadvantages at the international level as a result of the Kyoto obligations and the instruments involved."[63] The agreement was voluntary in nature and contained no penalties for nonfulfillment beyond the vague threat to impose regulations if industry should fail to achieve their joint target. The impressive industrial commitments are somewhat misleading because a significant portion of the reductions occurred as the result of either shutting down or replacing inefficient plants in the former East.

The cabinet gave final approval to the strategy in October 2000. The timing was designed to provide the government with maximum credibility entering negotiations in The Hague and deflect accusations that Germany would be unable to achieve its 25 percent target. Statistics released in early 2001, however, undermined Germany's claim to leadership. In 2000, total German CO_2 emissions actually rose by 1 percent over 1999 rates.[64] The primary cause was the growth in emissions from coal burning power plants in the former East. It appeared that the easy emission reductions from economic restructuring in the East were coming to a close.

The German Negotiating Position

The Kyoto Protocol created a number of challenges for the Kohl government. It had been opposed to a significant role for flexibility mechanisms and sinks in the Protocol, but it reluctantly accepted the provisions to secure American participation. On December 11, 1997, Environment Minister Angela Merkel put climate negotiators on notice that Germany would aggressively move to limit the role of these mechanisms in subsequent negotiations.

> Germany will only ratify the protocol if there are satisfactory rules on emission trading. The aim cannot be for industrialized countries to satisfy their obligations solely through emissions trading and profit, in particular, from substantial emission cuts achieved in the former Soviet Union following the collapse of its manufacturing base. For this reason, we insist that at least 50 percent of emission reductions pledged by industrialized countries come as a result of national measures.[65]

Germany once again reaffirmed the norm that national measures should be at the heart of climate policy. The government aggressively promoted the 50 percent requirement within the EU and in the multilateral negotiations. It also sought to limit the role for sinks in the final GHG accounting rules. Germany received significant support for these positions within the EU, but it also faced considerable opposition from the United States and the Umbrella Group, which established the core conflict that would drive the post-Kyoto negotiations.

The Kohl government established Germany's position in the negotiations, and this position did not change significantly when the SPD/Greens assumed power. Green Environment Minister Jürgen Trittin assumed responsibility for the climate negotiations after the 1998 elections. Trittin brought a much more vocal and confrontational approach to the negotiations. The German government, and particularly the Green Party, was reluctant to compromise on Germany's core demands, which greatly complicated the negotiations in The Hague. Trittin and the Greens would play a major role in the initial failure of the negotiations.

EUROPEAN UNION

The Kyoto Protocol created a number of new challenges for the European Union. The United States had succeeded in incorporating several new provisions into the Kyoto agreement that had not been a part of the EU's negotiating position. The most important of the additions were the inclusion of the flexibility mechanisms (joint implementation, the Clean Development Mechanism, and emissions trading) and the expansion of the number of controlled GHGs from three to six. The expansion in the number of GHGs forced the EU to revisit its burden sharing agreement, which produced a mad rush by most of the EU member states to weaken the emission targets they had agreed to prior to Kyoto. Additionally, the flexibility mechanisms opened a debate between the more environmentally proactive member states that wanted to force states to fulfill their commitments domestically and those that saw the flexibility mechanisms as a low-cost option to meet their commitments under the burden sharing agreement. European climate policy also continued to deadlock over proposals for common EU policies to reduce GHG emissions.

In June 1998, the Commission attempted to recast the EU's climate debate with the release of a communication entitled "Climate Change: Towards an EU Post-Kyoto Strategy" that outlined the EU's plans for cutting GHG emissions.[66] The communication called on all member states to submit their individual emission reduction plans to the EU by the end of 1998. The Commission would then coordinate the member state policies with common EU initiatives to meet the Union's emission reduction commitment. In particular, the Commission argued that common policies and measures would be required in the areas of energy, transport, agriculture, and industry. The communication also noted that the EU should play a major role in developing the rules that would govern the international flexibility mechanisms to prevent their abuse.

The internal policy debates leading up to The Hague meeting centered on three primary issues: the burden sharing agreement, common policies and measures versus domestic initiatives, and negotiating international rules to govern the use of flexibility mechanisms. In addition, the Commission launched its "European Climate Change Programme" (ECCP) in June 2000. The program was intended to establish a consultative process involving groups with an interest in climate policy to identify cost-effective measures to reduce GHG emissions that could be incorporated into EU legislation. The ECCP's June 2001 report identified a mix of existing and potential policy measures that could purportedly reduce GHG emissions by twice the amount necessary to meet the EU's target.[67] It remained to be seen whether the Commission could implement the changes necessary to realize the reductions, but given the contentious nature of past negotiations, the prospects for success were not compelling.

European Burden Sharing

The expansion of the number of regulated GHGs from three to six created a difficult situation for the Commission and the member states. The Kyoto agreement did not specify individual emission reduction targets for each of the gases. Instead, it provided an aggregate reduction target based upon the global warming potentials of the various gases. Prior to the Kyoto negotiations, the member states had agreed a burden sharing formula that provided reductions across three gases of approximately 10 percent for the EU as a whole. The Blair government, which assumed the rotating presidency of the EU in January 1998, made the negotiation of a new agreement one of its top priorities. The British had hoped to merely extend the existing formula to cover all six gases, but the strategy stalled in the face of demands to reopen the agreement at the March 1998 Environment Council meeting. Rather than reopen the agreement, British Deputy Prime Minister John Prescott agreed to undertake a tour of European capitals in an attempt to produce a viable agreement for the next Council meeting in June.[68]

The British government found itself in a difficult position. It had agreed to reduce its emissions by 10 percent under the pre-Kyoto burden sharing agreement, but the new Labour government had pledged to reduce British emissions by 20 percent. The United Kingdom's European partners argued that the Blair government should increase its contribution to the burden sharing agreement in light of the new commitments. Domestic critics charged that the government was not serious about the 20 percent target and was only using it for cynical political purposes. The government reaffirmed the domestic commitment, but it argued that the other states had to act more aggressively to fulfill the EU commitment, rather than rely on British reductions. The Blair government acknowledged that it would likely have to increase its contribution to the agreement, but it sought to minimize the additional commitment.

Following consultations with the member states, the British presidency put forward a burden sharing proposal that would produce an 8.9 percent emission reduction across the six gases. The proposal relaxed the commitments for the states demanding them, but most member states insisted that their commitments be reduced even further. The final agreement also became mired in arguments over the relationship between the burden sharing agreement and common policies and measures to achieve the reductions. The Netherlands, Denmark, and Austria argued that their competitive positions would be substantially harmed if they were forced to take the measures necessary to meet their emission reduction targets unilaterally. Environment ministers were finally able to hammer out an agreement after two days of difficult negotiations in June 1998. Every country that had committed itself to reducing its GHG emissions under the pre-Kyoto agreement (with the exception of the United Kingdom), received a reduction in their commitment. The burden-sharing negotiations demonstrated the lukewarm support among member states for substantial commitments to cut GHG emissions. Even in the case of Germany, there was reluctance to be legally bound to a higher commitment. British Environment Minister Michael Meacher noted the difficulties in securing the agreement, "[a]s we found out, there was a great deal of difference between aspirational targets and legally binding targets."[69]

Common Policies and Measures

The Commission had consistently argued that it would be necessary for the EU to adopt a set of common policies and measures to meet the EU target to avoid excessive competitive effects within the common market. Climate policy also created an opportunity for the Commission to expand its powers in fields that had previously been restricted. The most important proposals included the harmonization of energy taxes, the negotiation of voluntary commitments with the automobile industry, the promotion of energy efficiency investments, and the expansion of renewable energy sources. With the partial exception of the automobile industry negotiations, the rest of these initiatives languished for lack of support from the member states. The evolution of these initiatives provides important insights into the depth of support for reducing GHG emissions among the member states. As the Commission noted in a May 1999 communication, "[a]mbition . . . has to be complemented by concrete action and tangible results. . . . When assessing the current situation, the conclusions are not very positive."[70]

The initiative that held the greatest potential for reducing GHG emissions was the Commission's proposal to create minimum energy taxes within the EU. This proposal had its roots in the failed 1992 initiative to launch an EU-wide carbon tax. Launched in March 1997, the new proposal called for minimum levels of taxation to be applied to a range of energy sources. The tax levels were set low enough that they would require increases in only a few states. The intent of the measure was to establish a floor for energy taxes and create a mechanism for future tax increases. The initiative faced many of the same objections as the prior attempts to impose energy/carbon taxes. Several states jealously guarded the power to tax as strictly national. In addition, countries with low energy taxes, such as Spain and Greece, opposed the initiative because it would force unpopular tax increases and could spark inflation. The disparity in positions weakened the prospects for adopting the tax.

The Commission attempted to portray the tax initiative as a test of member state support for reducing GHG emissions. Environment Commissioner Ritt Bjerregaard openly challenged the rhetoric of the member states on climate policy. "It is quite clear from what member states say, they take climate change seriously. . . . I think the proposal is a modest one. It is just dealing with minimum standards, which for some countries would not mean that they would have to change anything. Now is the time to act on what we have agreed in Kyoto."[71] According to Commission estimates, the tax would provide a quarter of the emission reductions necessary to achieve the EU's emission reduction target.[72]

The European Parliament supported the proposal and attempted to strengthen it through a number of amendments, but the initiative languished before the Council. The 1998 British presidency failed to place the issue on the ECOFIN agenda. The Austrian presidency made the tax a priority during the second half of 1998, but it continued to run up against opposition from member states. The Schroeder government made the tax proposal a top priority for its 1999 presidency. It was particularly important to Germany because the new SPD/Green government had launched its own initiative to raise domestic energy taxes. A coordinated increase in EU energy taxes would help to minimize the competitive effects of the domestic initiative.

The German government put forth a compromise proposal in May 1999 that would introduce minimum taxes on natural gas, coal, electricity, and mineral oils. The proposal contained a multitude of special provisions to address member state concerns. For example, coal would be taxed at a minimum of 0 percent. While the other taxes would be positive, there were exemptions for energy intensive industries and home heating fuels. There were also a number of provisions for extended transition periods and exemptions if the taxes caused inflation or created negative competitive effects on domestic industries. Taxation issues required unanimity in the Council, and even with the numerous provisions—many added to satisfy Spain—the Spanish government nonetheless vetoed the proposal. Every other country expressed at least rhetorical support for the proposal, but it was unclear whether the German proposal would have been sufficient to achieve consensus because skeptical member states were able to hide behind the Spanish veto. The strong support for the energy tax from Germany, Austria, and the Nordic countries guaranteed that the issue remained on the EU agenda, but Spain's veto would make further negotiations extremely difficult.

The spike in oil prices during the summer and fall of 2000 further undermined support for the tax initiative. In the face of protests and rioting, France, the Netherlands, and Italy reduced their tax rates on transportation fuels. The Blair government canceled the annual automotive fuel escalator. The increasing oil prices cast a pall over further attempts to increase energy taxes. The window of opportunity for adopting a common European energy tax had closed.

EU-Automobile Industry GHG Negotiations

Between 1985 and 1995, EU CO_2 emissions from road transportation increased by 36 percent and air transport emissions increased by 57 percent.

The Commission estimated that by 2010 transport related emissions would increase by 40 percent, which would offset emission reductions in other areas.[73] The Commission developed a strategy based largely on existing initiatives, which it claimed would halve the predicted growth in transport emissions. The strategy involved the promotion of rail and sea transport and the transformation of transport pricing to better reflect its environmental impact. Most of these initiatives languished for lack of support. The one initiative that did receive broad support was the negotiation of a voluntary agreement with the automobile industry to cut CO_2 emissions in new cars.

The Commission and the Association of European Car Manufacturers (ACEA) had worked together on reducing automobile pollutant emissions for many years. However, negotiations to reduce CO_2 emissions had made little progress prior to 1998. The Commission's goal was to reduce CO_2 emissions in new cars by approximately 35 percent by 2005. This goal was to be met through a combination of improved fuel efficiency, fiscal incentives, and an information campaign to encourage the purchase of more efficient automobiles. ACEA rejected the goal as unrealistic and argued that a 20 percent reduction was the most that was technically and economically feasible by 2005.[74] The negotiations remained at an impasse until February 1998. The Commission, with at least rhetorical support from the Council, put the automobile industry on notice. If the automakers did not negotiate in good faith, the EU would propose a regulatory solution to achieve its desired outcome. ACEA responded with an offer to reduce average CO_2 emissions in new cars by 25 percent by 2008. The Commission finalized the agreement in July 1998, and the Council accepted it. American automakers were a part of the ACEA agreement through their European subsidiaries, but the Commission also committed itself to negotiating a similar agreement with Korean and Japanese automakers.

The voluntary agreements had the potential to significantly reduce the growth in automobile emissions. However, it lacked specific requirements for individual automakers, which created the potential free riding. The agreement also contained no penalties for missing the targets; although, there was an implicit threat that the EU would legislate if the automakers missed the targets. The voluntary agreement thus held potential for slowing transport emissions, but there was also significant risk that the target would not be met. Between 1995 and 1999, ACEA reduced the average CO_2 emissions of its new cars by 6 percent, but it would need to significantly increase the rate of improvement if it was to meet its EU commitments.[75]

Energy Policy

The 1999 deregulation of European electricity markets dominated European energy policy during this period. The purpose of the reform was to enhance the efficiency of the sector by introducing greater competition. The initiative succeeded, but falling electricity prices had unintended consequences for climate policy. Declining prices made combined heat and power (CHP) plants uncompetitive and reduced incentives for improving energy efficiency. Renewable energy technologies also faced difficulties due to their higher costs relative to the falling prices for fossil fuel electricity. These effects further undermined the EU's attempts to meet its climate goals. The Commission and the member states acknowledged the problems, but they struggled to find an acceptable mechanism to secure the economic benefits of deregulation while also promoting energy efficiency, CHP, and renewable energy.

The Commission, in particular, continued to tout the potential contributions of renewable energy toward the EU's GHG emission reduction target. In 1995 renewable energies filled approximately 6 percent of the EU's energy demand. In 1998, the Commission proposed and the Council approved a target of doubling the contribution of renewables by 2010. The target was not binding on the member states, but it was intended to provide the impetus for expanding investments in renewable energy. Despite the rhetorical support for renewables, there was little enthusiasm for expanding EU financial support. Instead, the Energy Council decided that the promotion of renewable energy should be the primary responsibility of national authorities.

The Commission attempted to create a common support mechanism for renewable energy that would promote fair access to national grids. However, the initiative became bogged down in negotiations with the member states. Initially, the directive would have required minimum levels of renewable electricity generation by each member state and would have created a common support mechanism for renewable energy. However, differences in national support schemes and substantial variation in the potential for developing renewable energy across the member states led to significant weakening of the proposal. The Commission continued to press the member states to commit themselves to the expansion of renewable energy.

Germany led a number of member states in an effort to head off Commission efforts to harmonize national renewable energy support schemes. In December 2000, the Council accepted nonbinding targets for each member state to expand its renewable energy output. For example, the United Kingdom agreed to raise its proportion of renewably generated electricity from 2 to 10 percent of total electricity production. However, the Council made it clear that these targets were contingent upon the maintenance of national support schemes. In a compromise adopted in 2001, the Parliament, Commission, and Council accepted the nonbinding goal of doubling the share of EU renewable energy in total energy production by 2010. The directive overcame the opposition of several states, including Germany, by dropping the common support scheme and protecting the existing national support systems for at least seven years. However, the lack of specific provisions to promote renewable energy made the target more aspirational than realistic.

The Commission also continued to press for the expansion of the SAVE program to encourage greater energy efficiency and the ALTENER program to support renewable energy development. After running for five years, the EU mandates for both programs expired, and the Council deadlocked with the Parliament and Commission over a directive to extend them. In 1998, the Council consolidated the SAVE and ALTENER programs, along with other minor energy programs, into the EU Multiannual Framework Energy Program. The move was intended to simplify the management of the programs and provide administrative cost savings. While the Council was willing to relaunch the programs, it did so with little additional funding. Environmental groups and members of the European Parliament charged the Council with hypocrisy for establishing ambitious goals to reduce EU GHG emissions but failing to fund policies to achieve those reductions. The member states continued to obstruct Commission efforts to expand EU level renewable support and energy efficiency programs, which made it increasingly unlikely that the EU as a whole would be able to achieve its Kyoto commitments.

The European Negotiating Position

The Kyoto Protocol created a number of interesting challenges for the EU. The operationalization of the flexibility mechanisms (joint implementation, carbon trading, and the Clean Development Mechanism) and the inclusion of sinks in the calculation of net emissions created significant internal debate as well as conflict with the United States and the Umbrella Group. Initially, the focus of the EU's negotiating position was limiting the use of flexibility mechanisms to meet national emission reduction targets. The Commission had opposed the inclusion of emissions trading in the final agreement and was skeptical of the extensive use of flexibility mechanisms to meet national targets. In the weeks following the Kyoto meeting, the Commission was adamant that the use of the flexibility mechanisms had to be capped so that domestic actions would provide the primary means of meeting national commitments. In April 1998, the Commission was able to elicit Environment Council approval of an EU negotiating position that underlined the importance of domestic action and mandated a cap on the use of flexibility mechanisms to meet domestic commitments. The Commission, with the support of several member states argued that the ceiling should be set at 50 percent of total GHG emission reductions. However, in a precursor to battles that would ensue among member states, Austria, Denmark, and Germany pressed for a hard emissions cap, but several other states, including the Netherlands and Italy, vigorously opposed it.[76]

Beginning in the spring of 1998, the Commission began to alter its long-standing opposition to the early implementation of emissions trading and the use of trading to meet the EU emission reduction target. The shift was in part a response to efforts by the Umbrella Group to dominate the development of rules for the flexibility mechanisms. In addition, many EU member states saw the flexibility mechanisms as important ingredients in their domestic strategies to meet GHG reduction commitments. The Commission asserted that it would be important to play a constructive role in the negotiations to create a legitimate trading mechanism. In addition, the participation of the EU in emissions trading would drive up the costs of emission credits and force the Umbrella Group to undertake more domestic action to reduce emissions.[77]

By September 1998, it was clear that the member states would be unable to achieve consensus on a quantitative cap. In the place of a quantitative cap, the Environment Council decided in October 1998 to include the following language in the EU negotiating mandate: a limit to the use of flexibility mechanisms "should be defined in quantitative and qualitative terms, based on equitable criteria."[78] The Commission asserted that it would continue to argue for the norm that states should meet at least 50 percent of their target through domestic actions. In June 1999, the Council finally agreed on a negotiating stance that would limit the total amount of emissions that could be traded, by using a formula to calculate the total credits that could be bought and sold by each country. The EU formula would allow those countries that had undertaken the most significant emission reduction measures domestically to purchase additional credits while limiting the purchases of other countries. Under the proposed formula, EU member states could on average secure 42 percent of their emission reductions through the flexibility mechanisms, while the United States would only be allowed 34 percent. Sweden and the Netherlands refused to accept the formula because they would be allowed to acquire only 30 percent of their goal through the flexibility mechanisms.[79] In a last minute compromise, the Council agreed to an unpublished declaration that would allow countries to use flexibility mechanisms to achieve up to 50 percent of their target. The compromise undermined any hope of the EU gaining international acceptance of its position. As one German official noted, "[t]he agreement is, quite frankly, rather ridiculous. I don't think anybody now seriously believes this EU position and the formula will be accepted at the climate change negotiations."[80]

Beyond the conflict over flexibility mechanisms, the issue of how to count emission credits for sinks became a major issue for the EU. In June 2000, the Council adopted a negotiating mandate, which stated that "[t]he Council has serious concerns about the scale and scientific and other uncertainties and risks associated with sinks. . . . [therefore] defined and limited activities associated with further sources of sinks shall not apply in the first commitment period except if these concerns are met."[81] However, internal opposition from Sweden, Finland, and Italy to the EU's stance on sinks further undermined the EU's negotiating position.

EU opposition to credits for sinks and limits on the use of flexibility mechanisms set up a contentious fight with the Umbrella Group at The Hague. The EU delegation was also led by a number of Green Party members, who took a very aggressive stand in the negotiations and refused to give in to American demands. Both the EU and the Umbrella Group believed that a compromise was possible at The Hague. However, the significant divide between the parties on numerous issues and the political posturing before and during The Hague meeting created an ominous atmosphere.

THE HAGUE NEGOTIATIONS

As the prior sections demonstrate, the Kyoto Protocol signatories approached the post Kyoto negotiations with widely divergent interests and strategies. The successful conclusion of the Kyoto talks masked the substantial differences in interests that would have to be accommodated in the ensuing negotiations. Resolution of three primary disputes among developed states would determine the future ratification of the Protocol. First, the states had to agree upon a set of rules governing the flexibility mechanisms. In particular, they had to define the proportion of national targets that could be met through the mechanisms. Second, the parties disagreed over how to account for carbon sequestration through sinks. What activities were eligible for credits? Should there be caps on the amount of a state's commitment that could be met through sinks? Third, would developing countries be required or permitted to undertake emission reduction commitments? These issues split the EU and the Umbrella Group.

It was initially believed that the issues left unresolved at Kyoto could be finalized by the 1998 COP–4 meeting in Buenos Aries. The UNFCCC secretariat sponsored frequent workshops and other meetings to promote progress on the various technical issues, but it quickly became apparent that the countries were not eager to compromise until a final deal could be achieved. At COP–4 the parties could only agree to complete a final agreement by the 2000 COP–6 meeting. During the two year interlude, the primary diplomatic activity revolved around attempts to fracture the opposing group's coalition and persuade members of the G–77/China to support one side or the other on the various points. Both sides also pursued public relations campaigns to shape the public perception of their policies. The primary issues dividing the countries are discussed below.

Emissions Trading

Emission trading was initially the most contentious issue dividing the developed world. It was a vital component of the Clinton administration's plans to meet its Kyoto emission reduction target. Japan, Canada, New Zealand, Australia, and to a slightly lesser extent Iceland and Norway, also saw trading as a central mechanism to achieve their targets. For Russia and the former Communist states, trading offered a significant source of income from the sale of their excess emission credits. However, international emissions trading potentially violated the norm requiring states to pursue emission reductions domestically. The EU emphasized that it would only support trading under strict provisions to guard against cheating, and trading had to be supplemental to domestic action. This split over the trading rules and the definition of "supplemental" dominated the early post-Kyoto negotiations.

The dispute between the Umbrella Group and the EU states, as well as the positions of the G–77/China, reflected important economic interests as well as divergent perceptions of emissions trading. The debate was as much about framing the issue as it was about the rules for emissions trading. The Umbrella Group portrayed trading as the most efficient mechanism to assure maximum emission reductions at minimum economic cost. Speaking for the Clinton administration, National Security Advisor, Sandy Berger argued that "[t]he president's view has been that a trading mechanism, where American industry is essentially able to swap its credits, is a way to get the gases down. It does not matter whether that unit of greenhouse gas is diminished in Thailand or Toledo from an environmental standpoint."[82] Many American environmental organizations actively supported this view and worked in cooperation with American businesses to promote a trading regime.

Most European Union member states depicted emissions trading as a crass attempt by the Umbrella Group to shirk their domestic responsibilities and achieve their commitments through "hot air" credits from the former Communist states. The EU, along with most European and some American environmental organizations, rejected trading as a primary mechanism for fulfilling national commitments. Most European states argued that domestic regulatory actions were the only legitimate mechanisms to achieve the majority of a state's emission reduction commitment. This fundamental normative conflict made compromise difficult and produced acrimonious exchanges among governments and NGOs alike.

The United States began to build a coalition in support of the early adoption of trading rules shortly after the end of the Kyoto negotiations. In March 1998, the United States convened a meeting of the Umbrella Group in Washington to coordinate the group's position on trading. The Umbrella

Group argued that the EU bubble was a form of emissions trading and that the non-EU developed states should have the right to pursue a similar mechanism. The member states adamantly rejected efforts by the Umbrella Group to exclude them from emission trading. Following a G–8 environment minister's meeting in April 1998, British Environment Minister, Michael Meacher, asserted that the EU member states were "in favor of emissions trading, and we expressed the view that it should be an open trading system and that there shouldn't be a cartel from which the [EU] is separated. That view was expressed very strongly because the EU is not a trading mechanism—it is a pledging mechanism, which is quite separate."[83] The EU states worried about the potential for the Umbrella Group to meet most, if not all, of its emission reduction commitments by relying on Russian "hot air" credits. The use of the 1990 baseline provided Russia with a potential economic windfall from the sale of excess credits that resulted from the collapse of its economy. These credits would allow the other Umbrella Group states to avoid costly domestic actions to reduce emissions.

Beyond the broad philosophical and political differences over trading, negotiators also faced a myriad of difficult technical issues. Would private parties be able to trade, or would trading be confined to governments? Would buyers or sellers be held liable for guaranteeing that credits bought or sold were actually achieved? How would domestic trading regimes be linked to the international market? Would credits derived from the JI or CDM programs be tradable? While many of these issues were technical, they were also central to the interests of the parties and would have to be resolved at the highest levels.

The Umbrella Group and the EU laid out their competing plans for an emission trading regime in June 1998. Under the Umbrella Group's proposal, national governments, corporations, brokers, and NGOs would be allowed to buy and sell emission allowances. There would be no limits on the proportion of the national emission target that could be met through purchasing credits from abroad. The EU proposal was much more restrictive in the amounts of credits that could be bought and sold. The EU also had much stricter rules for participation. The Umbrella Group rejected the EU's attempts to cap trading. In response, the United States proposed an alternative "bubble" encompassing the Umbrella Group countries. Undaunted by the Umbrella Group's attempts to exclude the EU and force unlimited emission trading, the Commission put forth a complex formula to restrict the amounts of credits achieved through flexibility mechanisms that parties could count toward their national targets. Under the EU proposal, Russia would only be able to sell a fraction of the credits arising out of its economic collapse.[84] The Umbrella Group rejected the approach. The United States accused the EU of attempting to rewrite the Kyoto Protocol. The American delegation argued that the EU was politically naïve to believe that increasing the costs of implementation would not undermine the prospects of American ratification and accused the Europeans of applying a double standard. Emission reductions from East German economic restructuring and British reductions from fuel switching were no different than Russian emission credits.

The Umbrella Group and the EU remained deadlocked on this issue until COP–6. The Umbrella Group successfully lobbied some G–77 countries to support its position, and it made headway in persuading some NGOs of the benefits of trading. In the end though, the rules for emission trading would have to await a final compromise.

Developing Country Participation

The Berlin Mandate had explicitly excluded developing country commitments from the first protocol negotiations. The G–77/China successfully deleted a provision in the draft Kyoto Protocol that allowed developing countries to voluntarily accept a commitment. However, the United States made it clear that it would not ratify the Protocol unless the largest and most economically advanced of the developing states (i.e., China, India, Korea, Mexico, and Brazil) accepted some sort of commitment. The EU member states were willing to work with the United States on this issue, though they continued to emphasize that the developed states had to lead by example by reducing domestic emissions.

Over the ensuing months, the United States successfully convinced a number of developing countries to accept some form of participation in the Protocol. However, China was unyielding in its opposition to additional commitments. "The position of the G–77 and China is clear: no new commitments in whatever guise or disguise. . . . [the industrial states] have to pay to the Earth the debt owed since the Industrial Revolution."[85] The United States received support for its position from Raul Estrada-Oyuela, the chairman of the negotiating group on the Kyoto Protocol. At the November 1998 COP–4 meeting, Estrada asserted that "[i]t doesn't make any sense to request a reduction in emissions from little developing countries, but there are key developing countries whose emissions have to be controlled or limited. You cannot have China, which is sitting at the UN Security Council; India, which is exploding a nuclear device; and Brazil, who is willing to sit at the Security Council as a permanent member, and have them not take the full responsibility in all sectors of this treaty."[86]

At American request, Argentina attempted to put voluntary developing country commitments on the COP–4 agenda in Buenos Aires. The attempt failed in the face of overwhelming opposition from China, India, and a large proportion of the G–77. The Americans then endeavored to include the issue through various backdoor maneuvers. The American delegation sought to require voluntary developing country commitments. In addition, Article 4.2 (*a*) and (*b*) of the FCCC requires that the parties periodically review the adequacy of commitments to achieve the goal of the convention. The United States attempted to use this review to force developing countries to accept national commitments at COP–4. The G–77/China adamantly opposed the attempt to link the review to developing country commitments. The Clinton administration continued to aggressively pursue mechanisms to include developing countries throughout the negotiations. However, the debate was framed in terms of the principle of responsibility for past actions versus the obligations to address future threats. Developing countries repeatedly affirmed the norm requiring developed countries to take domestic action first, and the United States was unable to undermine the norm.

Sinks

The final issue that would prove to be a major obstacle to agreement was the question of how to account for sinks in national emission balances. The Umbrella Group pursued a generous approach to emissions crediting for sinks, which included provisions for reforestation, land-use change, soil absorption, and afforestation. The proposal potentially offered very large credits for CO_2 removal from the atmosphere. The EU sought a much more limited approach. The sinks negotiations were highly technical, but the resolution of the technical issues could have profound effects on the costs of achieving national emission reduction targets. Some of the most important debates were over definitions and the development of a scientific methodology to account for CO_2 removals. For example, what is a forest? How much CO_2 do various types of forests remove? The EU and the G–77/China demanded that the IPCC address the issue and provide a scientific foundation to answer these questions. The past appeals to the IPCC provided the G–77 and the EU with the necessary leverage to force the Umbrella Group to acquiesce in an IPCC study to be completed prior to COP–6.

The IPCC held talks in May 2000 to finalize its "Special Report on Land Use, Land Use Change, and Forestry." The conclusions of the report had the potential to dramatically affect the costs of achieving national emission targets. According to the U.S. Department of Energy, American credits for sinks could be as high as 227 million metric tons per year or as low as a few million metric tons, depending on the definitions and methodologies adopted.[87] European nations challenged the inclusion of credits for sinks on scientific grounds. They argued that most forms of carbon sequestration were only temporary and that the carbon would eventually be released. They wanted to limit credits to a small number of clearly defined activities.

The Umbrella Group, on the other hand, sought to receive credits both for human activities and also for natural land-use changes that had the effect of sequestering carbon, such as natural forest expansion. The European position received significant support from NGOs and also fit well with European economic interests. The potential for European carbon sequestration was extremely limited relative to the American, Canadian, and Russian opportunities. Economic interests heavily influenced the supposedly scientific process. In the end, the IPCC provided a set of alternative definitions and accounting methods with their associated impacts on accounting for carbon sequestration. The IPCC left it to the climate negotiators in The Hague to choose their preferred set of definitions and accounting rules to incorporate into the treaty. Under the various scenarios, forests in the Northern Hemisphere could release up to 849 million tonnes or capture 483 million tons of carbon by 2010. Additional activities such as soil sequestration could offer an additional 287 mtc of sequestered carbon.[88] If all proposed credits were accepted, the sinks could completely offset the required emission reductions contained in the Kyoto Protocol.

When the United States finally presented its data on the effects of sinks on the American Kyoto commitments, it became immediately apparent why they were vital to the American position. The inclusion of all proposed sink activity would fulfill nearly one-third of the American commitment. For most EU countries, it would fulfill less than 10 percent of their commitments. The debate over accounting methods for sinks and their role in meeting national emission commitments would prove to be one of the most difficult issues to resolve in The Hague.

COP–6 PART I: THE FAILURE

As COP–6 approached, the climate negotiations continued to founder on the same set of priority issues left over from Kyoto: caps on the use of flexibility mechanisms and rules for their implementation, accounting rules and definitions for sinks, and developing country participation. National negotiating strategies undermined the resolution of these issues. All of the delegations took provisions important to other states "hostage" prior to COP–6 to use as bargaining chips in the final negotiations. All of these issues would have to be bundled into one final compromise.

There was little progress made during the first week and a half, and the negotiations remained deadlocked. In an attempt to bridge the divide, COP–6 President Jan Pronk put forward the outline of a final agreement. The proposal was negatively received by most delegations, and Pronk was roundly criticized for offering the proposal too late in the process and with insufficient detail to permit meaningful negotiations. As the negotiations drew to a close, there was a last minute attempt to put together a compromise agreement to salvage the negotiations.

Following a lengthy telephone discussion between President Clinton and Prime Minister Blair, British Deputy Prime Minister, John Prescott put together a draft agreement developed with input from the United States and members of the EU. The agreement would set quantitative limits on the credits that could be claimed from sinks. The limits were lower than the United States desired but higher than what the EU had been willing to accept. The two groups were essentially arguing over a few million tons of carbon—a relatively insignificant amount. While this small group of delegates (reportedly composed of officials from France, Sweden, the United Kingdom, Germany, and the United States) was able to reach agreement, the EU delegation as a whole later rejected it after further internal deliberations.[89] The rejection led to acrimonious accusations among British, French, American, and Commission officials. Commenting on the agreement, American negotiator, Frank Loy, asserted that following the negotiations with the EU representatives, "we physically shook hands. . . . I asked, 'Are we now in full agreement; is this a deal?' I was pointing to a piece of paper. They said 'yes.' " Loy presciently noted that "I think it is fair to say that that was a pretty important opportunity that was not cashed in on."[90] Commenting on the proposed compromise, French Environment Minister and head of the EU delegation, Dominique Voynet, argued that "this compromise is completely one-sided; it transfers the Protocol on reducing greenhouse gas emissions into a protocol that, on the contrary, would authorize an increase in emissions by 2010. If we accept it, it will open loopholes that would then be very difficult to close."[91]

Participants in the negotiations provided very interesting explanations for the failure. Voynet asserted that the problem was cultural. "It's extremely difficult to negotiate between groups where political cultures are so different."[92] The American insistence on free market principles in environmental control was perceived in France as the "law of the jungle." Europeans tended to expect regulatory and fiscal methods to achieve environmental goals. Both the German and French delegations were led by Green Party ministers, which created both cultural and political obstacles to achieving an agreement with the United States. Loy blamed the failure on the domestic political interests of important European actors. "We showed real willingness to compromise. But, too many of our negotiating partners held fast to positions shaped more by political purity than by practicality, more by dogmatism than pragmatism."[93] Following the failure of the negotiations, the delegates to COP–6 suspended the meeting rather than conclude it in failure and agreed to reconvene in the coming months to finalize a treaty.

COP–6 PART II: KYOTO WITHOUT THE AMERICANS?

Immediately following the demise of the negotiations, the Clinton administration approached the EU with a proposal to quickly resume the negotiations. At the time, there was a widespread belief that the gap between the EU and the Umbrella Group was so narrow that a few extra hours of negotiations at The Hague could have produced an agreement. The Clinton administration and the Europeans sought to hold a preparatory meeting in early December, to be followed by a ministerial meeting before Christmas, to finalize an agreement acceptable to all of the industrial states. The hope was that an agreement with the EU would make it more difficult for the incoming Bush administration to walk away from the protocol or pursue significant changes. It would also set the stage for a final agreement with the developing countries in May when COP–6 was initially set to resume.

The United States and the EU agreed to a mid-level diplomatic meeting in Ottawa, Canada on December 6 and 7. Umbrella Group representatives met with an EU delegation. The meeting was intended to narrow the differences between the two sides to provide the foundation for a ministerial conference of industrial states to be held in Oslo, Norway in mid-December. The meeting failed to resolve the major disputes, and the proposed ministerial meeting was cancelled. The meeting represented a retreat from the compromise rejected in The Hague. The EU took a hard-line on credits for sinks, and the Umbrella Group stepped back from some of the compromises that it had been willing to accept in November.[94]

The challenges surrounding a final agreement were put into stark terms by the correspondence between Voynet and Loy. In a letter to Voynet, Loy listed the minimum American requirements for an agreement. First, there should be no limits on the use of flexibility mechanisms to achieve GHG reduction commitments. Second, credits for carbon sink enhancement activities, both domestically and through the Clean Development Mechanism, should be permitted to offset national GHG emissions. Third, a strict compliance mechanism needed to be established to monitor national performance in meeting commitments, but there should not be any punitive measures for countries that do not fulfill their commitments. Voynet, in response, outlined the minimum requirements for an agreement acceptable to the EU. First, the EU was willing to permit limited crediting for domestic sinks during the first commitment period. Second, sinks should not be included in the CDM during the first commitment period. Third, there must be a strict compliance mechanism in place. Fourth, provisions must be established that limit the trading of carbon credits (specifically "hot air" credits from the former Communist states). Finally, domestic actions must represent the "primary" measures to meet domestic GHG emission reduction commitments (i.e., at least 50 percent of the national commitment).[95] Both sides accused the other of retreating from positions agreed in The Hague.

The reluctance of the Europeans to compromise with the Clinton administration is puzzling. Republicans disparaged the Clinton administration's attempts to achieve an agreement in its final days and warned the administration not to undermine American interests by caving in to European demands. As a candidate, George W. Bush had condemned the treaty as fundamentally flawed and unfair. It was extremely unlikely that the Europeans would be able to negotiate a better agreement with the new administration, but the European leaders were extremely reluctant to offer concessions to the Americans. Voynet in France and Jürgen Trittin in Germany had condemned the United States' final offer in The Hague on the grounds that it would undermine the integrity of the agreement. Accepting the concessions necessary to secure American participation may have been politically impossible. European leaders may also have judged that the Bush administration would not be satisfied with an agreement acceptable to the Clinton administration. The new administration could potentially demand even greater concessions in the future. Regardless of the rationale behind the European position, Green politicians capitalized on the failure as an opportunity to denounce American climate policy. The harsh political rhetoric made future concessions to the United States extremely difficult to justify. Any agreement would have to await a new administration in the United States.

BUSH, ENERGY, AND THE REPUDIATION OF THE KYOTO PROTOCOL

The victory of George W. Bush in the contested 2000 presidential elections produced substantial uncertainty both in American climate policy and in the international negotiations. A central element of the Bush campaign had been the development of a new national energy strategy. President Bush had focused on the need to reduce American dependence on foreign energy sources by expanding domestic production of fossil fuels. The Bush campaign had also called the Kyoto Protocol a flawed and unfair agreement. The international negotiations essentially stalled while the new administration contemplated its approach to the Kyoto Protocol.

The first indications emerging from the new administration created international concern. The administration requested that the scheduled resumption of COP–6 in May be pushed back to July. According to the State Department, the administration needed the additional time to reevaluate American climate policy. America's partners reluctantly acquiesced in the delay amid growing concern that the Bush administration would walk away from the agreement. The administration was sending mixed signals about its intentions. In February 2001, EPA Administrator Christine Todd Whitman announced that the administration was considering a plan to limit CO_2 emissions from power plants. Whitman noted that "[t]his president is very sensitive to the issue of global warming. . . . There is no question but that global warming is a real phenomenon, that it is occurring."[96] The proposal created significant anxiety within the energy industry, which launched an aggressive lobbying campaign to block it. The announcement came just days before Whitman was scheduled to meet her fellow G–8 environment ministers in Trieste, Italy. The suggestion that the United States would regulate CO_2 emissions provided evidence of American commitment to addressing climate change and helped to deflect some European criticism of American policy. In fact, the final declaration from the meeting affirmed a commitment to "strive to reach agreement on outstanding political issues and to ensure in a cost-effective manner the environmental integrity of the Kyoto Protocol."[97] It appeared that the Bush administration would be willing to engage in continued negotiations.

The optimism was fleeting. Shortly after the G–8 meeting, the administration announced that a cabinet-level review had determined that regulating CO_2 emissions was inconsistent with the administration's broader goals to increase domestic energy production. Energy industry lobbying and opposition from Vice President Cheney and Energy Secretary Spencer Abraham were apparently decisive in the shift in policy.[98] The decision signaled a retreat from meaningful domestic action to reduce GHG emissions. In a marked shift in tone, President Bush cast doubt on the need to undertake domestic measures to cut CO_2 emissions.

> At a time when California has already experienced energy shortages, and other western states are worried about price and availability of energy this summer, we must be very careful not to take actions that could harm consumers. This is especially true given the incomplete state of scientific knowledge of the causes of, and solutions to, global climate change and the lack of commercially available technologies for removing and storing carbon dioxide.[99]

The administration followed up on this policy announcement with a declaration in late March that it considered Kyoto "dead." National Security Advisor, Condoleezza Rice met with EU ambassadors in Washington to inform them that, while the administration would remain "engaged" on the issue of climate change, it would not support the Kyoto Protocol. In a letter to Senate Republicans, President Bush outlined his position. "I oppose the Kyoto Protocol because it exempts 80 percent of the world, including major population centers such as China and India, from compliance, and would cause serious harm to the U.S. economy."[100] Various administration spokespeople reiterated the administration's opposition over the ensuing weeks, which produced an avalanche of condemnation from environmental groups, Democrats, and foreign leaders. European leaders were furious that the administration would so abruptly walk away from an agreement produced through years of arduous negotiations. The administration announced that it would undertake a cabinet-level review to develop an alternative framework that would focus on new technologies and market incentives to reduce GHG emissions.

The Bush administration rejected the Kyoto Protocol even as the public appeared to offer broad support for it. An April 2001 poll found that 61 percent of Americans supported ratification of the Protocol with only 26 percent opposed.[101] The administration apparently calculated that climate change would not resonate with the American public and that the international response would be muted. The administration was surprised by the backlash that its position produced both domestically and internationally. The only support that it offered to the Kyoto negotiations was a pledge not to undermine them and to allow other countries to move forward without the United States. However, a State Department memo sent to American diplomatic posts noted that the goal in the international climate negotiations was to "maximize flexibility to craft a new approach to climate change that is not based on the Kyoto Protocol."[102]

In an attempt to address some of the criticisms of American climate policy, senior members of the administration initiated weekly briefings on climate science and policy issues from a broad range of scientists, economists, business representatives, and policy experts. The briefings were the first step in designing an alternative to the Kyoto Protocol. As part of the White House review, the administration requested in May 2001 that the National Academy of Sciences review the existing literature on climate change to guide the policy review. In June the panel, which included skeptics of climate change, produced its report.[103] They concluded that the atmosphere was indeed warming and that human activity was largely responsible. The report failed to spur any changes in the American position, and the administration continued to defer the formulation of an alternative to Kyoto.

The May 2001 release of the administration's new energy strategy further strained relations with the EU and cast doubt on the ability of the United States to slow its growing rate of CO_2 emissions. The strategy emphasized the importance of domestic oil and gas exploration, investment in energy infrastructure, and the building of new power plants. Some provisions in the strategy would reduce GHG emissions, but they were overshadowed by the overwhelming emphasis on energy security and supply. The strategy contained initiatives to promote highly efficient cars and energy conservation. It also called for the building of new nuclear power plants to reduce CO_2 emissions.

Energy policy continued to dominate the American domestic debate, but the political context for the debate shifted dramatically in 2001. At the beginning of 2001, Republicans controlled the House and the Senate, but the party controlled the Senate on the thinnest of margins. The Republicans and Democrats each controlled fifty seats, and Vice President Cheney provided the Republicans with the controlling vote. The Republicans had placed energy policy at the top of their legislative agenda. However, after a series of conflicts with the Bush White House, Vermont Republican Senator James Jeffords declared himself an independent. The defection shifted the balance in the Senate to a fifty to forty-nine advantage to the Democrats with Jeffords tacitly supporting the Democrats. The shift in control moved energy policy down the Senate's agenda. The Senate split complicated the energy debate and created additional uncertainty for American climate policy.

Kyoto without the United States?

The EU and its member states made numerous appeals to the United States to return to the negotiations, but they also resolved to conclude an agreement and pursue ratification of the Protocol without the United States if it could not be persuaded to return to the negotiations. An EU delegation undertook a world tour in April 2001 to secure sufficient international support to achieve ratification. The delegation traveled to the United States, Canada, China, Russia, Japan, and Iran (holder of the G–77 presidency). Following a meeting between the EU delegation and EPA Administrator Whitman, Whitman reiterated that the administration would not support the Protocol, but she asserted that it was willing to work with other states on an alternative approach.[104] With the continued American snubs, the EU's focus shifted to securing Russian and Japanese commitments to ratify the Protocol. If the United States did not ratify Kyoto, both Russia and Japan would have to ratify the Protocol for it to enter into force. This dramatically altered the international negotiations. Desparately seeking to salvage the agreement, the EU became much more willing to compromise on the Umbrella Group's demands. The EU received widespread support for the possibility of moving ahead without the United States, though the Umbrella Group members expressed a strong preference for moving forward with the United States if at all possible.

The new focus on Japan and Russia gave these countries considerable leverage over the negotiations, which both countries aggressively exploited. In April, Jan Pronk put forth a compromise plan based on the deal that was nearly agreed in The Hague. Japan rejected the plan and demanded larger sink credits. Japan had apparently been willing to accept the proposal in the last minute negotiations in The Hague, but it increased its demand for sink credits after the United States withdrew. As the negotiations continued toward the resumption of COP-6, Japan and its Umbrella Group partners aggressively pursued their demands and threatened to not ratify the Protocol if they were not met. By June 2001, it was apparent that the Bush administration would not return to the Kyoto negotiations. The EU quickly began to give in to Japanese and Russian demands.

President Bush's first visit to Europe in June 2001 confirmed the importance of moving forward without the United States if Kyoto was to be salvaged. Acknowledging the importance of climate change to the European states, the president addressed the issue in a speech the day before he left for Europe. He conceded that climate change was real and had to be addressed multilaterally, but he continued to reject the Kyoto Protocol as an unjust and unworkable solution to the problem. Emphasizing the uncertainties surrounding the effects of climate change, he asserted that additional research was needed prior to pursuing economically painful policy changes to reduce GHG emissions.[105] President Bush faced near universal condemnation of America's climate policy. The question was whether the rest of the world was willing and able to move forward without the United States.

The international negotiations accelerated leading up to the resumption of COP-6 in Bonn, where the core of the agreement was concluded. The final rules to govern the Kyoto Protocol were then completed in Marrakech, Morocco in November 2001. The first major advance in the negotiations was Jan Pronk's June 2001 completion of a single unified text that eliminated the hundreds of "brackets" that various parties had placed around contested language in the earlier texts. The revised text contained concessions to entice Japan and Russia. The EU responded favorably to the new text, and it appeared to offer the foundation for an agreement.

As the Bonn negotiations approached, it became apparent that Japan and Russia would drive a hard bargain. At a preparatory meeting in June, Russia demanded that it receive more sink credits in line with the concessions that Japan had received. The additional credits would allow Russia to sell more carbon credits in international markets. Japan also continued to be coy about whether it would proceed with ratification without the United States, which increased pressure on the EU to grant further concessions on Japanese sinks and other concerns. Japanese Prime Minister Koizumi met with President Bush in late June and backed off his earlier condemnations of American climate policy. The Japanese government asserted that it would seek changes in the Kyoto agreement that would allow the United States to return. Koizumi continued his tour with a visit with Prime Minister Blair in London. The two leaders publicly pledged to work together to bring the United States into the Kyoto agreement. An EU delegation went to Japan in early July in an attempt to elicit a Japanese pledge to ratify Kyoto even if the United States did not. Koizumi reiterated his preference to include the Americans if at all possible.

The Bush administration, after several months of cabinet reviews of climate policy, failed to propose an alternative plan before the Bonn meeting. The administration pledged to actively and constructively engage in the negotiations and promised not to obstruct an agreement among the other states, but it made it abundantly clear that it would not be a party to the Protocol. As the Bonn negotiations approached there was a widespread sense of impending failure. It would be up to the Europeans to accept enough compromises to entice the Umbrella Group to sign on to an agreement. As COP–6 resumed in Bonn, four issues dominated the negotiations: nuclear energy, funds for developing countries, credits for sinks, and compliance. The Umbrella Group aggressively sought to minimize the costs of meeting the Kyoto commitments. One of the most important measure for achieving this goal was a liberal distribution of credits for sink activities. The EU had entered the negotiations with a proposal to use a common equation to determine the maximum amounts of credits that each country could use to offset domestic emissions. Japan, Canada, Russia, and Australia rejected this approach and demanded the right to individually negotiate maximum credits on a country by country basis. Initially, the EU attempted to hold the line on sink credits. However, the primary goal was to achieve an agreement, even if it meant that the EU would have to yield to the Umbrella Group.[106]

The second primary area of conflict involved the role of nuclear energy in the Kyoto mechanisms. The EU demanded that nuclear energy be excluded from the joint implementation and Clean Development Mechanisms. The Umbrella Group argued aggressively for its inclusion. The high profile of nuclear energy reflected the prominent role of Green Party members in the European delegation. The head of the EU delegation, Olivier Deleuze, was a former head of Greenpeace Belgium, and the German and French delegations both had prominent Green representation. During the negotiations, the EU apparently offered to acquiesce in the Umbrella Group's demands on sinks in return for the exclusion of nuclear energy from the flexibility mechanisms. While such an agreement would achieve one of the Greens' core interests, it would be detrimental to the cause of reducing GHG emissions. First, the concession on sinks would reduce the GHG emission reductions required of the Umbrella Group, and second, the prohibition on investments in nuclear power, which produces no GHGs, would likely result in more fossil fuel based power plants.

The final compromise contained a number of concessions to the Umbrella Group. Japan and Canada received very generous allowances for sink credits due to "national circumstances." In addition, countries could count carbon absorption resulting from better management of cropland and grassland, and there was no defined limit to these credits. It was unclear how this provision would affect national emission reduction commitments. Finally, limited credits would also be available for sink enhancement through the CDM. The EU had fought against all of these proposals in The Hague, but it was forced to yield to the demands to secure an agreement. According to WWF calculations, the sink credits would force states to reduce emissions by only 1.8 percent instead of the 5.2 percent implied by the Kyoto commitments.[107] Depending on the size of credits for cropland and grassland management, it was possible that states could meet their Kyoto targets with no emission reductions. In another concession by the EU, there would be no quantitative caps on the use of flexibility mechanisms to achieve national commitments. The only restriction in the agreement was that "the use of mechanisms shall be supplemental to domestic action, and that domestic action shall thus constitute a significant element of the effort made by each Party included in Annex I to meet its quantified emission limitation and reduction commitments. . . . "[108] The vague requirements for domestic action would allow states to rely heavily on the flexibility mechanisms to achieve their commitments. In one of the few Umbrella Group concessions to the EU, the Bonn agreement excluded emission reduction credits for investments in nuclear energy through the CDM and JI mechanisms.

Despite the weakened text, European leaders reveled in the ability to achieve an agreement without the United States. EU Environment Commissioner Margot Wallstrom asserted that "[w]e've really started something so important here today. . . . We've shown the United States, our citizens, communities, and NGOs that we could have an agreement without the US."[109] British Environment Minister Michael Meacher concurred. "This is a brilliant day for the environment. I think it is very significant that the rest of the world, despite the enormous setback when the United States took its own decision, has nevertheless rallied, supported the Protocol, and demonstrated to the United States that its death is a little premature."[110] While the congratulations flowed, it was impossible not to contemplate what the agreement might have looked like if the compromises had been made in The Hague instead of in Bonn. Michael McCarthy, writing in the British newspaper, *The Independent*, perhaps best expressed the lingering doubts regarding the EU's negotiating strategy. "In The Hague the European Union wanted a good deal, and threw out what it perceived to be a bad one; last night in Bonn the EU wanted any sort of deal and was grasping at something much worse than the one it rejected in November."[111] There is a strong possibility that the Bush administration would have walked away from the agreement even if the Clinton administration had signed on to it. However, it would have been more difficult for it to do so, and it would have also been more difficult for the other Umbrella Group countries to reopen the negotiations.

The Bonn agreement provided the foundation to operationalize the Kyoto Protocol, and an agreement at the November 2001 COP–7 meeting tied up the remaining issues. The focus then shifted to ratification. The EU and its member states committed to ratify the Protocol by the end of 2002. Japan, Russia, and Canada asserted that they would be willing to ratify without the United States, though they also expressed a strong desire to bring the United States into the agreement. The Bonn agreement also set the stage for states to begin to implement the various mechanisms included in the Protocol. With Russia's ratification in 2004, the Protocol entered into force in February 2005. The larger question that remained was whether the Kyoto Protocol would prove to be a viable mechanism to address climate change, or whether it would merely be a false façade that would allow countries to claim that they were actively addressing climate change while continuing with a business as usual domestic policy response. Kyoto represented overwhelming acceptance that climate change had to be addressed multilaterally, but its provisions would have a limited effect on global emissions. The critical next steps were to negotiating an agreement to cover the post-2012 period and assure that Kyoto's requirements for domestic action were translated into domestic policy changes. This would depend on the degree to which the climate policy norms achieved political salience in each of the countries.

CHAPTER SEVEN

Conclusion

The case studies of German, British, and American climate policy support the argument that material interests and relative power positions alone cannot explain the evolution of domestic and international climate policy. It is necessary to integrate normative debates with material forces to explain national responses to climate change. However, if international norms are to be analytically useful for explaining and predicting national behavior, then it is essential to evaluate the causal pathways through which norms are translated into and alter the domestic political process. The case studies suggest that scholars should focus their attention on the interplay among international normative debates, associated domestic normative debates, the material interests of affected actors, and the relative power positions of major states.

The climate policy case studies focused on two normative debates that played critical roles in defining international and domestic climate policy. This chapter evaluates the forces affecting the domestic political salience of these norms and offers suggestions for further research in this area. The first normative debate centered on who should bear primary responsibility for reducing global GHG emissions. Should developed states be forced to act first because they are historically responsible for the vast majority of GHG emissions, or should all states bear a common responsibility to reduce emissions? The second normative debate focused on the principles that would guide global emission reductions. Should individual states be held to a principle of national accountability, which would require every state to commit to a common domestic GHG emission reduction target, or should the principle of economic efficiency guide global emission reductions? Most environmental NGOs, developing countries, as well as most European states argued for a norm requiring national responsibility. The United States argued that the important point was to reduce global emissions, and that these emission reductions should be achieved wherever they were most cost-effective. These normative debates were at the heart of the climate negotiations, and they were integrated to varying degrees into the domestic and foreign climate policy positions of Germany, the United Kingdom, and the United States.

Chapter 1 identified a set of four hypotheses that the literature on the effects of international norms on domestic political dialogue and policy suggests should influence the domestic salience of international norms. First, the greater the congruence between an international norm and domestic political norms, the greater will be the potential for the norm to be integrated into domestic political dialogue and achieve a high degree of political salience. Second, the greater the congruence between the domestic policy implications of the international norm and the material interests of influential actors, the more likely the norm will achieve political salience. Third, the stronger the perception that a norm serves the "general interests" of humanity and environmental protection rather than the pursuit of narrow self-interest, the more likely that it will be perceived as legitimate by a broad coalition of interested actors. Finally, normative debates that are more public in nature and require domestic policy changes expand the number of relevant actors and create greater potential for private actors to force political actors to accept a norm regardless of their convictions related to the appropriateness of the norm.

Combining these hypotheses produces a set of conditions that should dictate the likelihood that a nascent international norm will achieve significant domestic political salience. International norms that resonate with existing domestic political norms and which are also consistent with the material interests of significant domestic actors should rapidly achieve domestic salience. Cases in which the international norm does not resonate with existing domestic political norms and which would adversely affect significant domestic economic actors will be least likely to achieve domestic salience. The potential domestic salience of international norms where either the norm resonates with existing domestic norms but negatively affects domestic economic actors or where the norm does not resonate with existing domestic norms but positively affects the material interests of domestic economic actors is more difficult to predict. In these cases, the level of salience should be affected by the domestic political structure and the relative influence of important domestic actors. The broader perception of the legitimacy of the norm should also be critical to determining whether it will achieve domestic salience.

The index of domestic norm salience presented in chapter 1 provides a mechanism to measure changes in international norm salience as well as evaluate the forces shaping norm salience. In particular, the index helps to differentiate between the effects of international norms on the positions of leaders as well as the broader public's perception of the appropriateness of the contested normative claims. As discussed in chapter 1, the starting point for studying norm salience is the analysis of domestic political rhetoric. Rhetorical norm affirmation provides early evidence of the promotion of a preferred norm or the acknowledgement of an emergent international norm, which may later be more fully transcribed into domestic institutional structures and policies. However, it may also represent the cynical use of norm affirmation to deflect political pressure and avoid concrete action. It is thus necessary to evaluate behavior as well as rhetoric to gauge the domestic salience of the emergent norm.

One conclusion that flows from this study is that future research on the domestic effects of international norms should measure domestic political salience by analyzing both rhetoric and associated policy initiatives. Each of the chapters analyzed the relationship between climate policy and energy, transportation, taxation, and foreign policies. Rhetoric, while important, was not a sufficient indicator of norm salience. Rhetoric may indicate support for—or at least acknowledgement of—an emerging norm, but it does not necessarily provide evidence of persuasion of the appropriateness of the norm or evidence that national behavior will change. Rhetoric can be cynically manipulated to bolster a state's image or to postpone costly policy changes. Many states affirmed the norm requiring a domestic emission reduction commitment and then failed to make any attempt to alter domestic policies to meet that commitment. The rhetorical affirmation deflected charges that the government was undermining efforts to address climate change, but the norm did not achieve sufficient domestic salience to induce domestic policy changes to reduce GHG emissions. The combination of national rhetoric and behavior provides stronger evidence of norm salience. Has the government justified policy changes with reference to international norms? Are other policy initiatives consistent with the norm? Domestic norm salience can be arrayed along a continuum from domestic irrelevance to a "taken for granted" status, and this is where the eight-point scale of norm salience provides an index to compare norm salience across countries and issue areas to evaluate the role of norms in the domestic and foreign policies of states.

CLIMATE POLICY: MEASURING THE DOMESTIC SALIENCE OF INTERNATIONAL NORMS

Evaluating the two primary normative debates provides an opportunity to assess the level of domestic political salience that these international norms achieved in Germany, the United Kingdom, and the United States and evaluate the hypotheses discussed above. The debate surrounding the relative responsibility of developed and developing countries to reduce GHG emissions largely affected the foreign policy positions of the states rather than directly influencing domestic policy. However, it does have implications for domestic policy. Requiring developing states to accept emission reduction commitments would reduce negative competitive effects of GHG reduction policies pursued by the developed states alone. If combined with the flexibility mechanisms, it would also allow developed states to pursue less costly emission reductions in the developing states. The developed states should thus share a common material interest in requiring developing countries to accept emission reduction commitments.

As climate change emerged as a political issue, norm entrepreneurs argued that the developed states had to accept responsibility for their past emissions and act first. Developing countries should only be obliged to accept international commitments after developed states had significantly reduced their emissions. Environmental NGOs and developing countries broadly perceived this norm as providing a legitimate foundation for international negotiations. The EU and its member states also endorsed the norm. This norm quickly achieved level eight, "Taken for Granted Status," on the index of norm salience in both Germany and the United Kingdom. Neither country challenged the norm internationally, nor did it face significant domestic opposition. There were no immediate domestic policy implications that flowed from this norm so the direct economic effects on domestic actors were minimal, though it created the potential for adverse competitive effects. The norm also seemed to fit well with existing political norms related to the polluter pays principle and perceptions of justice for developing countries. In addition, the norm was broadly perceived as legitimate. The hypotheses discussed above would suggest that this norm would rapidly achieve a high-level of domestic salience, which it did.

The American case, however, is more problematic. It was primarily the United States that challenged this norm, and the norm failed to resonate with the American people. The same conditions that led Germany and the United Kingdom to affirm the norm should have held for the American case; and yet, the norm never moved beyond the second level on the salience index, "Rejection." American political leaders repeatedly condemned the exemption of developing countries. The Senate's ninety-five to zero vote in a resolution rejecting the exemption in the Kyoto Protocol is perhaps the clearest example of the broad denunciation of this norm.

The American position presents a puzzle. In light of the substantial responsibility of the developed world (and particularly the United States) for past emissions, why did broad sections of the American public perceive the exemption of developing countries as completely unjust? The American position seems to point to the importance of the early framing of a normative debate. The American debate was never framed in terms of past responsibility. It was overwhelmingly focused on the costs of addressing the potential threat of climate change. From the beginning, the developing country commitment became intertwined in the other normative debate related to economic efficiency of GHG reductions, which will be discussed below. Industrial interests aggressively attacked the exemption of developing countries as economically inefficient and unjust. American industry and the American people would pay the price for reducing emissions through lost jobs and deindustrialization as developing countries absorbed jobs and investment because they would not face the same emission reduction requirements. This argument resonated with the American people and American political leaders, who repeatedly rejected the developing country exemption as unjust. Material interests thus played an important role, but the framing of the issue in terms of economic efficiency and global responsibility also seemed to fit well with broader American political norms.

The second primary normative debate related to the question of national accountability for domestic emission reductions versus the economic efficiency of global emission reductions. As climate change emerged as a major political issue, norm entrepreneurs began to call on all developed states to accept binding domestic emission reduction commitments. This movement gathered force at the Toronto Conference in 1988. From this point forward, the mechanism by which states could identify themselves as supporters of action on climate change was to accept a domestic emission reduction commitment. Those states who failed to do so were castigated as irresponsible and antienvironment. Germany and most of the EU member states as well as the developing world affirmed this norm as appropriate and just. Each developed state should be held accountable for achieving a domestic emission reduction commitment. The United States rejected this approach and argued that states should focus on cost-effective emission reductions on a global scale. Individual countries should be obliged to contribute toward addressing the problem, but the actual emission reductions should be achieved where the marginal cost was lowest. This required a mechanism to permit market forces to allocate emission reductions. States that supported this alternative formulation were castigated for obstructing international consensus and delaying action to address climate change.

The domestic emission reduction commitment norm achieved a high degree of political salience in Germany from the very beginning. The more prominent position of the precautionary principle in German environmental policy predisposed the government to more aggressively act on the potential threat of climate change. The German position also speaks to the importance of the initial framing of the problem. The Enquete Commission framed climate change as a human induced problem that required a multilateral international response, but it was also possible to dramatically reduce CO_2 emissions utilizing existing technologies with limited economic costs. This framing of the problem settled the domestic debate regarding whether Germany should act. The domestic emission reduction commitment norm achieved level five ("Foreign Policy Impact") on the salience index almost immediately. The government affirmed the norm and advocated immediate international negotiations to enshrine the commitment in a treaty. Germany adopted this position before reunification and thus before the potential for easy CO_2 emission reductions became apparent. The implication was that Germany would have to reform its domestic policies to reduce emissions, which would impose some economic costs.

After accepting that domestic reductions were necessary, the question then became how best to achieve the reductions; thus, the norm rapidly moved to level six ("Domestic Policy Impact") on the salience index. The government justified a large number of domestic policy changes on the grounds that they were necessary to meet the German 25 percent CO_2 emission reduction commitment. Again, this occurred prior to reunification. However, actors who would be significantly adversely impacted by the measures were typically able to block the new policies or substantially weaken their adverse effects as was the case with the carbon tax proposal and later the weakened energy tax. The norm thus had not achieved "Norm Prominence" (level seven), and it is likely that this will continue to be the case until the norm achieves greater domestic political salience among other developed states. The German people and their government are genuinely persuaded by the need to reduce GHG emissions and are committed to pursuing policies to achieve this outcome. However, there is also recognition that German reductions by themselves will not have a significant effect on the path of climate change. Germany will be unlikely to sacrifice domestic economic competitiveness to unilaterally reduce GHG emissions, though it has demonstrated a willingness to impose some costs to achieve emission reductions.

The British case is perhaps the most interesting in terms of this norm. The British government rejected quantitative commitments from the very beginning and argued that such commitments lacked scientific justification. The government was also concerned by its potential inability to meet such a commitment. There was thus a material interest that reinforced its opposition to quantitative commitments. While the British government was an early leader in promoting international efforts to address climate change, it was unwilling to commit to a specific emission reduction commitment. The norm remained at level two ("Rejection") during the pre-INC negotiating period. However, the opposition Labour Party seized on the norm and pressed the government to accept it, which raised the norm to level three ("Domestic Relevance") fairly early in the international negotiations. As a result of growing domestic and international pressure, the Thatcher government eventually affirmed the norm that states should accept a domestic emission reduction commitment, but it rejected the 2000 date that most other states had accepted and made it contingent upon the United States accepting a similar commitment. The government thus affirmed the norm, but economic interests led it to support a 2005 date for stabilizing British emissions, which appeared likely to occur without additional domestic activity. The norm achieved a "Foreign Policy Impact" (level five), but the government was not prepared to accept the domestic implications of policies that would be necessary to meet a 2000 stabilization target.

Under the Major government the norm began to achieve a "Domestic Policy Impact" (level six). The government justified VAT increases on domestic heating fuels and increases in gasoline taxes on the basis of reducing CO_2 emissions, but these measures were primarily focused on raising revenue. After campaigning on a platform of more aggressively addressing climate change, the new Blair government put the emission reduction commitment much more to the forefront of its domestic policy. Under Labour the norm clearly achieved a "Domestic Policy Impact," but it did not rise to "Norm Prominence" as economic interests repeatedly delayed or weakened emission reduction policies to avoid costly actions. The Labour government and the British public were convinced by the need to address climate change and were committed to reducing British emissions, but they shared the economic concerns that restrained the Germans.

The British case seems to fit well with the hypotheses regarding domestic norm salience. The norm requiring a domestic emission reduction commitment did not immediately resonate with other domestic political norms. The precautionary principle was weaker in the British case. The British also lacked the framing of the problem that the Enquete Commission provided in Germany. In addition, the norm could adversely affect a number of important economic actors, so it should be expected that it would not immediately achieve a high degree of salience. The British government proposed a number of alternatives to quantitative commitments, but the growing prominence of the norm largely doomed its efforts. Growing international pressure, particularly within the EU, as well as rising acceptance within the British public and the Labour Party that the norm was appropriate eventually forced the Conservative government to affirm it. However, it was only when it became apparent that the United Kingdom could achieve the necessary emission reductions without significant additional domestic actions that the government accepted a domestic commitment (and even then it was five years later than the date that others had accepted). While material forces played a critical role in shaping norm salience, international pressure and public support for the norm also played an important role in shaping the government's position and forcing it to abandon its preferred strategies. Once the norm achieved a domestic policy impact, the government began to pursue a number of policies to reduce GHG emissions that entailed some economic costs to domestic actors such as the voluntary CO_2 emission reductions agreements with industry and the industrial energy taxes.

The American case again seems to indicate the importance of the initial framing of an issue for the later political response. From the beginning, the Reagan and Bush administrations framed climate change as an uncertain, potential long-term threat that was worthy of additional study but which lacked the scientific certainty to justify costly policy changes. In addition, both administrations argued that policies to dramatically reduce CO_2 emissions were economically costly and had the potential to devastate the American economy. Reducing emissions thus carried substantial economic trade-offs. This framing of the problem made acceptance of an emission reduction commitment very difficult.

While the Reagan administration largely focused on the uncertainties of climate science, the Bush administration accepted that climate change should be addressed multilaterally, but it rejected the emission reduction commitment norm. Instead, it argued that addressing climate change required global emission reductions, which should be based on the principle of cost-effectiveness. States should pursue "no-regrets" measures, which could reduce emissions but that were also justified on economic grounds. This focus on cost-effectiveness evolved into the American championing of an alternative normative framework. The United States championed joint implementation and emissions trading as mechanisms capable of reducing global emissions in a cost-effective manner. States should have an obligation to pursue GHG emission reductions, but those reductions should be achieved wherever they were most cost-effective. However, this approach was not fully compatible with the dominant normative framework based on national responsibility and domestic emission reductions. For the United States to secure an agreement on international emissions trading and JI, it needed to alter the normative debate to accommodate the principle of economic efficiency and the use of market mechanisms to achieve environmental goals. The debate over national responsibility versus economic efficiency in the reduction of GHG emissions created the normative divide that propelled the negotiations leading up to Kyoto and through the Marrakech agreement to implement the Kyoto Protocol.

The emissions trading debate provides a good example of how this normative debate shaped both the international negotiations and domestic policies. Emissions trading fit well with American domestic norms. The Bush and later the Clinton administrations increasingly emphasized market-based strategies to achieve the most efficient solutions to regulatory problems. The Clinton administration argued that the American experience with its sulfur trading program demonstrated the potential to achieve cost-effective emission reductions through carbon trading. However, the American approach did not fit well with EU environmental policy norms. From the European perspective, emissions trading represented an American attempt to buy its way out of reducing domestic emissions. Dutch Environment

Minister, Margaretha De Boer, alluded to the difficulties that the United States faced in gaining acceptance for emissions trading. "[Emissions trading] might be fine for the U.S, but the cultures are different, and what will work for the U.S. will not necessarily work for Europe."[1]

The United States and its allies succeeded in utilizing their power positions within the Kyoto negotiations to coerce European acceptance of international emissions trading. Nonetheless, Germany and the European Union were not convinced of the legitimacy of the strategy for reducing emissions, and they worked aggressively to limit the ability of the United States and its allies to utilize international emissions trading to meet their Kyoto commitments. However, by 1998 the Commission and the member states had largely been persuaded that emission trading at a *national or European level* was a legitimate and desirable mechanism to reduce the costs of emission reductions. In spite of this, the international negotiations over emissions trading remained ensconced in the normative debates relating to the importance of domestic emission reductions through regulatory and taxation changes versus the use of international flexibility mechanisms.

The emissions trading debate demonstrates that the resonance of international norms with domestic norms is an important variable influencing the domestic salience of international norms. If an international norm does not resonate with domestic norms, it will be difficult for that norm to achieve domestic political salience and produce domestic policy changes. Political pressure from abroad or from within may force norm affirmation, but the pressure will have to be maintained to produce domestic political change. It is also possible that persuasion and learning could alter the domestic normative context to bring it into line with emerging international norms. The EU experience with emissions trading provides an example of this phenomenon. EU leaders gradually accepted that emissions trading provided a legitimate and desirable mechanism to efficiently achieve emission reductions. However, the prior norm-based opposition to trading made it extremely difficult to alter their position. The EU faced a situation of "norm entrapment" as discussed in chapter 1.[2] It took a revolutionary change such as the American repudiation of Kyoto to permit the EU to alter its position. The affirmation of the norm requiring all states to adopt a domestic emission reduction commitment and to achieve this commitment primarily through domestic policy changes as well as the condemnation of the extensive use of international emissions trading trapped the EU and prevented it from altering its negotiating position even though the preferences of member states had begun to shift. However, once the international emissions trading proposal was separated from American sponsorship, the European Union was in position to adopt the mechanism and pursue international negotiations to implement it under a mantle of legitimacy.

The public perception of the intentions of the sponsor was critical to the acceptability of emissions trading. Following the failure of The Hague negotiations, environmental NGOs, European green parties, and the European public did not perceive EU support of international emissions trading as the pursuit of narrow self-interest at the expense of the environment, but rather as a necessary compromise to bring Kyoto into force in the face of American opposition. If the United States had not rejected Kyoto, American sponsorship and the perception of American attempts to buy its way out of its commitments would have continued to taint the emissions trading debate. The EU did not face this perception and was thus free to undertake a leadership position in the development of the emissions trading mechanism. This case study points to the important interactions between the strategic pursuit of national interests and the limitations that international norms and normative debates can place on the pursuit of those interests.

CONCLUSIONS AND SUGGESTIONS FOR FURTHER RESEARCH

The case studies support the hypotheses identified in chapter 1. The interplay among international and domestic normative debates, the material interests of affected actors, and the relative power positions of major states structure the domestic policy processes of states and the international negotiating environment. The combination of ideational and material factors is critical to explain national and international responses to emerging international environmental problems. Scholars need to focus on the degree to which nascent international norms resonate with existing domestic political norms in important countries or at a minimum can be framed in a way that makes them compatible with existing domestic norms. In addition, it is essential to evaluate the domestic policy implications of international norms and their redistributive consequences and perceived effects on economic competitiveness. The material consequences of accepting a norm will affect its potential salience. Domestic actors that are perceived to oppose a norm based purely on narrow self-interest will find it difficult to stop the norm from achieving domestic political salience if the public broadly perceives it as legitimate. However, if these actors are able to frame the norm as inappropriate or unjust, then they may create obstacles to the norm achieving domestic salience. The American rejection of the exclusion of developing countries from emission reduction commitments appears to fit this model.

The case studies suggest that particular attention should be given to the initial normative framing of emergent environmental problems. The initial framing helps to establish the boundaries within which international negotiations and domestic policy debates will occur. The early framing of climate change had a significant impact on subsequent international negotiations and on domestic policy debates. As new environmental problems emerge there is typically uncertainty about the nature of the problem and possible solutions. The uncertainty creates opportunities for scientists to influence the initial framing and the normative context within which the problem will be addressed. The international scientific community operating within the World Meteorological Organization's World Climate Program (WCP) played a critical role in framing the threat of climate change for the public and for policy makers. WCP scientists presented climate change as a human induced phenomenon that had the potential for catastrophic environmental effects. They advocated a multilateral reduction in global GHG emissions to slow and eventually halt the process of climate change. The WCP scientists framed climate change as a problem that had to be stopped rather than merely adjusted to. This is important because it was possible to view climate change as providing potential benefits as well as costs. A clearer specification of the costs and benefits of climate change could have altered the debate, but the scientific community largely rejected adaptation as a primary response and thus placed it outside of the acceptable normative debate on how to respond to climate change.

Once a scientific consensus began to emerge on the threat posed by climate change, the United Nations Environment Program (UNEP) and the World Meteorological Organization (WMO) assumed primary responsibility for promoting climate change on the international diplomatic agenda. Governments had to respond to a consensus among scientists and associated IGOs that climate change was a serious problem that required coordinated multilateral action to resolve it. The question essentially moved from whether the international community should address the problem to how and when it should respond.

The international framing of the problem then had to be translated into a domestic context. The initial domestic framing of the problem in each of the countries established the parameters for the domestic political debate, which proved to be extremely resistant to change. The European Union, Germany, and the United Kingdom largely absorbed the international framing of the issue. The German Enquete Commission affirmed that climate change was a human-induced phenomenon that required multilateral emission reductions. In addition it asserted that the problem could be addressed at minimal cost with existing technologies. This framing of the issue made it more difficult for opponents of initiatives to reduce GHG emissions to argue that German economic competitiveness would be significantly harmed. It also created a positive environment for the translation of the emerging international climate norms into the domestic political debate. The British government and the major political parties also accepted the international framing, but there was a greater focus on the economic implications of efforts to reduce GHG emissions. There was an explicit recognition that emission reductions could be costly, and the government was more sensitive to the cost-benefit calculations of initiatives to reduce GHG emissions. The United Kingdom thus supported international efforts to address the problem, though it was reluctant to immediately accept emission reduction commitments.

The Reagan and Bush administrations rejected the international framing of the problem and instead argued that climate change was an uncertain, long-term threat that deserved greater scientific study. The lack of an entity equivalent to the Enquete Commission to definitively interpret the scientific evidence for the policy community meant that opponents of initiatives to reduce GHG emissions were able to stress the uncertainty of the science and offer competing scientific research to undermine support for policy changes. Opponents of action thus argued that reducing GHG emissions in the short-term was costly and unjustified given the uncertainty of the science. The initial American framing of the problem made it much more difficult for the emerging international norms to achieve domestic political salience. This was especially true because both of the major political parties broadly shared this framing of the issue.

The effects of the early international framing of the problem on the development of international norms and domestic policy responses to the problem suggests that scholars should further evaluate the effects of norm entrepreneurs and the translation of the international framing into the domestic political debate. The early framing of a problem should have significant effects on subsequent political debates and policy outcomes. The United States fought throughout the negotiations to alter the normative debate to focus on economic efficiency and market mechanisms to achieve emission reductions, but it was consistently blocked by the consensus that the only legitimate policy response was to achieve domestic emission reductions through regulatory and taxation changes. It was only in the period leading up to the Kyoto agreement that the United States secured acceptance of market mechanisms, and these only achieved broad recognition as legitimate strategies after the United States withdrew from Kyoto.

These case studies also suggest that norms can have an insidious effect on international policy. Supporters of international climate policy overwhelmingly focused on forcing states to adopt emission reduction commitments, which then became a major focus for media coverage. The normative requirement for states to accept a quantitative emission reduction commitment established a benchmark against which support for climate policy would be judged. Quantitative commitments offered a clear indicator of support for addressing climate change, and NGOs used them effectively to shame states that rejected such commitments. Over time, the vast majority of developed states accepted a commitment, though the sincerity of the commitments is questionable. The norm achieved a "Foreign Policy Impact" (the fifth level of norm salience). Many states affirmed the norm and supported its inclusion in international agreements but did not internalize it and failed to enact the domestic policy changes implied by the norm. For example, the Thatcher government opposed the norm and faced significant international and domestic pressure to affirm it. It eventually accepted it—though only when it became apparent that it was achievable with existing policies. The international power position of the United States and the lower domestic political salience of climate change provided American leaders with greater leeway to withstand international pressure and avoid what they regarded as an economically devastating international commitment. However, even the United States eventually acceded to international pressure and accepted the norm, but it did not have a significant effect on domestic policy. Essentially, it had a "Foreign Policy Impact" (level five) until the second Bush administration rejected the norm in 2001. The norm remained an important part of the domestic political dialogue on climate change, but it had a very limited effect on policy.

States may rhetorically affirm a norm. They may agree to the institutionalization of the norm in an international agreement. However, if state commitments do not reflect a consensus among political leaders and broad sections of the public that a norm is appropriate and just, compliance with the norm's domestic policy implications is unlikely—unless there are significant penalties for noncompliance. The commitment by developed countries to individually stabilize their GHG emissions at 1990 levels by 2000 provides a good example of a norm achieving international prominence without achieving widespread domestic salience. Many states affirmed the norm because rejecting it would produce domestic and international political costs. However, few states internalized the norm. They affirmed it rhetorically, but they did little to reduce their emissions. The overwhelming focus on establishing a norm requiring a commitment to quantitative emission reductions distracted attention from the problems associated with meeting those targets. This problem continues to bedevil international climate negotiations. The headline debates mask the complexity of implementation. Acceptance of a norm under political pressure does not ensure compliance unless there are sufficient incentives to induce compliance. In these cases, the norm has not achieved a "Domestic Policy Impact" (level six), and it is unlikely to alter domestic behavior in the short-term.

Kyoto's enforcement mechanism is weak, and it is fairly easy for states to plausibly justify missing emission reduction commitments on the grounds of rapid economic growth, cold winters, or the need to burn additional coal to replace more costly natural gas or oil rather than admitting a failure to pursue policies to reduce emissions. It is not clear that the acceptance of emission reduction commitments will provide a viable foundation to force emission reductions. Inducing widespread adoption of policies to reduce emissions may require a shift in the normative framework. The case studies suggest that aligning the economic interests of important actors with a normative framework that can compel emission reductions is critical to success. The EU's acceptance of emissions trading internally and connecting the EU markets to an international market may provide a firmer foundation for emission reductions. Alternatively, a focus on the adoption of common policies across developed states such as a global carbon tax could produce a similar outcome. The emission reduction commitment by itself does not appear to provide a sufficient foundation for meeting Kyoto's objectives.

It is the combination of ideational and material factors that is critical to explaining national and international responses to the problem of climate change. It would appear that this approach should provide a firmer foundation for explaining and predicting national responses to other international environmental issues as well as other issue areas where international norms contain requirements for domestic policy changes.

Notes

CHAPTER 1: CLIMATE POLICY AND THE DOMESTIC SALIENCE OF INTERNATIONAL NORMS

1. Jepperson, Wendt, and Katzenstein, "Norms, Identity, and Culture," 54.

2. See for aexample Cortell and Davis, "Understanding Domestic Impact of International Norms," 65–87; Klotz, "Norms Reconstituting Interests," 451–478; and Gurowitz, "Mobilizing International Norms," 413–445.

3. Jepperson, Wendt, and Katzenstein in "Norms, Identity, and Culture (54–55) argue in footnote 69 that "a distinction between collectively 'prominent' or institutionalized norms and commonly 'internalized' one, with various 'intersubjective' admixtures in between, is crucial for distinguishing between different types of norms and different types of normative effects."

4. Cortell and Davis, "Understanding Domestic Impact of International Norms" (68) develop the concept of norm "salience" to evaluate the forces "that promote an international norm's attaining the status of an 'ought' in the domestic political arena."

5. For a discussion of catalytic events, see Birkland, *After Disaster.*

6. Checkel, "International Norms and Domestic Politics," 473–474.

7. For a discussion of constitutive and regulative norms see Ruggie, "What Makes World Hang Together" 855–886; and Katzenstein, "Introduction: Alternative Perspectives," 1–32.

8. On norm emergence, see Kowert and Legro, "Norms, Identity, and Their Limits," 451–497.

9. Barnett, "Culture, Strategy and Foreign Policy," 15.

10. Finnemore and Sikkink. "International Norm Dynamics," 887–917; Checkel, "Norms, Institutions, and National Identity," 83–114; and Payne, "Persuasion, Frames," 37–61.

11. Finnemore and Sikkink, "International Norm Dynamics," 887–917.

12. Checkel, "International Norms and Domestic Politics," and Checkel, "Norms, Institutions, and National Identity," 83–114.

13. Checkel, "Norms, Institutions, and National Identity," 83–114.

14. Cortell and Davis, "Understanding Domestic Impact of International Norms," 65–87.

15. Checkel, "Norms, Institutions, and National Identity," 83–114.

16. Cortell and Davis, "Understanding Domestic Impact of International Norms," 73–75.

17. Risse, " 'Let's Argue!,' " (1–39) claims that argumentation and deliberation provide the mechanisms through which competing truth claims can be explored.

18. See for example: Cortell and Davis, "Understanding Domestic Impact of International Norms," 65–87; Ikenberry, "Creating Yesterday's New World Order," 57–86; and Ikenberry, "World Economy Restored," 289–322.

19. For a discussion of the strategies and influence of environmental NGOs, see Newell, *Climate for Change*; Princen and Finger, *Environmental NGOs in World Politics*; Gulbrandsen and Andresen, "NGO Influence," 54–75; and Betsill and Corell, "NGO Influence," 65–85.

20. Risse, " 'Let's Argue!,' " 22.

21. Schimmelfennig, "The Community Trap," 63.

22. Ibid.

23. Risse-Kappen: "Bringing Transnational Relations," 3–36, and "Ideas Do Not Float Freely,"185–214.

24. Intergovernmental Panel on Climate Change, *Climate Change 2001*, 8.

25. Ibid., 9.

26. See data from the UNFCCC website: http://ghg.unfccc.int/.

27. Legro, "Culture and Preferences," 118–137.

28. Boehmer-Christiansen and Skea, *Acid Politics*; and Spretnak and Fridtjof, *Green Politics*.

29. See, for example, Lundqvist, *The Hare and the Tortoise*; Boehmer-Christiansen and Skea, *Acid Politics*; Brickman, et. al., *Controlling Chemicals*; and Vogel, *National Styles of Regulation*.

30. On the precautionary principle in German policy, see Boehmer-Christiansen and Skea, *Acid Politics*.

CHAPTER 2: ISSUE FRAMING, NORM EMERGENCE, AND THE POLITICIZATION OF CLIMATE CHANGE

1. Rowlands, *Politics of Global Atmospheric*; and Kellogg, "Mankind's Impact," 170–192.

2. Bodansky, "United Nations Framework Convention," 460.

3. Hecht and Tirpak, "Framework Agreement," 380–381.

4. UN General Assembly, *Protection of Global Climate for Present and Future Generations of Mankind*, A/RES/43/53 (December 6, 1988).

5. "Delegates to UNEP Meeting Say Treaty on Global Change Should Be Top Priority," *International Environment Reporter* 12, no. 6 (June 14, 1989): 279.

6. Bodansky, "United Nations Framework Convention," 466.

7. Edward Cody, "Environment to Take Center Stage at Summit," *Washington Post*, July 13, 1989; http://www.lexis-nexis.com.

8. John Hunt, "Action Call on Global Warming," *Financial Times*, April 6, 1989.

9. "U.K. Representative to United Nations Proposes Global Convention to Council," *International Environment Reporter* 12, no. 6 (June 14, 1989): 281.

10. "Delegates to UNEP Meeting," 279.

11. "Recommendations Call for Transformation of Both Economic and Environmental Issues," *International Environment Reporter* 12, no. 9 (September 13, 1989): 428.

12. John Mason, "The Labour Party at Brighton," *Financial Times*, October 5, 1989.

13. "Patten Promises 'White Paper' on Agenda for Remainder of Century," *International Environment Reporter* 12, no. 11 (November 8, 1989): 538.

14. John Hunt "The Race for the Greener Ground," *Financial Times*, October 13, 1989.

15. Greg Neale and David Wastell, "Britain Fights Green Demands from EEC," *Sunday Telegraph* (London), November 5, 1989, http://www.lexis-nexis.com.

16. Laura Raun, "States to Back Global Warming Convention," *Financial Times*, November 11, 1989.

17. Rudy Abramson, "U.S. and Japan Block Firm Stand on Global Pollutants," *Los Angeles Times*, November 11, 1989; http://www.lexis-nexis.com.

18. Labour MP Elliot Morley quoted in "House of Commons Members Attack Stance of U.K. at Noordwijk Meeting," *International Environment Reporter* 12, no. 12 (December 13, 1989): 580.

19. Peter Riddell, "Thatcher Unveils New Strategy for Environment," *Financial Times*, November 8, 1989.

20. John Hunt, "Patten Proposes EC Limitations on Emissions of Carbon Dioxide," *Financial Times*, March 24, 1990.

21. Paul Brown and Nigel Williams, "UK: Thatcher's Global Warming Plan Criticised by Opposition MPs," *Guardian* (London), May 26, 1990; http://www.lexis-nexis.com.

22. John Hunt, "Opposition to EC on Environment," *Financial Times*, September 21, 1990.

23. "Presidency Puts CO_2 Tax, Emissions Stabilisation on Agenda," *EC Energy Monthly*, September 1, 1990; http://www.lexis-nexis.com.

24. Bodansky, "United Nations Framework Convention," 464.

25. Hecht and Tirpak, "Framework Agreement," 371–402.

26. Guy Darst, "Greenhouse Effect Will Bring More Droughts, Hot Weather, Scientists Say," Associated Press, June 24, 1988; www.lexis-nexis.com.

27. John C. Topping Jr., "Where Are We Headed in Responding to Climate Change?" *International Environment Reporter* 11, no. 10 (October 12, 1988): 555.

28. "Administration Seeks Cuts in EPA Funds; Boost for International Environmental Action," *International Environment Reporter* 11, no. 3 (March 9, 1988): 179.

29. House Subcommittee on Human Rights and International Organizations of the Committee on Foreign Affairs, *Global Climate Changes: Greenhouse Effect*, 100th Cong., 2d sess., March 10, 1988, 42.

30. "UNEP/WMO Panel from 30 Countries to Work Toward Global Warming Treaty," *International Environment Reporter* 11, no. 12 (December 14, 1988): 644.

31. Hecht and Tirpak, "Framework Agreement," 383.

32. Philip Shabecoff, "Joint Effort Urged to Guard Climate," *New York Times*, January 31, 1989.

33. Leslie H. Gelb, "Sununu vs. Scientists," *New York Times*, February 10, 1991.

34. EPA, *Policy Options for Stabilizing Global Climate*, Draft Report to Congress, March 1989.

35. Philip Shabecoff, "Scientist Says Budget Office Altered His Testimony," *New York Times*, May 9, 1989.

36. Philip Shabecoff, "U.S., in a Shift, Seeks Treaty on Global Warming," *New York Times*, May 12, 1989.

37. Philip Shabecoff, "E.P.A. Chief Says Bush Will not Rush into a Treaty on Global Warming," *New York Times*, May 13, 1989.

38. Shabecoff, "U.S. in a Shift."

39. Glenn Frankel, "U.S. Moves to Block Pact on Emissions; Group Seeks Ceiling for Carbon Dioxide," *Washington Post*, November 7, 1989; http://www.lexis-nexis.com.

40. Philip Shabecoff, "U.S. to Urge Joint Environmental Effort at Summit," *New York Times*, July 6, 1989.

41. Peter Riddell, "Bush Seeks to End Split on Global Warming Issue," *New York Times*, February 5, 1990.

42. Michael Weisskopf, "Bush Pledges Research on Global Warming," *Washington Post*, February 6, 1990; http://www.lexis-nexis.com.

43. Ibid.

44. Philip Shabecoff, "Bush Asks Cautious Response to Threat of Global Warming," *New York Times*, February 6, 1990.

45. Economic Report of the President, (February 1990), GPO, 214 and 223 cited in Rowlands, *Politics of Global Atmospheric.*

46. David Nicholson-Lord, "Global Warming Plan Creates Climate of Mistrust," *The Independent* (London), February 4, 1990; http://www.lexis-nexis.com

47. Terry Atlas, "Bush: Wait and See on Warming," *Chicago Tribune*, April 18, 1990; http://www.lexis-nexis.com.

48. Philip Shabecoff, "European Officials Dispute Bush over Global Warming," *New York Times*, April 18, 1990, section B.

49. Philip Shabecoff, "Bush Denies Putting Off Action on Averting Global Climate Shift," *The New York Times*, April 19, 1990, section B.

50. Ibid.

51. Philip Shabecoff, "Critics Say Draft Report on Climate Shift Ignores Urgency of Problem," *New York Times*, June 2, 1990.

52. Ibid.

53. "Nations' Goals on CO$_2$ Emissions Cuts Lack Specifics, U.S. Environment Chief Says," *International Environment Reporter* 13, no. 11 (October 10, 1990): 416.

54. "Agreements to Reduce Carbon Dioxide Based on Rhetoric, U.S. Official Says," *International Environment Reporter* 13, no. 16 (December 23, 1990): 540.

55. "U.S. Senator Accuses Bush Administration of Trying to 'Sabotage' Geneva Conference," *International Environment Reporter* 13, no. 12 (October 24, 1990): 433.

56. Jasanoff, *The Fifth Branch.*

57. Rest and Bleischwitz, "Policies and Legal Instruments," 159–177.

58. Ibid., 161.

59. Hatch, "Politics of Global Warming," 415–440.

60. Rudy Abramson, "U.S. and Japan Block Firm Stand on Global Pollutants," *Los Angeles Times*, November 8, 1989; http://www.lexis-nexis.com.

61. David Thomas, "West Germans Hopeful on Carbon Dioxide Emissions," *Financial Times*, February 14, 1990.

62. "Souberere Kraftwerke ohne Gewalt und Dennoch Wirkungsvoll," *Frankfurter Allgemeine Zeitung*, February 21, 1990; http://www.lexis-nexis.com.

63. Lionel Barber, "Bush Defends Wait-and-See Approach on Global Warming," *Financial Times*, March 18, 1990.

64. "Toepfer: Lack of Knowledge No Excuse for Inaction," *The Week in Germany*, March 20, 1990; http://www.lexis-nexis.com.

65. "Klimaschutzsteur gegen das Kohlendioxyd?" *Frankfurter Allgemeine Zeitung*, June 8, 1990; http://www.lexis-nexis.com.

66. Roberto Suro, "The Houston Summit; Europeans Accuse the U.S. of Balking on Plans to Combat Global Warming," *New York Times*, July 10, 1990.

67. David Nicholson-Lord, et. al., "Kohl Heads for Clash with US over Environment," *The Independent* (London), July 8, 1990; http://www.lexis-nexis.com.

68. Suro, "Houston Summit."

69. "EC Confrontation Expected on Carbon Dioxide Emissions," *Financial Times*, December 29, 1990.

70. Marcus Kabel, "Germany Claims World Leader Role with Anti-Greenhouse Plan," *Reuter Library Report*, November 7, 1990; http://www.lexis-nexis.com.

71. The Greens damaged their electoral chances by opposing German reunification. This had a larger effect on their electoral performance than their environmental positions.

CHAPTER 3: INTERNATIONAL NORMS AND THE POLITICS OF EMISSION REDUCTION COMMITMENTS

1. Michael Weisskopf, "Global Warming Conferees to Focus on Carbon Dioxide," *Washington Post*, February 15, 1991; http://www.lexis-nexis.com.

2. "Garbage," *ECO* (May 1, 1992): 2.

3. David Goodhart, "Energy Efficiency 2; Carbon Cloud Over Reunification—Germany," *Financial Times*, November 14, 1990, survey.

4. Hatch, "Politics of Global Warming," 421.

5. Ibid.

6. Leach, "Policies to Reduce Energy," 921.

7. "Nuclear Power Given Priority in New Energy Plan," *Europe Energy*, no. 366 (October 31, 1991); http://www.lexis-nexis.com.

8. Ibid.

9. David Young, "Energy Campaign Reaches Boiling Point," *The Times* (London), January 20, 1992; http://www.lexis-nexis.com.

10. International Energy Agency, *Energy Policies of IEA Countries: 1993 Review* (Paris: OECD, 1993), 255.

11. International Energy Agency website, http://www.IEA.org.

12. International Energy Agency, *Energy Policies of IEA Countries: 1990 Review* (Paris: OECD, 1990), 214.

13. "International Energy Agency Recommends Strategies for Improving National Policy," *International Environment Reporter* 14, no. 6 (March 27, 1991): 168.

14. "Fiscal Instruments for CO_2 Reduction Should be Last Resort," *EC Energy Monthly*, May 8, 1992; http://www.lexis-nexis.com.

15. BMU report quoted in Hatch, "Politics of Global Warming," 431.

16. Jochem, "Reducing CO_2 Emissions," 369.

17. Collier, "Global Warming and the Internal Energy Market," 917.

18. CEC, *A Community Strategy to Limit Carbon Dioxide Emissions and Improve Energy Efficiency: Communication from the Commission*, COM(92) 246 Final, 1992.

19. "Commission Recommends CO_2 and Energy Consumption Tax," *European Report*, no. 1707 (September 28, 1991); http://www.lexis-nexis.com.

20. "CO_2 Tax: Scrivener Leads Cautious First Reactions," *Europe Environment*, no. 373 (October 15, 1991); http://www.lexis-nexis.com.

21. David Gardner and John Hunt, "Brussels Calls for EC Tax on Energy," *Financial Times*, September 26, 1991.

22. "Commission Asked to Make Formal Proposal on Energy Tax to Address Climate Change," *International Environment Reporter* 14, no. 25 (December 18, 1991): 670.

23. "ECC Delays Actions Concerning Carbon Tax to Address Climate Change Issues," *International Environment Reporter* 15, no. 9 (May 6, 1992): 255

24. Ibid.

25. "Environment Council: Ministers Put up a Poor Show," *Europe Environment*, no. 388 (June 2, 1992); http://www.lexis-nexis.com.

26. "Rip di Meana to Boycott Summit, Cites EC Inaction on Energy Tax," *EuroWatch* 4, no. 5 (May 9, 1992); http://www.lexis-nexis.com.

27. National Academy of Sciences, *Policy Implications of Greenhouse Warming* (Washington, DC: National Academy Press, 1991).

28. "Strict Energy-Saving Urged To Combat Global Warming," *Washington Post*, April 11, 1991; http://www.lexis-nexis.com.

29. William K. Stevens, "New Studies Predict Profits in Heading Off Warming," *New York Times*, March 17, 1992, section C.

30. Ibid.

31. Repetto, *The Costs of Climate Protection*.

32. "America at the Crossroads: A National Energy Strategy Poll," *ECO* (February 19, 1991).

33. "Special Report on Industry Disinformation," *ECO* (June 25, 1991).

34. Thomas W. Lippman, "Energy Legislation Proliferates on Hill," *Washington Post*, February 8, 1991; http://www.lexis-nexis.com.

35. Thomas W. Lippman, "Bush Unveils Energy Strategy Emphasizing Fossil, Nuclear Power Production," *Washington Post*, February 21, 1991; http://www.lexis-nexis.com.

36. William Stevens, "Hopeful E.P.A. Report Fans a Debate as Talks on Warming Near," *New York Times*, January 13, 1991.

37. "Climate Change Strategy: US Says No with a Smile," *ECO* (February 6, 1991): 1.

38. Intergovernmental Negotiating Committee for a Framework Convention on Climate Change, *Set of Informal Papers Provided by Delegations*, A/AC.237/Misc/Add.1, 94 (May 22, 1991), 94.

39. Tom Kenworthy and Ann Devroy, "Memo Shows Emission Cuts By U.S. Are Within Reach," *Washington Post*, April 25, 1992; http://www.lexis-nexis.com.

40. Michael Weisskopf, "Bush to Attend Rio 'Earth Summit' in June," *New York Times*, May 13, 1992.

41. Leach, "Policies to Reduce Energy," 921.

42. Ibid.

43. Nicholas Schoon and Stephen Castle, "Petrol Tax Rise Urged by Business Leaders," *The Independent* (London), November 3, 1991; http://www.lexis-nexis.com.

44. Nicholas Schoon, "Heseltine Brings Global Warming Closer to Home," *The Independent* (London), November 5, 1991; http://www.lexis-nexis.com.

45. British Climate Change Impacts Review Group, *The Potential Effects of Climate Change in the United Kingdom* (London: HMSO, 1991).

46. Nicholas Schoon, "Pollution is Blamed for Warmest Year on Record," *The Independent* (London), January 11, 1991; http://www.lexis-nexis.com.

47. Robinson, "Electricity Privatization," 22–26.

48. Martin Jacques, "The Humbling of Heseltine," *Sunday Times* (London), December 27, 1992; http://www.lexis-nexis.com.

49. International Energy Agency, *Energy Policies of IEA Countries: 1992 Review* (Paris: OECD, 1992), 41.

50. Ibid., 443.

51. Nicholas Schoon, "Cabinet Row Brews over 'Greenhouse' Gas Cuts," *The Independent* (London), December 7, 1991; http://www.lexis-nexis.com.

52. David Young, "Energy Campaign Reaches Boiling Point," *The Times* (London), January 20, 1992; http://www.lexis-nexis.com.

53. Nicholas Schoon, "Ministers Fail to Agree Target for 'Greenhouse Gas,'" *The Independent* (London), March 14, 1992; http://www.lexis-nexis.com.

54. Ibid.

55. Paul Brown, "Britain Fails to Heed EC Deadline on Emissions," *The Guardian* (London), April 1, 1992; http://www.lexis-nexis.com.

56. "U.K. Government Says It Will Stabilize CO_2 Emissions by 2000 if Others Follow," *International Environment Reporter* 15, no. 9 (May 6, 1992): 259.

CHAPTER 4: THE DOMESTIC POLITICAL SALIENCE OF INTERNATIONAL NORMS?

1. Michael Weisskopf, "Rival Running Mates Clash on Shades of Green," *Washington Post*, August 8, 1992.

2. "The US (Re) Action Plan," *ECO INC6*, no. 1 (December 7, 1992).

3. Jeremy Gaunt, "Clinton Plans Review of Global Warming Policy," *Reuter European Union Report*, March 16, 1993; http://www.lexis-nexis.com. Italics added.

4. Keith Schneider, "Gore Meets Resistance in Effort for Steps on Global Warming," *The New York Times*, April 19, 1993.

5. Ruth Marcus, "U.S. to Sign Earth Pact; Clinton Also Backs Emissions Targets," *Washington Post*, April 22, 1993; http://www.lexis-nexis.com.

6. "EPA Draft Emissions Tally for 1990 Said Lacking Some Greenhouse Gas Sources," *International Environment Reporter* 16, no. 17 (August 19, 1993): 621.

7. "Three Advisers to Next President Back Gasoline, Carbon Taxes in Report," *International Environment Reporter* 15, no. 25 (December 16, 1992): 824.

8. Dan Balz and Ann Devroy, "Clinton Navigates Politics, Deficit to Craft Plan," *Washington Post*, February 21, 1993; http://www.lexis-nexis.com.

9. Thomas Lippman, "Energy Tax Proposal Has 'Green' Tint," *Washington Post*, March 2, 1993; http://www.lexis-nexis.com.

10. Agis Salpukas, "Going for the Kill on the Energy Tax Plan," *New York Times*, June 5, 1993.

11. Eric Pianin and David S. Hilzenrath, "Hill Agrees to Raise Gas Tax 4.3 Cents," *Washington Post*, July 30, 1993; http://www.lexis-nexis.com.

12. "U.S. Action Plan to Cut Emissions Relies Mainly on Voluntary Industry Actions," *International Environment Reporter* 16, no. 22 (October 19, 1993): 797.

13. Ibid.

14. Jaya Dayal, "U.S. Ready to Lead Fight Against Climate Change," *Inter Press Service*, March 15, 1993; http://www.lexis-nexis.com.

15. Nicholas Schoon, "Tough Policies Needed to Keep Emissions Pledge," *The Independent* (London), October 10, 1992; http://www.lexis-nexis.com.

16. Ibid.

17. Tom Wilkie and Nicholas Schoon, "Britain Lags behind in Action on Global Warming," *The Independent* (London), December 15, 1992; http://www.lexis-nexis.com.

18. Bronwen Maddox and David Gardner, "Paler Shade of Green: The UK Budget Adds Obstacles to an EU Carbon Tax," *Financial Times*, March 18, 1993.

19. Bronwen Maddox, "Off on the Wrong Foot," *Financial Times*, February 16, 1994.

20. OFGAS is responsible for regulating the natural gas industry. The director general is appointed by the government but serves a five year term independent of political control.

21. Bronwen Maddox, "Business and the Environment: Off on the Wrong Foot," *Financial Times*, February 16, 1994.

22. Nicholas Schoon, "Families Urged to Cut Use of Energy in the Home," *The Independent* (London), October 13, 1992; http://www.lexis-nexis.com.

23. Nick Nuttall and Tim Jones, "Commission Offers 'Greenprint' to end Tyranny of the Car," *The Times* (London), October 27, 1994; http://www.lexis-nexis.com.

24. Nick Nuttall, "Gummer Seeks to Make Life Difficult for the Motorist," *The Times* (London), March 16, 1994; http://www.lexis-nexis.com.

25. "Germany Unlikely to Meet Goal of Cutting CO_2 by 2005, Researcher Says," *International Environment Reporter* 15, no. 21 (October 21, 1992): 682.

26. "CO_2 Emissions Reduction Said Slowed by Bickering, Economy, Lack of New Policies," *International Environment Reporter* 16, no. 2 (February 2, 1993): 64.

27. Guenter Heismann, "Die grosse Illusion," *Die Woche*, August 4, 1994; http://www.lexis-nexis.com.

28. "Re-Elected Christian Democratic Government Agrees to Pursue 'New Ecological Direction," *International Environment Reporter*, 17, no. 23 (November 17, 1994): 931.

29. Petra Kaminsky, "Germans Argue over Using Coal vs Nuclear Power," *Deutsche Presse-Agentur*, February 1, 1995; http://www.lexis-nexis.com.

30. "Environment Council: Tangible Progress on Reduction of CO_2 Emissions," *Europe Environment*, no. 407 (March 30, 1993); http://www.lexis-nexis.com.

31. David Gardner, "Germany Leads Push for EC Energy Tax," *Financial Times*, March 23, 1993.

32. "Commission to Produce Study on Burden-Sharing of CO_2 Reduction," *International Environment Reporter* 16, no. 13 (June 30, 1993): 465.

33. "Energy Ministers' Action on Energy Programs Cited as Major Step in Reaching CO_2 Goal," *International Environment Reporter* 16, no. 14 (July 7, 1993): 501.

34. "Environment Ministers Claim Progress on Union-Wide Carbon Dioxide/ Energy Tax," *International Environment Reporter* 17, no. 7 (April 7, 1994): 299.

35. "Ministers Agree on Cuts in Substances Harming Ozone Layer, Fail to Move on CO_2 Tax," *International Environment Reporter* 17, no. 12 (June 15, 1994): 499.

36. "Environment Ministers Claim Progress."

37. UN, *United Nations Framework Convention on Climate Change* (New York: UN Press, 1992), 9.

38. Ibid, 13.

39. German proposal quoted in "Germany Tests the Water," *ECO INC10*, no. 2 (August 24, 1994).

40. "JI: Countries Miss the Boat at Southampton," *ECO INC9*, no. 2 (February 9, 1994).

41. William Stevens, "Nations to Consider Toughening Curbs on Global Warming," *New York Times*, February 21, 1995.

42. Ibid.

43. Haig Simonian, "UN Conference on Climate Change: Determined to Force the Pace," *Financial Times*, March 28, 1995.

44. "EC Mandate Trashed?" *ECO COP 1*, no. 3 (March 30, 1995).

45. "Don't Trade Tech. Transfer for JI," *ECO COP 1*, no. 4 (March 31, 1995).

46. UNFCCC, *Report of the Conference of the Parties on Its First Session*, FCCC/CP/1995/7/Add.1 (June 6, 1995), 5.

47. Kevin Liffey, "U.N. Climate Deal Clinched, But What Does It Mean?" *Reuter European Union Report*, April 7, 1995; http://www.lexis-nexis.com.

48. Ibid.

49. UNFCCC, *Report of the Conference of the Parties on Its First Session*, FCCC/CP/1995/7/Add.1 (June 6, 1995), 4.

CHAPTER 5: DOMESTIC CONFLICT AND INTERNATIONAL NORMATIVE DEBATES

1. "Wirth Questions about U.S. Commitments to Cut Greenhouse Gas Emissions after 2000," *International Environment Reporter* 18, no. 11 (May 31, 1995): 407.

2. Paul Lewis, "U.S. Industries Oppose Emission Proposals," *New York Times*, August 22, 1995.

3. Dan Morgan, "Strengthened U.S. Commitment Lights a Fire Under Global Warming Debate," *Washington Post*, September 13, 1996; http://www.lexis-nexis.com.

4. Ibid.

5. "Administration Working to Prevent Overestimates of Emission Control Costs," *International Environment Reporter* 19, no. 22 (October 30, 1996).

6. Annex I refers to developed countries bound by the FCCC commitments. UNFCCC, *Report of the Conference of the Parties on Its First Session*, FCCC/CP/1995/7/Add.1 (June 6, 1995), 4.

7. "Gore Pledges Support for Talks on Warming; Calls for Flexible Targets," *International Environment Reporter* 20, no. 7 (April 2, 1997).

8. Ibid.

9. Kathleen McGinty, Chair of the Council on Environmental Quality, quoted in Leyla Boulton, "Clinton Aide Sees Big Threat in Climate Change," *Financial Times*, March 27, 1997.

10. "Success of Voluntary Emission Curbs Said to Fortify U.S. Stance in Negotiations," *International Environment Reporter* 20, no. 7 (April 2, 1997).

11. "World Wildlife Fund Study Released," *Reuters*, September 29, 1997; http://www.lexis-nexis.com.

12. "President's Science Advisor Says Time Key Element in U.S. Stance at Negotiations," *International Environment Reporter* 20, no. 16 (August 6, 1997).

13. Joby Warrick, "Clinton Outlines Global Warming Education Plan," *Washington Post*, July 25, 1997; http://www.lexis-nexis.com.

14. Ibid.

15. Ibid.

16. *Expressing the Sense of the Senate Regarding the United Nationsl Framework Convention on Climate Change*, S. Res. 98, 105th Cong., 1st sess., *Congressional Record* 143 (June 12, 1997): S 5623.

17. Helen Dewar, "Senate Advises Against Emissions Treaty that Lets Developing Nations Pollute," *Washington Post*, July 26, 1997; http://www.lexis-nexis.com.

18. Ibid.

19. Howard Kurtz, "CNN Stops Airing Ad Campaign," *Washington Post*, October 3, 1997; http://www.lexis-nexis.com.

20. Vicki Allen, "Technology Could Offset Climate Treaty Costs," *Reuters*, July 25, 1997; http://www.lexis-nexis.com.

21. "World Wildlife Fund Study Released," *Reuters*, September 29, 1997; http://www.lexis-nexis.com.

22. Repetto, *Costs of Climate Protection*.

23. "Kyoto Apt to Produce Framework, Call for Further Talks, U.S. Official Says," *International Environment Reporter* 20, no. 21 (October 15, 1997).

24. "No U.S. Support for Deep Emission Cuts in Short Time, Clinton Tells Conference," *International Environment Reporter* 20, no. 21 (October 15, 1997).

25. Joby Warrick, "Clinton Urges Action on Emissions," *Washington Post*, October 7, 1997; http://www.lexis-nexis.com.

26. "EU Scheme Fuzzy, Japan Plan Specific, Top U.S. Official Tells Senate Subcommittee," *International Environment Reporter* 20, no. 21 (October 15, 1997).

27. Joby Warrick and Peter Baker, "Clinton Details Global Warming Plan," *Washington Post*, October 23, 1997; http://www.lexis-nexis.com.

28. Mark Felsenthal, et al., "Clinton Proposes Stabilizing at 1990 Levels by 2012, Require Developing Countries' Role," *International Environment Reporter* 20, no. 22 (October 29, 1997).

29. Nicholas Timmins, "US Lifts Carbon Gas Emission Forecast," *Financial Times*, November 13, 1997.

30. Peter Baker and Joby Warrick, "Gore to Go to Climate Conference; Visit Is Meant to Show Commitment to Issue," *Washington Post*, December 2, 1997; http://www.lexis-nexis.com.

31. "Voluntary Accords Seen as Way to Protect Environment While Remaining Competitive," *International Environment Reporter* 18, no. 16 (July 28, 1995).

32. "UK Chemical Industry Pact on Energy Advances," *ENDS Daily*, June 26, 1997; http://www.environmentdaily.com.

33. "UK Chemical Firms Sign Energy Efficiency Deal," *ENDS Daily*, November 19, 1997; http://www.environmentdaily.com.

34. "Richard Page Turns up the Heat for Renewable Electricity," M2 *Presswire*, February 7, 1997; http://www.lexis-nexis.com.

35. "List of Successful Renewable Electricity Bidders Published," M2 *Presswire*, March 11, 1997; http://www.lexis-nexis.com.

36. Leyla Boulton, "Big Cuts in Greenhouse Gas Emissions Wins Support," *Financial Times*, November 11, 1997.

37. "Greater Use of Renewable Energy Sources to Be Part of U.K. Climate Change Strategy," *International Environment Reporter* 20, no. 24 (November 26, 1997).

38. Leyla Boulton and Liam Halligan, "Ministers Prepare Climate Change Strategy," *Financial Times*, November 13, 1997.

39. *First Report of the Government of the Federal Republic of Germany Pursuant to the United Nations Framework Convention on Climate Change*, (September 1994); http://unfccc.int/resource/docs/natc/gernc1.pdf, 214–260.

40. Leyla Boulton, "A Trailblazer Fizzles Out," *Financial Times*, December 4, 1996.

41. "Government Study Says Pledge to Reduce CO_2 Emissions Will Cost 270,000 Jobs," *International Environment Reporter* 19, no. 25 (December 11, 1996).

42. "Official Coalition Government Urges Nations to Join Germany in CO_2 Cuts," *International Environment Reporter* 20, no. 20 (October 1, 1997).

43. "Draconian Measures on Ozone, Benzene, CO_2 and Waste," *Europe Environment*, no. 456 (June 13, 1995); http://www.lexis-nexis.com.

44. "Greens Propose Energy Tax, Income Tax Reform and Cuts in Working Hours as Antidotes to Economic Doldrums," *The Week in Germany*, March 8, 1996; http://www.lexis-nexis.com.

45. "Plans to Cut Coal Subsidy Prompt Massive Protest," *The Week in Germany*, March 14, 1997; http://www.lexis-nexis.com.

46. Ralph Atkins, "Hacking out a Future for Germany's Coal Industry," *Financial Times*, February 13, 1997.

47. "Kohl Cancels Coal Subsidy Talks amid Massive Bonn Miner Protest," *Deutsche Press-Agentur,* March 11, 1997; http://www.lexis-nexis.com.

48. International Energy Agency, *Energy Policies of IEA Countries: Germany 1998 Review* (Paris: OECD, 1998), 24.

49. "Bonn Minister Defends Nuclear Power, Stresses European Safety," *Deutsche Press-Agentur,* April 26, 1995; http://www.lexis-nexis.com.

50. IEA, *Germany 1998 Review,* 123.

51. "Industry Cut CO_2 Emissions by 42 Million Tons between 1990–1996, Research Group Study Says," *International Environment Reporter* 20, no. 24 (November 26, 1997).

52. Stephan Singer and Delia Villagrasa, "EC—Where's the Beef?" *ECO* 92, no. 2 (March 5, 1996): 3.

53. "Commission Report Finds Current Policies on CO_2 Emissions 'Clearly Insufficient,'" *International Environment Reporter* 19, no. 7 (April 3, 1996).

54. "Dutch Presidency Proposes 10 Percent Cut in Greenhouse Gases by 2005 over 1990 Level," *International Environment Reporter* 20, no. 3 (February 5, 1997).

55. "Commission Hopeful Climate Change Accord Will Help Boost Effort for CO_2/Energy Taxes," *International Environment Reporter* 20, no. 5 (March 5, 1997).

56. "EU Climate Target 'Credible and Achievable,'" *ENDS Daily,* September 1, 1997; http://www.environmentdaily.com.

57. "Commission in Volte Face on Climate Target," *ENDS Daily,* October 2, 1997; http://www.environmentdaily.com.

58. Joe Kirwin, "EU's Claim to Meet Stabilization Goal for Greenhouse Gases Met with Skepticism," *International Environment Reporter* 20, no. 21 (October 15, 1997).

59. "Two Energy-Saving Measures Clear Assembly amid Concern about Climate Change Pledges," *International Environment Reporter* 19, no. 24 (November 27, 1996).

60. "Energy Efficiency: Parliament Votes to Strengthen Standards in Refrigeration," *Europe Environment,* no. 464 (October 31, 1995); http://www.lexis-nexis.com.

61. "European Commision: Energy Efficiency Requirements for Electric Fridges," *Europe Energy,* no. 442 (March 8, 1995); http://www.lexis-nexis.com.

62. "Proposal on Energy Efficiency Rules for Refrigerators Clears Second Reading," *International Environment Reporter* 19, no.13 (June 26, 1997).

63. "EU Climate Talks Yield Little Progress," *ENDS Daily,* May 28, 1997; http://www.environmentdaily.com.

64. "Finance Ministers Reject Latest Proposals on Carbon Tax to Curb Greenhouse Emissions," *International Environment Reporter* 18, no. 22 (November 1, 1995).

65. "Commission Calls for Minimum Level Taxes on Oil, Coal, Natural Gas, Electricity," *International Environment Reporter* 20, no. 6 (March 19, 1997).

66. "EU Energy Tax Suffers Swift Rebuke," *ENDS Daily*, March 17, 1997; http://www.environmentdaily.com.

67. "EU Energy Tax 'Would Have Triple Dividend,'" *ENDS Daily*, October 13, 1997; http://www.environmentdaily.com.

68. "Bjerregaard Said to Oppose Enlargement as Way for EU to Meet Climate Change Goals," *International Environment Reporter* 20, no. 15 (July 23, 1997).

69. Ibid.

70. "Joint Implementation Scheme Said Necessary if CEECs Are to Join in EU Commitment at COP–3," *International Environment Reporter* 20, no. 19 (September 17, 1997).

71. Frances Williams, "US Seeks Target for Reducing Greenhouse Gases," *Financial Times*, July 18, 1996.

72. "U.S. Statement Breaks Logjam in Talks on Speeding Up Phaseout of Gas Emissions," *International Environment Reporter* 19, no. 15 (July 24, 1996).

73. UNFCCC, "Report of the Conference of the Parties on Its Second Session, Held At Geneva from 8 to 19 July 1996," FCCC/CP/1996/15/Add.1 (October 29, 1996), 73.

74. Daniel Lashof, "US 'Non-Paper' Falls Short," *ECO* 94, no. 1 (December 9, 1996): 1.

75. "Conference Reports," *ECO* 94, no. 3 (December 13, 1996): 5.

76. "Report of the Sixth Session of the Ad Hoc Group on the Berlin Mandate," *Earth Negotiations Bulletin* 12, no. 45 (March 10, 1997): 9.

77. "Report of the Meetings of the Subsidiary Bodies to the Framework Convention on Climate Change," *Earth Negotiations Bulletin* 12, no. 55 (August 11, 1997): 12.

78. "Japanese Climate Plan Undermines EU Targets," *ENDS Daily*, October 6, 1997; http://www.environmentdaily.com.

79. "European Commission Calls U.S. Proposal 'Inadequate,' Step Back from Commitment," *International Environment Reporter* 20, no. 22 (October 29, 1997).

80. "USA Scuppers EU Plan for Climate Talks . . . " *ENDS Daily*, October 23, 1997; http://www.environmentdaily.com.

81. The gases were byproducts of aluminum smelting, used in semiconductor manufacturing, and used as CFC substitutes. Their global warming potential was up

to twenty thousand times that of CO_2. Reductions in these gases could thus offset significant amounts of other GHG emissions.

82. Author's calculation based on data from Bureau of Oceans and International Environmental Scientific Affairs, "Climate Action Report: 1997 Submission of the United States of America Under the United Nations Framework Convention on Climate Change," Department of State Publication 10496 (July 1997), table 3.2: 56.

CHAPTER 6: RHETORIC AND REALITY: THE UNITED STATES VS. THE WORLD?

1. The EU was responsible for 24.2 percent of developed country emissions, Japan 8.5 percent, and Russia 17.4 percent for a total of 50.1 percent of the necessary 55 percent. The United States was responsible for 36.1 percent, which left countries representing 13.8 percent of the emissions to provide the final 5 percent.

2. "Testimony of Janet Yellen Chair, Council of Economic Advisers before the House Commerce Committee on the Economics of the Kyoto Protocol," March 4, 1998; http://clinton3.nara.gov/WH/EOP/CEA/html/19980304.html.

3. "White House Analysis Calls Cost of Kyoto Protocol Reductions Modest," *International Environmental Reporter* 21, no. 16 (August 5, 1998*).

4. "Table 4.1: Environmental/Natural Resources High Priority Programs," *Budget of the United States Government: Fiscal Year 1999* (Washington, DC: GPO, 1998), 81.

5. GAO, "Global Warming: Administration's Proposal in Support of the Kyoto Protocol," (June 4, 1998), T-RCED–98–219.

6. William Branigin, et. al., "Give-and-Take in the Bowels of the Budget," *Washington Post*, October 16, 1998; http://www.lexis-nexis.com.

7. "Table S–6: Effect of Proposals on Receipts," *Budget of the United States Government: Fiscal Year 2001* (Washington, DC: GPO, 2000), 372.

8. "Browner Questioned on Fate of Superfund, Plans by Agency to Implement Kyoto Pact," *Environment Reporter* 28, no. 44 (March 13, 1998).

9. John H. Cushman, Jr., "House Spending Bill Dictates Delay in Action on Climate Treaty," *New York Times*, June 26, 1998.

10. Cheryl Hogue, "Gore Knocks Congress on Provision to Block Discussion of Global Warming," *Environment Reporter* 29, no. 12 (July 17, 1998).

11. Ibid.

12. *Departments of Veterans Affairs and Housing and Urban Development, and Independent Agencies Appropriations Act of 1999*, Public Law 105–276, *U.S. Statutes at Large* (1998): 2496.

13. Vicki Allen, "White House at Odds over Electricity Plan," *Reuters*, March 15, 1998; http://www.lexis-nexis.com.

14. Ibid.

15. There were a number of similar corporate-NGO climate initiatives. The World Resources Institute established the "Safe Climate, Sound Business" project to identify ways to utilize energy more efficiently and promote renewable energy. The WWF and the Center for Energy and Climate Solutions created the "Climate Savers" to help businesses reduce energy consumption and adopt voluntary emission reduction targets.

16. John Cushman, "Industrial Group Plans to Battle Climate Treaty," *New York Times*, April 26, 1998.

17. John Cushman, "Industries Press Plan for Credits in Emissions Pact," *New York Times*, January 1, 1999.

18. This assumes a price of $23 per ton of carbon equivalent, which was a part of the administration's estimates on the cost of climate policy.

19. Energy Information Agency, Department of Energy, "table ES1. Reporting Indicators for the Voluntary Reporting of Greenhouse Gases Program, Data Years 1994–1999"; http://www.eia.doe.gov/oiaf/1605/vrrpt/tbles1.html.

20. GAO, *Review of DOE's Voluntary Reporting Program for Greenhouse Gas Emissions Reductions*, RCED–98–107R (March 24, 1998).

21. Resources for the Future, "DOE Announces Appliance Energy Efficiency Agreement," May 25, 2000; www.weathervane.rff.org/archives/News&Notes/archive_may00.html.

22. Pamela Najor, "Northeast States, Industrial Sources Seek Early Action Credits for Emission Cuts," *Environment Reporter* 30, no. 32 (December 17, 1999), 1491.

23. Andrew Revkin, "7 Companies Agree to Cut Gas Emissions," *New York Times*, October 18, 2000.

24. "Republican Platform 2000: Renewing America's Purpose. Together," C-Span, August 2000; http://www.c-span.org/campaign2000/gopplatform.asp.

25. "The 2000 Democratic National Platform: Prosperity, Progress, and Peace," Democratic Convention, August 2000; http://www.dems2000.com/AboutThe Convention/03_partyplat.html.

26. "Joint Declaration with President Eduardo Frei of Chile, April 16, 1998," *Weekly Compilation of Presidential Documents* (Washington, DC: GPO, 1998), 655.

27. "Clinton Urges China to Launch Effort to Limit Greenhouse Gas Emissions," *International Environmental Report* 21, no. 14 (July 8, 1998).

28. "India, U.S. Sign Accord to Team up on Alternative Energy, Clean Coal Technology," *International Environmental Report* 22, no. 23 (November 10, 1999).

29. "Eizenstat Says U.S. to Retain Option of Umbrella Group for Emission Trading," *Environment Reporter* 29, no. 20 (September 18, 1998).

30. "U.S. Says Doing All It Can to Fight Global Warming," *Reuters*, May 22, 2000; http://www.lexis-nexis.com.

31. "Consultation on Climate Change Leaves Holes in Jigsaw," *ENDS Report*, no. 285 (October 1998); http://www.endsreport.com.

32. Department of the Environment, Transport, and the Regions, *Climate Change: The UK Programme* (London: Her Majesty's Stationary Office, 2000), 124–125.

33. "Energy Policy in the Melting Pot as Agency Clamps Down on Emissions," *ENDS Report*, no. 276 (January 1998); http://www.endsreport.com.

34. "Environment Takes a Back Seat in Government's Energy Review," *ENDS Report*, no. 281 (June 1998).

35. "Renewables Win Major Boost under Largest ever NFFO Order," *ENDS Report*, no. 284 (September 1998); http://www.endsreport.com.

36. "Whitehall Sets First Targets for Buying 'Green Electricity,' " *ENDS Report*, no. 292 (May 1999); http://www.endsreport.com.

37. Ibid.

38. "Battle Backs Offshore Wind as Row Brews on 10% Renewables Target," *ENDS Report*, no. 284 (September 1998); http://www.endsreport.com.

39. "Electricity Trading Reforms Bad for Environment, DTI Admits," *ENDS Report*, no. 297 (October 1999); http://www.endsreport.com.

40. Stewart Boyle, "Wind Taken Out of Renewables' Sails," *Financial Times*, March 21, 2000.

41. "Concessions on Fuel Duty and Climate Levy Spell Trouble on CO_2," *ENDS Report*, no. 298 (November 1999); http://www.endsreport.com.

42. Ibid.

43. Leyla Bolton, "Companies May Face Green Tax on Energy Use," *Financial Times*, March 18, 1998.

44. "Talks on Energy Efficiency Deals with Major Users," *ENDS Report*, no. 291 (April 1999); http://www.endsreport.com.

45. George Parker, "Big Energy Users Warn Prescott on Impact of New Fuel Tax," *Financial Times*, March 30, 1999.

46. "Concessions on Fuel Duty and Climate Levy Spell Trouble on CO_2," *ENDS Report*, no. 298 (November 1999); http://www.endsreport.com.

47. "Climate Levy Talks Race against the Clock," *ENDS Report*, no. 300 (January 2000); http://www.endsreport.com.

48. Dan Bilefsky, et. al., "Green Image May Wash off in Stream of Compromises," *Financial Times*, March 15, 2000.

49. Peter Norman, "SPD Anger as Greens Split over Nato," *Financial Times*, March 27, 1998.

50. Ibid.

51. Ralph Atkins, "SPD and Greens Reach Deal on Tax Reform," *Financial Times*, October 9, 1998.

52. Ralph Atkins, "Schroder Faces Split with Greens," *Financial Times*, November 9, 1998.

53. Ralph Atkins, "Nuclear Dispute Deepens in Germany," *Financial Times*, July 6, 1999.

54. Ralph Atkins, "German Greens See Red over Nuclear Power Deal," *Financial Times*, June 16, 2000.

55. Verena Schmitt-Roschmann, "Government to Introduce New System to Push Renewable Energy Sources," *International Environmental Reporter* 23, no. 6 (March 15, 2000).

56. "Partial Liberalisation 'A Disaster' for CHP," *Energy Newsletters—Power in Europe*, June 9, 2000; http://www.lexisnexis.com.

57. "Rift over German Cogeneration Policy Deepens," *ENDS Environment Daily*, February 13, 2001; http://www.environmentdaily.com.

58. Ibid.

59. Verena Schmitt-Roschmann, "Country Considering Speed Limit, Levy on Air Traffic in Climate Change Strategy," *International Environmental Reporter* 23, no. 9 (April 26, 2000): 355.

60. Ibid.

61. Federal Ministry for the Environment, Nature Conservation, and Nuclear Safety, *Umweltbewusstsein in Deutschland 2000: Ergebnisse einer reprasentiven Bevolkerungsumfrage* (Berlin: n.p., 2000), 37.

62. Federal Ministry for the Environment, Nature Conservation, and Nuclear Safety, *Germany's National Climate Protection Programme: Summary* (Berlin, n.p.: 2000), 12–13.

63. Federal Ministry for the Environment, Nature Conservation, and Nuclear Safety, "Agreement on Climate Protection between the Government of the Federal Republic of Germany and German Business," November 11, 2000; www.bmu.de/english/topics/climateprotection/agreement.php.

64. "Carbon Dioxide Emissions in Germany Increase," Resources for the Future, February 7, 2001; http://www.weathervane.rff.org/archives/News&Notes/archive_feb01.html.

65. "Special Report," *International Environmental Reporter* 21, no. 3 (February 4, 1998).

66. Commission of the European Communities, "Climate Change—Towards an EU Post-Kyoto Strategy," 1998, COM(98)353.

67. ECCP, "European Climate Change Programme: Long Report," July 2001; http://europa.eu.int/comm/environment/climat/pdf/eccp_longreport_0106.pdf.

68. "Ministers Take Stock of EU Climate Policy," *ENDS Daily*, March 24, 1998; http://www.environmentdaily.com.

69. Joe Kirwin, "EU Agrees Burden-Sharing Plan for Emission Cuts under Kyoto Protocol," *International Environment Reporter* 21, no. 13 (June 24, 1998).

70. "EU Warned of Climate Policy Credibility Gap," *ENDS Daily*, May 19, 1999; http://www.environmentdaily.com.

71. "Bjerregaard Blasts Member States for Stalling Harmonized Energy Tax Proposal," *International Environment Reporter* 21, no. 10 (May 13, 1998).

72. Ibid.

73. European Commission Press Release, "Commission Outlines Measures to Reduce Carbon Dioxide Emissions from Transport," IP/98/307, March 31, 1998.

74. "EU Car-Makers to Make New CO_2 Offer," *ENDS Daily*, February 19, 1998; http://www.environmentdaily.com.

75. "First Progress Report on Reducing CO_2 Emissions from Cars," *European Report*, no. 2533 (October 7, 2000); http://www.lexisnexis.com.

76. "EU Begins Planning Strategy to Prevent 'Loopholes' in Kyoto Protocol," *International Environmental Reporter* 21, no. 7 (April 1, 1998).

77. Joe Kirwin, "EU Divided on Whether to Limit Use of Emission Trades for Meeting Targets," *International Environmental Reporter* 21, no. 11 (May 27, 1998).

78. "EU Agrees Climate Trading Negotiations Stance," *ENDS Daily*, October 6, 1998; http://www.environmentdaily.com.

79. "IEA's Preliminary Analysis of EU Proposal on the Kyoto Mechanisms," *Energy Europe*, no. 538 (June 11, 1999); http://www.lexisnexis.com.

80. Joe Kirwin, "EU to Push for Limit on Use of Kyoto's 'Flexible Mechanisms' During Bonn Talks," *International Environmental Reporter* 22, no. 11 (May 26, 1999).

81. "EU to Call for Restrictions in Use of Carbon Sinks to Offset GHG Emissions," *International Environmental Reporter* 23, no. 14 (July 5, 2000).

82. Susan McInerney, "G–8 Approves 'Flexible Mechanisms' to Cut Greenhouse Gas Emissions," *International Environment Report* 21, no. 11 (May 27, 1998).

83. Jacqueline Paige, "Strong Domestic Action to Reduce Emissions Urged at G–8 Environment Ministers' Summit," *International Environment Reporter* 21, no. 8 (April 15, 1998).

84. "Slow Progress Down the Rocky Road from Kyoto," *ENDS Report*, no. 293 (June 1999); http://www.endsreport.com.

85. Cheryl Hogue, "Developing Countries Reject Possibility of Emission Limits in 1992 Treaty Review," *International Environment Reporter* 21, no. 12 (June 10, 1998).

86. James Langman, "Climate Change Chair Predicts No Dramatic Results in Buenos Aires," *International Environment Reporter* 21, no. 21 (October 14, 1998).

87. James Kennedy, "High Stakes Seen in IPCC Negotiations on Carbon Sequestration by Forests, Lands," *Environment Reporter* 31, no. 18 (May 5, 2000).

88. "UN Global Warming Talks Bogged Down in Technical Tussle," *Agence France Presse*, June 13, 2000; http://www.lexisnexis.com.

89. Stephen Fidler and Vanessa Houlder, "Europeans Defend Rejection of Climate Deal," *Financial Times*, November 28, 2000.

90. Andrew C. Revkin, "Treaty Talks Fail to Find Consensus in Global Warming," *New York Times*, November 26, 2000.

91. "EU/UN: Unholy Compromise to Drag Climate Talks out of the Mire," *European Report*, no. 2547 (November 25, 2000); http://www.lexisnexis.com.

92. Andrew C. Revkin, "Treaty Talks Fail to Find Consensus in Global Warming," *New York Times*, November 26, 2000.

93. William Drozdiak, "Global Warming Talks Collapse; U.S., EU Fail to Resolve Dispute over Curbing Emissions," *Washington Post*, November 26, 2000; http://www.lexisnexis.com.

94. Patrice Hill, "Warming Alert; GOP Upset by Attempt to Revive Gases Treaty," *Washington Post*, December 9, 2000; http://www.lexisnexis.com.

95. "Kyoto Protocol Suffers Serious Setback," *European Report*, no. 2544 (December 20, 2000); http://www.lexisnexis.com.

96. Eric Pianin, "EPA Mulls Limits for Power Plant Emissions," *Washington Post*, February 28, 2001; http://www.lexisnexis.com.

97. "G–8 Nations Unfreeze Global Warming Talks," *Deutsche Presse-Agentur*, March 4, 2001; http://www.lexisnexis.com.

98. Douglas Jehl, and Andrew Revkin, "Bush, in Reversal, Won't Seek Cut in Emissions of Carbon Dioxide," *New York Times*, March 14, 2001.

99. Ibid.

100. White House Press Secretary, "Text of a Letter from the President to Senators Hagel, Helms, Craig, and Roberts," March 13, 2001; www.usinfo.state.gov/topical/global/climate/01031401.htm.

101. Dalia Sussman, "Six in 10 Say U.S. Should Join Kyoto Treaty," *ABC News*, April 17, 2001; http://abcnews.go.com/sections/us/DailyNews/poll010417.html.

102. "US Pessimistic on any Global Climate Change Pact," *New York Times*, April 21, 2001.

103. National Academy of Science, *Climate Change Science: An Analysis of Some Key Questions* (Washington, DC: National Academy Press, 2001).

104. Douglas Jehl, "U.S. Rebuffs European Plea Not to Abandon Climate Pact," *New York Times*, April 4, 2001.

105. White House, "President Bush Discusses Global Climate Change," June 11, 2001; http://www.whitehouse.gov/news/releases/2001/06/print/20010611-2.html.

106. Richard Ingham, "Ministers Try to See Kyoto through the Trees," *Agence France Presse*, July 20, 2001; http://www.lexisnexis.com.

107. WWF, "Analysis of the Pronk Proposal of 21 July 2001," July 22, 2001; http://www.panda.org/climate/summit2001/pronk_prop.doc.

108. UNFCCC, "Report of the Conference of Parties on the Second Part of Its Sixth Session , Held at Bonn from 16 to 27 July 2001," September 25, 2001, FCCC/CP/2001/5, p. 42.

109. "Kyoto Climate Protocol Comes Back to Life," *ENDS Daily*, no. 1036 (July 23, 2001); http://www.environmentdaily.com.

110. Michael McCarthy, " 'Watered Down' Kyoto Deal Is Hailed by World Leaders but Angers Green Groups," *Independent* (London), July 24, 2001; http://www.lexisnexis.com.

111. Michael McCarthy, "So Just Why Can't These Men Agree to Save the Planet?" *Independent* (London), July 23, 2001; http://www.lexisnexis.com.

CHAPTER 7: CONCLUSION

1. "Ministers Agree to 7.5 Percent Cut in Greenhouse Gas Emissions by 2005," *International Environment Reporter* 20, no. 13 (June 25, 1997).

2. Cass, "Norm Entrapment and Preference Change."

Bibliography

Barnett, Michael. "Culture, Strategy and Foreign Policy Change: Israel's Road to Oslo." *European Journal of International Relations* 5, no. 1 (1999): 5–36.

Betsill, Michele M., and Elisabeth Corell. "NGO Influence in International Environmental Negotiations: A Framework for Analysis." *Global Environmental Politics* 1, no. 4 (2001): 65–85.

Birkland, Thomas. *After Disaster: Agenda Setting, Public Policy, and Focusing Events.* Washington, DC: Georgetown University Press, 1997.

Bodansky, Daniel M. "The United Nations Framework Convention on Climate Change: A Commentary." *Yale Journal of International Law* 18 (1993): 451–558.

Boehmer-Christiansen, Sonja and Jim Skea. *Acid Politics: Environmental and Energy Policies in Britain and Germany.* New York: Belhaven Press, 1991.

Brickman, Ronald, Sheila Jasanoff, and Thomas Ilgen. *Controlling Chemicals: The Politics of Regulation in Europe and the United States.* Ithaca, NY: Cornell University Press, 1985.

Cass, Loren. "Norm Entrapment and Preference Change: The Evolution of the European Union Position on International Emissions Trading." *Global Environmental Politics* 5, no. 2 (2005): 38–60.

Checkel, Jeffrey T. "International Norms and Domestic Politics: Bridging the Rationalist-Constructivist Divide." *European Journal of International Relations* 3, no. 4 (1997): 473–495.

———. "Norms, Institutions, and National Identity in Contemporary Europe." *International Studies Quarterly* 43, no. 1 (1999): 83–114.

Collier, Ute. "Global Warming and the Internal Energy Market: Policy Integration or Polarization." *Energy Policy* 21, no. 9 (1993): 915–925.

Collier, Ute and Ragnar E. Lofstedt, eds. *Cases in Climate Change Policy: Political Reality in the European Union.* London: Earthscan, 1997.

Cortell, Andrew and James Davis, Jr. "Understanding the Domestic Impact of International Norms: A Research Agenda." *International Studies Review* 2, no. 1 (2000): 65–87.

Finnemore, Martha and Kathryn Sikkink. "International Norm Dynamics and Political Change." *International Organization* 52, no. 4 (1998): 887–917.

Gulbrandsen, Lars H., and Steinar Andresen. "NGO Influence in the Implementation of the Kyoto Protocol: Compliance, Flexibility Mechanisms, and Sinks." *Global Environmental Politics* 4, no. 4 (2004): 54–75.

Gurowitz, Amy. "Mobilizing International Norms: Domestic Actors, Immigrants, and the Japanese State." *World Politics* 51, no. 3 (1999): 413–445.

Hatch, Michael T. "The Politics of Global Warming in Germany," *Environmental Politics* 4, no. 3 (1995): 415–440.

Hecht, Michael T., and Dennis Tirpak. "Framework Agreement on Climate Change: A Scientific and Policy History." *Climactic Change* 29 (1995): 371–402.

Ikenberry, G. John. "Creating Yesterday's New World Order: Keynesian 'New Thinking' and the Anglo-American Postwar Settlement." In *Ideas and Foreign Policy: Beliefs, Institutions, and Political Change.* Edited by Judith Goldstein and Robert O. Keohane, 57–86. Ithaca, NY: Cornell University Press, 1993.

———. "A World Economy Restored: Expert Consensus and the Anglo-American Post-War Settlement." *International Organization* 46, no. 1 (1992): 289–322.

Intergovernmental Panel on Climate Change. *Climate Change 2001: Synthesis Report, Summary for Policymakers.* 2001: http://www.ipcc.ch/pub/un/syreng/spm.pdf.

Jachtenfuchs, Markus. *International Policy-Making as a Learning Process? The European Union and the Greenhouse Effect.* Brookfield, VT: Aldershot, 1996.

Jasanoff, Sheila. *The Fifth Branch: Science Advisers as Policymakers.* Cambridge, MA: Harvard University Press, 1990.

Jepperson, Ronald L., Alexander Wendt, and Peter J. Katzenstein "Norms, Identity, and Culture in National Security." In *The Culture of National Security: Norms and Identity in World Politics.* Edited by Peter Katzenstein, 33–75. New York: Columbia University Press, 1996.

Jochem, Eberhard. "Reducing CO_2 Emissions—the West German Plan." *Energy Policy* 19, no. 2 (1991): 119–126.

Katzenstein, Peter J. "Introduction: Alternative Perspectives on National Security." In *The Culture of National Security: Norms and Identity in World Politics.* Edited by Peter J. Katzenstein, 1–32. New York: Columbia University Press, 1996.

Kellogg, William W. "Mankind's Impact on Climate: The Evolution of Awareness." *Climatic Change* 10 (1987): 170–192.

Klotz, Audie. "Norms Reconstituting Interests: Global Racial Equality and U.S. Sanctions against South Africa." *International Organization* 49, no. 3 (1995): 451–478.

Kowert, Paul and Jeffrey Legro. "Norms, Identity, and Their Limits: A Theoretical Reprise." In *The Culture of National Security: Norms and Identity in World Politics.* Edited by Peter J. Katzenstein, 451–497. New York: Columbia University Press, 1996.

Leach, Gerald. "Policies to Reduce Energy Use and Carbon Emissions in the UK," *Energy Policy* 19, no. 10 (1991): 918–925.

Legro, Jeffrey W. "Culture and Preferences in the International Cooperation Two-Step." *American Political Science Review* 90, no. 1 (1996): 118–137.

Lundqvist, Lennart. *The Hare and the Tortoise: Clean Air Policies in the United States and Sweden.* Ann Arbor, MI: University of Michigan Press, 1980.

Luterbacher, Urs and Detlef F. Sprinz, eds. *International Relations and Global Climate Change.* Cambridge, MA: MIT Press, 2001.

Newell, Peter. *Climate for Change: Non-State Actors and the Global Politics of the Greenhouse.* Cambridge: Cambridge University Press, 2000.

O'Riordan, Tim and Jill Jäger, eds. *Politics of Climate Change: A European Perspective.* New York: Routledge and Kegan Paul, 1996.

Paterson, Matthew. *Global Warming and Global Politics.* New York: Routledge and Kegan Paul, 1996.

Payne, Rodger A. "Persuasion, Frames, and Norm Construction." *European Journal of International Relations* 7, no. 1 (2001): 37–61.

Princen, Thomas and Matthias Finger. *Environmental NGOs in World Politics: Linking the Local and the Global.* London: Routledge and Kegan Paul, 1994.

Repetto, Robert. *The Costs of Climate Protection: A Guide for the Perplexed.* Washington, DC: World Resources Institute, 1997.

Rest, Alfred and Raimond Bleischwitz. "Policies and Legal Instruments in FRG to Combat Climate Change and the Greenhouse Effect." In *Policies and Laws on Global Warming: International and Comparative Analysis.* Edited by Toru Iwama, 159–177. Tokyo: Environmental Research Center, 1991.

Ringius, Lasse. "The European Community and Climate Protection: What's Behind the 'Empty Rhetoric'?" CICERO Report 1999:8 (October 20, 1999).

Risse, Thomas. " 'Let's Argue!': Communicative Action in World Politics." *International Organization* 54, no. 1 (2000): 1–39.

Risse-Kappen, Thomas. "Bringing Transnational Relations Back In: Introduction." In *Bringing Transnational Relations Back In: Non-State Actors, Domestic Structures and International Institutions.* Edited by Thomas Risse-Kappen, 3–36. Cambridge: Cambridge University Press, 1995.

————. "Ideas Do Not Float Freely: Transnational Coalitions, Domestic Structures and the End of the Cold War," *International Organization* 48, no. 2 (1994): 185–214.

Robinson, Colin. "Electricity Privatization: What Future Now for British Coal?" *Energy Policy* 17, no. 1 (1989): 22–26.

Rowlands, Ian H. *The Politics of Global Atmospheric Change*. New York: Manchester University Press, 1995.

Ruggie, John Gerard. "What Makes the World Hang Together? Neo-Utilitarianism and the Social Constructivist Challenge." *International Organization* 52, no. 4 (1998): 855–886.

Schimmelfennig, Frank. "The Community Trap: Liberal Norms, Rhetorical Action, and the Eastern Enlargement of the European Union." *International Organization* 55, no. 1 (2001): 47–80.

Spretnak, C., and C. Fridtjof. *Green Politics*. London: Paladin, 1984.

Victor, David G. "On Writing Good Histories of Climate Change and Testing Social Science Theories." *Climatic Change* 29, no. 4 (1995): 363–370.

Vogel, David. *National Styles of Regulation: Environmental Policy in Great Britain and the United States*. Ithaca, NY: Cornell University Press, 1986.

Index